POSTMODERNISM
AND THE
SOCIAL SCIENCES

CONTEMPORARY SOCIAL THEORY

Series Editor:
Mark Gottdiener
University of California, Riverside

CONTEMPORARY SOCIAL THEORY books are brief, introductory texts designed to make current trends in social theory accessible to undergraduate students in the social sciences.

VOLUMES IN THIS SERIES

1. Tom Mayer, ANALYTICAL MARXISM
2. Sondra Farganis, SITUATING FEMINISM: From Thought to Action
3. Raymond A. Morrow with David D. Brown, CRITICAL THEORY AND METHODOLOGY
4. Robert Hollinger, POSTMODERNISM AND THE SOCIAL SCIENCES: A Thematic Approach

SERIES EDITORIAL BOARD

POSTMODERNISM AND THE SOCIAL SCIENCES
A THEMATIC APPROACH

ROBERT HOLLINGER

CONTEMPORARY SOCIAL THEORY

VOLUME 4

SAGE Publications
International Educational and Professional Publisher
Thousand Oaks   London   New Delhi

For information address:

 SAGE Publications, Inc.
2455 Teller Road
Thousand Oaks, California 91320

SAGE Publications Ltd.
6 Bonhill Street
London EC2A 4PU
United Kingdom

SAGE Publications India Pvt. Ltd.
M-32 Market
Greater Kailash I
New Delhi 110 048 India

Printed in the United States of America

Library of Congress Cataloging-in-Publication Data

Hollinger, Robert.
    Postmodernism and the social sciences : A thematic approach /
Robert Hollinger.
        p. cm. — (Contemporary social theory; 4)
    Includes bibliographical references and index.
    ISBN 0-8039-4637-6. — ISBN 0-8039-4638-4 (pb)
        1. Postmodernism–Social aspects. 2. Social sciences–Philosophy.
I. Title. II. Series: Contemporary social theory (Thousand Oaks, Calif.) ; 4.
HM73.H584 1994
300'.1–dc20   94-6852

        95 96 97 98 10 9 8 7 6 5 4 3

For Pat and Lisa

CONTENTS

Acknowledgments   ix

**Introduction: Toward an Understanding
of Postmodernism**   xi

**1. Modernity, the Enlightenment, and
the Social Sciences**   1
The Rise of the Social Sciences   3
The Agenda of the Social Sciences in Modernity   4
What Is the Enlightenment?   7
History of the Enlightenment Debates   9
The Failure of the Enlightenment Project   14
The Ethos of Enlightenment   15

2. Modernity   21
Modernity as a Philosophical Concept   21
Modernity in the Age of Enlightenment   22
Modernity as a Sociological/Historical Category   25

3. Modernism   40
Cultural Modernism and Its Ambiguities   40
Modern Ideas of the Self   42

4. Reason, Methods, Values   57
A Brief History of the Concept of Reason   57
Values   59
Methods   60
Naturalism and Antinaturalism   61
Pro- and Anti-Enlightenment Views   63
Relativism and the Sociology of Knowledge   66
Value Freedom in the Social Sciences   71

5. **From Critical Theory to Poststructuralism** **79**
Critical Theory Versus Structuralism 80
Western Marxism and the Frankfurt School:
Early Critical Theory 81
Critical Theory and Freud 82

6. **Postmodernism, Identity, and the Self** **95**
Textuality and Deconstruction 96
Truth, Knowledge, and Reality:
Nietzschean Themes 104
Antihumanism 111
Habermas, Humanism, and the Philosophy
of Consciousness 113
Postmodernism and Self-Identity 113
Implications for the Social Sciences 116

7. **Postmodernism and Society** **122**
Postmodernist Social Science
Versus the Social Sciences of Postmodernity 124
Postindustrial Society and Postmodernism 131
Marxism, Postmodernism, Post-Marxism,
and Postindustrial Society 135
Toward a Social Science of Postmodernity 140

8. **The Challenge From Critical Theory** **153**
Habermas and Critical Theory 154
Habermas on Modernity 159
Postmodern Feminism
Versus Feminist Critical Theory 162

9. **Postmodernism: An Overview** **169**

10. **How Postmodernism Is Changing
the Social Sciences** **178**
The Normative Structure of the Social Sciences 179
Conflict Versus Consensus 180
The Corporate State and Liberal Social Science 181
The Americanization of the Iron Cage 183
Postmodernism and the Social Sciences 184

Index **191**

About the Author **192**

ACKNOWLEDGMENTS

I am grateful to Mark Gottdiener (Department of Sociology, University of California, Riverside), the editor of this series, for inviting me to write this book, and to Bernd Magnus (Department of Philosophy, University of California, Riverside) for suggesting my name to Mark. Mark was enormously helpful in making constructive editorial suggestions and in assisting me at every stage in the preparation of the manuscript. I also wish to thank Doug Kellner (Department of Philosophy, University of Texas, Austin) for reading the penultimate version of the manuscript, and for his comments and suggestions.

I received incalculable editorial assistance from Gretchen Topp (Department of English, Iowa State University), David Dickens (Department of Sociology, University of Nevada, Las Vegas), and Larry Olsen and Mitch Allen (Sage Publications).

I would also thank my wife, Pat, and our daughter, Lisa, for providing me with the love and encouragement necessary to complete this book, as well as many other things. My late mother, Ruth Hollinger, and my parents-in-law, Virginia and Henry Pinkert, have provided immeasurable support and concern for many years. My debt to all of them is incalculable.

INTRODUCTION

Toward an Understanding of Postmodernism

P*ostmodernism and the Social Sciences* is part of a series that seeks to make a variety of current approaches to social theory accessible to social scientists, on the assumption that recent perspectives in feminist studies, critical theory, and postmodernism are directly relevant to standard traditions and research problems within the social sciences.

The literature on postmodernism is so vast, diverse, and unwieldy that even the initiated cannot keep up with it, let alone make coherent sense of it all. Moreover, the literature encompasses philosophy, literary criticism, culture studies, economics, sociology, cultural anthropology, history, psychology, and various combinations of these, and is written in a variety of styles and perspectives.

The difficulty of much of this literature, combined with an indeterminacy about postmodernist writers' shared assumptions and goals, has not fostered the understanding and intelligent criticism that this body of literature deserves. The various social and behavioral sciences, particularly sociology, political theory, and cultural anthropology, are becoming the sites of debates about postmodernism, and the number of books, articles, journals, and conferences on postmodernism is steadily increasing.

Postmodernism and the Social Sciences attempts to make postmodernism intelligible to social scientists by focusing on the main themes and issues in the modern social science traditions and addressing the issues that postmodernism raises that are relevant to sociology, cultural anthropology, history, economics, political science, and psychology. It promotes a critical understanding of the leading postmodernists—Foucault, Lyotard, Baudrillard, Deleuze and Guattari, Derrida, and (as leading critic) Habermas—who are the most directly relevant to the traditions, history, and current agendas of the social sciences.

Among the main themes considered are the following: What is postmodernism? How are postmodernist writings relevant to the social sciences? What are the main strengths and weaknesses of these writings? What are some recent postmodernist developments within the social sciences? The approach to these themes is thematic and historical. The book shows how postmodernism is addressing some of the basic assumptions and traditions within the modern social sciences.

Plan of the Book

Chapter 1 introduces a number of key issues and themes. The social sciences are the product of assumptions about human beings, society, community, methodology, values, and history that are rooted in the cultural context of modernity. Alternative ways of understanding modernity that have influenced the social sciences are discussed in terms of ongoing debates between Enlightenment and counter-Enlightenment thought. Postmodernism claims that the social sciences as they are now constituted are irrelevant to the cultural context of postmodern society and must be radically transformed if they are to help us understand the new world order.

A central debate surrounding postmodernism and the social sciences is the extent to which postmodernism seeks to counter the aims of the Enlightenment project, the modern program that seeks to extend the uses of reason—especially science, technology, and applied science—to promote the growth of a rational civilization. Critics of postmodernist writers accuse them of being against the Enlightenment and of favoring some form of irrationalism or mysticism. Yet postmodernist writers such as Foucault and Derrida are clearly not anti-Enlightenment. To sort out this key issue, Chapter 1 examines texts from Kant, Derrida, Foucault, and others to see exactly what the postmodernists have to say about the Enlightenment project.

Modernity

Following common application, the term *modernity* is used to denote the type of society that arose in the West during the Enlightenment: A society that is highly differentiated from a structural-functional point of view, dominated by a capitalist (market) economy, with a complex division of labor, industrialization and urbanization, science and technology, political and ethical individualism, liberal utilitarianism and social contract theory, a certain set of ideas about the self, and a conception of human history that is implicitly teleological and explicitly optimistic.

Chapter 2 explores several key questions about modernity: Is it good or bad, ambivalent, or merely different? The chapter begins with the conflict between the Enlightenment and Romanticism and moves to the writings of Hegel, Nietzsche, Marx, Tonnies, Weber, Simmel, Durkheim, Freud, Heidegger, and the Frankfurt theorists for defenses and criticisms of modernity. The question "What is modernity?" is a preface to the question of whether postmodernism rejects modernity in favor of a postindustrial society. However, the postmodernists are ambivalent in their diagnoses of modernity, and their views about the connections between modernity and postmodernity are neither uniform nor unambiguous. Being against modernity means both a nostalgic longing for premodernity and a call for an entirely new type of society and culture.

Modernism

The term *modernism* is difficult to define because writers in different fields, such as philosophy and literature, define modernism in different ways. Bacon and Descartes are usually considered the philosophical founders of modernism, whereas Baudelaire is considered the first self-consciously literary modernist. Is modernism a period or a style?

Chapter 3 follows such writers as Berman, Simmel, Foucault, and Bell in treating modernism as a kind of rebellious ethos or attitude toward the modern world. Modernism is a style stressing subjectivity or consciousness over objectivity. Modernism stems from the romantic reaction against the Cartesian and Hobbesian idea of the rational self.

Reason, Methods, Values

Chapter 4 sketches the history of the concept of rationality in the context of the Enlightenment and modernity. It explores the confrontation between modernists and postmodernists. The distinction between the natural and human sciences and the various conflicts about methods and values that shape the social sciences are the focus of these discussions.

From Critical Theory to Poststructuralism

Chapter 5 sketches the theoretical development of Marxism in an effort to situate this important line of thought in modernism. It outlines the ideas of structuralist and poststructuralist theorists as a preparation for later discussions of key ideas of postmodernism.

Postmodernism, Identity, and the Self

Chapter 6 discusses some basic motifs of postmodernism by focusing on the roots of Derrida's writings in Nietzsche and Heidegger. Following a discussion of Derrida and his relevance in the social sciences, various approaches to the self in postmodernist writings are surveyed.

Postmodernism and Society

Chapter 7 takes up the themes of society and community. It begins with Baudrillard's theme of the end of society and the silence of the masses, then moves into a discussion of postindustrial society and its relations with postmodernism. Postmodernist concerns about plurality, otherness, and legitimation are then taken up. The issue of nihilism is discussed, and various recent themes and movements (the end of history, feminism, post-Marxism, new social movements, post-Fordism, postcolonialism, cultural and media studies, technoculture) are touched on in an effort to bring out recent studies within the social sciences that exhibit postmodernist trends. The goal of understanding the conditions of postmodern society clearly requires changes in social science methods and concepts. A social science of postmodernity rather than just a postmodernist social science is needed.

The Challenge From Critical Theory

Chapter 8 discusses the controversy between the postmodernists and a key critic, Habermas, with a view toward bringing out current agendas and themes in the social sciences. It focuses on problems surrounding postindustrial society and its politics and on recent debates about the role of intellectuals in the so-called new world order.

Postmodernism: An Overview

Chapter 9 provides a general review of postmodernist themes. Against the backdrop of earlier discussions about the Enlightenment, modernity, modernism, reason, values, and methods, it attempts to answer the following questions.

1. Is postmodernism against the Enlightenment?
2. Is postmodernism a form of irrationalism or nihilism?
3. Does postmodernism abandon the ideas of society and the social?
4. Does postmodernism reject the idea of the self?
5. Does postmodernism relinquish the search for community?
6. Does postmodernism attack the modern ideas of freedom, reason, and emancipation?
7. What becomes of politics within a postmodernist outlook?
8. Is postmodernism the cultural ideology of late capitalism and postindustrial society?
9. Does postmodernism take anything seriously, or does it turn everything into a game?
10. Does postmodernism reject the ideas of objective reality, truth, and knowledge and thus try to overthrow modern science and technology?

**How Postmodernism
Is Changing the Social Sciences**

Chapter 10 discusses the ideological context of the modern social sciences and argues that the social scientists of postmodernity should not be universal intellectuals who legislate for society or launch totalistic criticisms of it, but instead should be specific intellectuals whose vocation is to interpret the current scene with the aim of promoting the Enlightenment ethos of probity.

1

MODERNITY,
THE ENLIGHTENMENT,
AND THE SOCIAL SCIENCES

Many postmodernist critics of the social sciences question the assumptions and concepts on which the social sciences are based. Simply put, postmodernists maintain that the ways in which the social sciences have been conceived and practiced involve assumptions and frameworks that are largely outdated. Postmodernists assert that the cultural and historical context within which the social sciences have developed since the 18th century is no longer operative. To understand postmodernism and its relevance to the contemporary social sciences, we must begin with a historical overview of the context in which the social sciences have developed.

The social sciences arose within a larger social and cultural context called modernization. *Modernization* refers to the process by which traditional societies were transformed into modern societies. The discussion here is restricted to the modernization process in Western culture.

The terms *modern* and *modernity* denote the types of societies that developed from modernization. The terms *traditional* and *premodern* refer to the types of societies that preceded modernization. The transformation to modern society began approximately in the 17th century and took 2 centuries to reach its zenith. Factors contributing to modernization included the Reformation, the Renaissance, the rise of the modern European state, the Scientific Revolution, the French Revolution, the Industrial Revolution, and the rise of mass urban societies.

1

Traditional European societies were largely rural, agricultural, authoritarian, religious, relatively small in population, relatively homogeneous, and precapitalist or early capitalist. Modern societies are characterized by the growth of urban areas, various forms of capitalism, democracy, science and technology, massive population growth and concentration, and cultural, political, and religious heterogeneity.

The process of modernization involved tremendous upheavals, thus causing anxiety for many people. The old order was disappearing, and a new, modern world was emerging. How was it possible to understand, let alone assess, such major changes? Was the modern world going to be better, worse, or just different than traditional society? How could it be possible to see what kind of world would result from all the changes? Was there cause for regret for the disappearance of some parts of the old order? Were some parts of the new order worrisome, even dangerous? These are some of the questions that dominated the thoughts and writings of philosophers, novelists, poets, political and social theorists, theologians, and other concerned people for generations.

The Enlightenment was a prominent intellectual movement that emerged in the late 18th century. This movement, which began in France, broached a set of doctrines stating that the source of all human misery is ignorance, especially superstition. Only knowledge, reason, and science can destroy ignorance and superstition and help improve the human condition.

What are the main sources of ignorance and superstition? Generally, they are the mainstays of traditional societies: religion, authoritarian government, customs, the simple outlook of farmers and peasants, traditions, and myths. In other words, according to the writers of the Enlightenment, traditional societies are rotten to the core and are an obstacle to freedom, happiness, and human progress. In many respects, the Enlightenment became a focus for debates about the advantages and disadvantages of traditional and modern society.

While the advocates of the doctrines and values of the Enlightenment were defining and defending key aspects of modernization, other writers were not as sanguine about the uniform benefits of the new or the ubiquitous evil of the old. A movement known as the counter-Enlightenment arose at the beginning of the 19th century, first in German romanticism and later in a variety of other movements, including existentialism in philosophy, modernism in literature and the arts, and anarchism in politics.

The counter-Enlightenment defended religion, traditions, customs, myths, and common experiences and values against the Enlightenment attacks and in turn severely criticized the Enlightenment's emphasis on science, reason, secularization, capitalism, and modern economic individualism.

The debates over Enlightenment and counter-Enlightenment themes have characterized much of European culture and politics since 1800. More is said about these debates in later chapters. For now, it is important to note that both movements have played a major role in the social sciences from the outset and that postmodernists are often accused of being against the Enlightenment or part of the counter-Enlightenment.

The Rise of the Social Sciences

Questions and problems about modernity are discussed by philosophers such as Rousseau, Kant, and Hegel. But philosophical speculation was not the only kind of writing that concerned itself with such questions. Writers throughout society asked question such as: What factors were responsible for modernization? How were they related to each other? What features of modern societies were in need of understanding and perhaps control? Such questions were motivated by the desire to understand and to assess the transformations of modernization, but they called for responses that required more specific and often more empirical approaches than that which concerned the philosophers, even though most of the early social scientists were also philosophers.

The social sciences thus began with the need to understand modernization. The rise of market capitalism and the modern state and the growing influence of science, especially Newtonian physics, in all areas of life called for understanding and also for prediction, because predictability meant some stability and control in tumultuous times. Moreover, the Enlightenment ideals for transforming society required this sort of knowledge and power, which philosophy could not provide by itself.

The social sciences arose within the larger context of modernization, including the debates initiated by the early proponents of the Enlightenment and the later counter-Enlightenment thinkers. Furthermore, the concepts, methods, and approaches developed in the social sciences were both shaped by this context and designed to understand society within this context. Presumably, major changes in the context of modernity would require changes in the social sciences if the social sciences were to understand subsequent changes. Postmodernists believe that we now live in a world that is postmodern, so the concepts and approaches of the social sciences are no longer relevant, or at least require modification.

The Agenda of
the Social Sciences in Modernity

This book argues that the social sciences developed in modernity and are thus constrained by this context. The agenda of the social sciences—the various concepts, methods, assumptions, and aspirations of economics, psychology, cultural anthropology, history, political science, and sociology—is designed to promote the understanding and control of modern society. The basic goals and assumptions of the various social sciences are discussed briefly to set the stage for later discussion.

Human Nature

An interest in the human individual, defined as the self, and in the "laws of human behavior" was fostered by the adoption of assumptions from Newtonian physics as early as the 17th century. A scientific study of human behavior could allow social scientists to understand, predict, and control human behavior. The Enlightenment emphasis on science—on rational methods to discover knowledge—made the scientific study of human nature mandatory.

Society

Scientific methods were similarly applied to the study of society. Two different models are discussed at length in later chapters: The atomistic model, derived from Newtonian physics and defended by advocates of the Enlightenment, especially by liberals and utilitarians, views society as an aggregation of individuals governed by the laws of nature, particularly the law of the maximization of one's rational self-interest. The organic model, derived from Plato and Aristotle, is defended by romantics and other counter-Enlightenment figures, including many political and cultural conservatives and reactionaries, but also by Marx. In this view, individuals are products of their community and can only realize themselves in it. (These two models are discussed in Chapter 2.)

Debates in the social sciences about human rationality, the nature of society, the possibilities of altruistic behavior, human history and progress, and the most rational forms of politics and economics are all predicated on one of these two models of society—on either the selfish idea of the individual endorsed by atomism or on the Aristotelian "self-realization" idea taken up by the romantics, Hegel, Marx, and other advocates of the organic model.

History

The study of history is similarly related to assumptions about society and the individual. Within the context of modernity, questions about historical progress, historical determinism, and the ends or goals of history stem from a scientific approach to knowledge. Is history governed by laws? Is it predictable and controllable? What role do individuals play in history? Are human beings making progress, or are things getting worse? The 19th century was dominated by theories of human development and stories about human progress. The idea of "primitive societies," used by early cultural anthropologists and others to justify European colonialism abroad and Social Darwinism at home, is rooted in the idea that modern European culture is more advanced because it is more rational and enlightened than others. Modernization became a guiding model for the study of history.

Methodology

Modernity produced the ideas of objectivity and subjectivity and value neutrality. The atomistic model of society as a self-regulating machine explainable by the laws of psychology is an adaptation of modern philosophy and Newtonian science. Other methodologies that rejected Newtonian models in the social sciences were influenced by the counter-Enlightenment, which was also part of modernity.

Ideology, Politics, Truth Versus Power

The concern in modernity with truth, power, liberation, and authenticity also rests on various assumptions and agendas in the social sciences. Ideologies such as Marxism, liberalism, and conservatism and issues about the possibilities of revolution and reform stem from mixtures of value judgments and scientific analyses that are rooted in the specific contexts of modernity.

Suppose that postmodernism is in part the idea that our present new world order is as radical a departure from modernity as modernity was from premodernity. The present age is characterized by a global economy, the end of the Cold War, the rise of the postindustrial information society, the worldwide triumph of liberal democracy and market capitalism, the death of Marxism and socialism, and the end of the welfare state. Suppose, further, that postmodernists urge the following: We must understand and assess these phenomena; the concepts, assumptions, and approaches of the social sciences, rooted as they are in modernity, will not help us do this; so the social sciences must either be revised to become capable of understanding postmodernity or become irrelevant or extinct.

How is one to assess such bold claims? Is the new world order a radical departure from modernity or continuous with it? Does postmodernism rely on modern ideas as modernity relied on philosophical assumptions from traditional society? We need a broader and deeper understanding of modernity, the Enlightenment, and the counter-Enlightenment, and their influences on the theories and practices of the social sciences to assess these postmodernist claims.

What Is the Enlightenment?

The European Enlightenment of the 18th century marks a high point in Western history. Although its roots go much farther back in Western history and it continued to develop long after the 18th century, a program for improving human life was worked out. The *Enlightenment project*, as it has recently been called, is based on the assumption that ignorance is the basic source of all human misery and that the elimination of ignorance, and its replacement with scientific knowledge, would pave the way for endless human progress.

The basic ideas of the Enlightenment codified major developments in early modern European thought and provided a rallying point for future cultural and political struggles. The Enlightenment project can be expressed in several claims.

1. The epistemological unity of humankind is the claim that everything worth knowing can be unified into a set of beliefs that all human beings can rationally assent to and rationally accept on the basis of a universally valid set of methodological assumptions.

2. The moral unity of humankind is the claim that universal rational moral principles are binding on all rational beings everyhere and provide guides and standards for conduct and judgment.

3. Any beliefs, values, claims, or factors that contradict or impede these two (connected) goals is an obstacle to human progress and happiness. Only a society based on science and universal values is truly free and rational; only its inhabitants can be happy.

4. The truth shall make us free. The more we know about ourselves and the world, the better human life will become, because ignorance is the cause of unhappiness and immorality.

In a recent paper, Rosen claims that "postmodernism is the Enlightenment gone mad."[1] Rosen's intriguing remark is posed in terms of the idea that moderns have lost the virtues of moderation and nobility and thus are prone to extremes: Something is either provable or it is false, dangerous, and immoral. To Rosen, the excesses of the Enlightenment idea of reason culminate in postmodernism.

Bennett claims that:

> In Enlightenment the urge to strip away all illusion and mystery, uncover truth through reason, finds its purest expression. Contemporary practices of deconstruction have roots in Enlightenment; this is true despite serious differences between Enlightenment critique and deconstructive technique—the most obvious is deconstruction's repudiation of the pursuit of a unified, rational replacement for the disassembled social and theoretical myths. But Enlightenment, in its early stage, devotes itself almost exclusively to the destruction of Faith, putting off its positive project until later. In this destructive effort it functions as a precursor of deconstruction, and, like its more recent progeny, it depends upon its adversary for its own energy and direction.[2]

Nietzsche criticizes the idea that truth, knowledge, and rationality are more important than anything else.[3] When carried to extremes, this idea destroys what is most important in life, even life itself. Indeed, what is most important and valuable may not be "provable" by science. Science itself may rest on faith. Nietzsche believes that the Enlightenment can be very destructive, perhaps even irrational, if it destroys everything that fails to meet its own standards, especially if those standards cannot themselves be proven.

Thus, there are two conflicting perspectives: The view that Enlightenment's goals are rational and enhance human life versus the view that the Enlightenment's goals are matters of faith that destroy life and all that we hold dear and can do nothing but destroy. What is of most value may be what cannot be proven, and what is most important is rooted in those very factors that the Enlightenment sees as the source of misery: culture, traditions, customs, myths. Is one of these views right? Are both of these views wrong? Are they both too one-sided?

History of the Enlightenment Debates

Historians are still debating many issues about the 18th-century Enlightenment.[4] Discussions by postmodernists such as Derrida and Foucault, as well as by their main critic, Habermas, take their departure from Kant. This section raises some of the issues that divide postmodernists from their opponents. In so doing, it also begins to explore the meanings of postmodernism. The immediate aim is to show that postmodernism is not the enemy of the Enlightenment, although whether it is the culmination of the Enlightenment is not clear. To say that some writers who have been called postmodernists, notably Foucault and Derrida, are ambivalent about the pros and cons of the Enlightenment, and are not "against" it is closer to the truth. On the other hand, Habermas, the most vociferous current defender of the Enlightenment, may in some ways be less sympathetic to certain aspects of the spirit of Enlightenment defended by Foucault and Derrida.

Kant

Kant's seminal essay "An Answer to the Question: 'What Is Enlightenment?' "[5] has become the canonical text of recent discussions, but his other, so-called political writings[6] need to be examined, as do *Contest of the Faculties*,[7] *Anthropology from a Pragmatic Point of View*,[8] and *Critique of Judgment*.[9]

Kant's conception of Enlightenment, which anticipates Mill's *On Liberty*,[10] focuses on the idea of "maturity," which is glossed as the use of reason. "The motto of Enlightenment is therefore *Sapere aude*! Have courage to use your own understanding!"[11] Kant believes that the masses have not yet developed to the point where they can make use of this advice; hence, we do not live in an enlightened age but rather in an age of Enlightenment.[12] Education of the masses by the few "guardians" who have thrown off the "yoke of immaturity" and achieved the proper level of "understanding" define the ethos of the times as one of Enlightenment, even though society has a long way to go to achieve progress and "perpetual peace."[13]

Another wrinkle is added to Kant's story when he introduces an important distinction between the "public" and the "private" uses of reason.[14] Kant wants to connect the Enlightenment as a social, political, and cultural ideal to dialogue and thus to publicity. Insofar as political freedom and Enlightenment are concerned, any and all matters must be subject to publicity and debate. But the "private" use of reason is restricted; in this realm one must not argue but obey.[15] By the private use of reason, Kant seems to mean the roles that theorists would call one's social roles. Thus, in Kant's view, a professor is not permitted to debate certain issues as an instructor, but only as a citizen or a human being. This view is partly inspired by Kant's republican allegiance to a polity governed by law, and partly by his notion of universality in the practical realm. To put the point in Habermasian terms,[16] one's remarks as an instructor may not represent the "generalized interest" and hence may be ideological, and thus are unqualified to serve as the locus of public debate.

Aside from well-known scruples about role theory's fragmentation of the self, Kant's claims, which are representative of the modern liberal tradition, raise serious questions about the extent of permissible debate and the limits of "practical reason." Kant seems ambivalent about a certain kind of enlightened despotism.[17] He is clearly against the right to rebel: He praises the Germans for being the least inclined of peoples to question the established order,[18] and his democratic sympathies are not, to say the least, very keen. So Enlightenment proceeds (largely through education) "from the top downward,"[19] another basic motif in modern liberalism.

Kant's distinction between the public and private uses of reason raises questions about the limits of discussion and critique, the role of institutions such as universities in politics, and the role of authorities in focusing and limiting discussion. Foucault, Lyotard, and Derrida explore these aspects of Kant's doctrine, which form a large part of the debate with Habermas concerning the political implications of the Enlightenment.

In *The Contest of the Faculties*, a work discussed by Derrida,[20] Kant connects the public use of reason with the philosophy faculty of the university, the lower faculty, and the vocation of seeking the truth through discussion. Kant believes that all citizens of an open society must eventually play this sort of role if public discourse is to make progress.

The "higher" university faculties—law, medicine, and theology—are related to the "civil," private use of reason. They are agents for the state and must obey, not argue. But the philosophy faculty has as its mission the thematization of issues taken for granted both by government and by the civil servants in the higher faculty. It is in the state's interest to let philosophers discuss the truth of the various claims that fall under its auspices; their mission is to employ the public use of reason in the hope that this will lead to more progress and freedom and less despotism, enlightened or not. (Even enlightened despotism can play a role in furthering these goals.)[21]

Kant's remarks may at first appear to be a defense of some kind of Platonic guardian role for philosophers or some version of the ruling elite idea that is so characteristic of modern liberalism. To a certain extent, they are. But writers such as Gay[22] and O'Neill,[23] as well as Derrida, Foucault, and Lyotard, give Kant's discussion a more radical meaning. Gay sees Kant as moving toward a certain kind of relativism. O'Neill sees Kant as emphasizing a kind of indeterminacy about political and other practical matters that moves away from an "algorithmic" model of practical/political reasoning to one of a "tribunal."

Recent works on Kant's *Critique of Judgment*, notably by Arendt,[24] Beiner,[25] Caygill,[26] Cohen and Guyer,[27] Ingram,[28] Lyotard,[29] and Saner,[30] interpret Kant as providing a model of judgment that moves away from a rigid conception of political reasoning, often associated with the Enlightenment, toward the sort of connections between aesthetics and politics, judgment and plurality, discussed by postmodern writers such as Lyotard.[31] In this reading of Kant, the philosophy faculty can play the role of undermining existing authority and dogma. When used as a model for general public dialogue, this view can be truly liberating.

Postmodernist Criticisms of Kant

Despite their radical potential, Kant's doctrines lend themselves to an alternative reading. Kant emphasizes the universal aspects of judgment and dialogue.[32] To some critics, Kant appears to defend bourgeois society.[33] His ambivalence comes out clearly in his belief that the philosophy faculty is, in effect, an agent of the state, yet he hopes that political leaders, including enlightened despots, will become less despotic and more reasonable as a result of this relationship.[34] In *Origins of Modernity*,[35] Rundell argues that Kant's doctrines about publicity and political judgment have the effect of narrowing the range of the public sphere, owing to his distrust of the masses. According to some authors,[36] this pessimism about the intelligence of the masses is a political weakness in the Enlightenment. Postmodernist misgivings about the Enlightenment's concepts of totality, universal reason, and the progress of humanity reflect their apprehension about this sort of Enlightenment elitism.

Foucault

Foucault is not against the Enlightenment, nor is he a romanticist or "irrationalist." In "What Is Enlightenment?" he makes this very clear.

> But that does not mean that one has to be "for" or "against" the Enlightenment. It even means precisely that one has to refuse everything that might present itself in the form of a simplistic and authoritarian alternative: you either accept the Enlightenment and remain within the tradition of its rationalism...or else you criticize the Enlightenment and then try to escape from its principles of rationality....And we do not break free of this blackmail by introducing "dialectical" nuances in the Enlightenment.[37]

In another work, Foucault writes:

> Let us leave in their piety those who wish to preserve alive and intact the heritage of *Aufklarung*. Such piety is doubtless the most touching of treasons. It is not the legacy of the *Aufklarung* which it is our business to preserve, but rather the very question of this event and its meaning, the question of the historicity of the thought of the universal, which ought to be kept present and retained in mind as that which has to be thought.[38]

Despite the fact that Foucault talks about "the blackmail of reason,"[39] he is sympathetic to some aspects of the Enlightenment found in Kant's writings. Foucault proceeds by distinguishing between the "ethos" of the Enlightenment and its dogmas. As he puts it, "The thread that may connect us with the Enlightenment is not faithfulness to doctrinal elements, but rather the permanent reactivation of an attitude—that is, of a philosophical ethos that could be described as a permanent critique of our historical era."[40]

The fact that Kant's political writings are sometimes radical and often elitist is, according to Foucault, the result of a failure to separate these two distinct, but historically related, strands of the Enlightenment. Foucault sees the culmination of the ethos of Enlightenment in Marx, Weber, the Frankfurt school, and his own work,[41] whereas the dogmas of the Enlightenment lead to positivism, scientism, and the emphasis on technological reason.[42] Although doctrine and ethos may have coincided at certain moments in modern history, for example, in the 18th century, at other times they may have been in conflict.

Foucault also distinguishes between the Enlightenment and modernity and humanism.[43] He rejects the latter concept as one of the dogmas of the Enlightenment.

What Foucault finds important about Kant's work and the ethos of Enlightenment is Kant's discussion of the limits of reason and the possibilities of transgressing them. Foucault claims that his own work, which he calls "the ontology of the present,"[44] embodies this aspect of Kant. This ethos must be continually practiced, and the dogmas that prevent us from doing so (for example, scientism) must be overcome.

What are these "dogmas"? The most prevalent are the belief that knowledge, notably in the form of the empirical sciences, can be applied to society to increase human progress and happiness; the idea that the human sciences, modeled on Newtonian physics, will contribute to knowledge about human life to transform society into a scientific, totally rational culture; the emphasis on utilitarian models of action, with the attendant need for experts to govern; the belief in rational universal values and human progress toward one or another utopian goal; and the belief that humanity will continually realize the Enlightenment goal of a society based exclusively on knowledge that liberates people from oppression.

Derrida

Derrida is more emphatic than Foucault. He says, "Of course I am in favor of the Enlightenment. But there are certain historical forms of Enlightenment, certain things in this tradition that we need to criticize or deconstruct. So it is sometimes in the name of. . . a new Enlightenment that I deconstruct a given Enlightenment." Derrida claims that "deconstructionism in its most active or intense form, and not what we inherit in the name of *Aufklarung*, *kritik*, *siecles des lumieres*, which are already very different things, may constitute his new Enlightenment."[45] Derrida is clearly not against the Enlightenment ethos.

The Failure of the
Enlightenment Project

For many thinkers, both modern and postmodern, the dogmas of the Enlightenment are either naive or have been falsified by events in the 20th century. Some writers are pessimistic and see modernity in entirely negative terms: the Romantics, Heidegger, the Existentialists, Weber, and many conservatives. Others think that the Enlightenment project can be reclaimed, even though modernity has betrayed its ethos. This is essentially Habermas's view. Postmodernists such as Derrida, Lyotard, and Foucault are not as sanguine as Habermas, but neither are they irrationalists. Instead, they move beyond the optimism/pessimism dualism of modern Western history to reject both utopianism and romanticist gloom. In Nietzschean terms, postmodernism may be moving toward "completed," "active" nihilism, beyond Mannheim's ideology and utopia, to a vision of history and human life that is closer to Freud's: Neither human life nor history has a grand purpose, meaning, or message; there is no cause for despair or for utopian hopes; and there are no sources of consolation anywhere. This is where the ethos of the Enlightenment, stripped of all dogmas and doctrines, leads: from Nietzsche through Weber and Freud to Foucault and other postmodernists.

The Ethos of Enlightenment

The theme of the "ethics of honesty," a phrase Rieff uses to characterize Freud's view that he can offer no consolation or recipes about life,[46] can be traced to Nietzsche's remarks about "our probity."[47] The development of this theme can be traced from Nietzsche through Weber to Freud and to Derrida, Lyotard, and Foucault. The ethos of the Enlightenment, teaches us that our dogmas and doctrines are not as "rational" as we had thought. But, despite Rosen and Habermas, this does not mean madness or irrationalism or nihilism. It means that we need to question the limits of our current dogmas, explore ways of transgressing them, and continually test the scope and limits of reason.

This sort of ruthless honesty can and does lead to pessimism; perhaps Weber and Freud are the clearest examples. But it need not. Foucault adopts a kind of pessimism, but a pessimism involving action, a "hyper and pessimistic activism," as he calls it.[48] Nietzsche attempts to revitalize the pessimism of strength of the Greeks. One might argue, as Megill does,[49] that Derrida's rejection of the assumptions that generate utopian optimism and historical pessimism permits us to move beyond passive, destructive nihilism altogether, in favor of a kind of "playfulness."

Derrida, Lyotard, and Foucault explore the limits of reason in a different way. Each relies to some extent on those aspects of Kant's work that stress indeterminacy, the need for judgment without determinate ideals or rules, the rejection of apocalyptic pronouncements,[50] and continual critique of existing dogmas and practices.

A variety of issues are at stake here for the social sciences, the policy sciences, the role of social scientists in universities and government, the connections between the social sciences and politics, and the role of "experts" in society. The postmodernists critically examine many of the assumptions and practices that grew out of the Enlightenment that have informed the social and policy sciences. Among these assumptions are beliefs and presumptions about reason and rationality, about normality and deviance, and about the best ways of dealing with practical issues of life and society.

The postmodernist theme of "the unsayable,"[51] for instance, can be read as a criticism of the idea that everything important can be articulated and proved or disproved by the social or natural sciences, and that whatever cannot be articulated by them is worth nothing. This assumption of the social sciences reinforces a mentality that treats moral, political, and even personal problems as problems calling for technical or applied science solutions. There is something narrow, impoverished, indeed, dangerous about this mentality. However, modernity may have lost the resources to articulate an alternative to rational policies such as cost-benefit analysis. One alternative is an appeal to "the unsayable," to indeterminate rather than precise solutions, to judgments that are rooted in dialogue, experience, and practical wisdom. Human values must not be reducible to social engineering rationalized by science, technology, and cost-benefit analysis.

If we consider what social scientists often say about "normality," "rationality," "the public good," "rational preferences," and similar concepts in fields ranging from the policy sciences to medicine to psychology, we find very narrow assumptions that lead to practices that have untoward consequences for many people. The assumptions that psychotherapists make about normality are a case in point. In their view, people who are too "deviant"—for example, too shy—are dysfunctional and need therapy. Obviously the assumptions one makes about "normal" behavior lead to programs and policies for controlling deviant behavior, with important consequences for many people.

At the same time, those who hold certain utopian visions of human progress and who need to be able to understand and control everything are vulnerable to despair when their programs fail. Others may ignore what cannot be controlled in favor of what can be. The postmodern emphasis on "playfulness" is intended to remedy this desire to control everything and the despair about not being able to. Life, in all its richness and messiness, is more important than the impoverished conception of life that we often find in psychology, economics, and other social sciences. Postmodernism, which rejects the optimism of cost-benefit analysis as well as the despair of existentialism, may give rise to forms of understanding and criticism that preserve the ethos of the Enlightenment against its dogmas in contemporary society.

Notes

1. Rosen, S. (1988). A modest proposal to rethink enlightenment. In S. Rosen, *Ancients and moderns* (pp. 1-21). New Haven, CT: Yale University Press, p. 17. See also Rosen, S. (1993). Postmodernism and the possibility of critical reasoning. In R. A. Talaska (Ed.), *Critical reasoning in contemporary culture* (pp. 231-250). Albany: State University of New York Press.

2. Bennett, J. (1987). *Unthinking faith and enlightenment.* Albany: State University of New York Press. (p. 24).

3. Nietzsche, F. (1967) *Birth of tragedy* (W. Kaufmann, Trans.). New York: Random House; Nietzsche, F. (1967) What is the meaning of ascetic ideals? In W. Kaufmann (Trans.), *Genealogy of morals* (pp. 97-163). New York: Random House, 1967; See also Hegel, G. W. F. (1977). *Phenomenology of spirit.* New York: Oxford University Press; and Hinchman, L. (1984). *Hegel's critique of the enlightenment.* Tampa: Florida University Press.

4. Anchor, R. (1967). *The enlightenment tradition* Berkeley: University of California Press; Cassirer, E. (1951). *Philosophy of the enlightenment.* Boston: Beacon Press; Gay, P. (1969). *The enlightenment: Vol. 2.* New York: Norton; Goldmann, L. (1973). *The philosophy of the enlightenment.* Cambridge: MIT Press; Jacob, M. C. (1991). The enlightenment redefined. *Social Research, 58*(2), 475-495; Kunneman, H., & de Vries, H. (Eds.). (1992). *Enlightenments.* Kamper, The Netherlands: Books International; Porter, R. (1990). *The enlightenment.* New York: Macmillan; Yolton, J. W., Porter, R., Rogers, P., & Stafford, B. (Eds.). (1992). *The Blackwell companion to the enlightenment* Cambridge, MA: Blackwell.

5. Kant, I. (1970/1991). An answer to the question:"What is the enlightenment?" New York/Cambridge, UK: Cambridge University Press.

6. Kant, I. (1991). *Political writings* (2nd enlarged ed.) (H. Reiss, Ed.). New York/Cambridge, UK: Cambridge University Press.

7. Kant, I. (1979). *Contest of the faculties* (M. Gregor, Trans.). Pleasantville, NY: Abaris Books.

8. Kant, I. *Anthropology from a pragmatic point of view* (M. Gregor, Trans.). Hingham, MA/The Hague, The Netherlands: Martinus Nijhoff.

9. Kant, I. (1951). *Critique of judgement.* New York: Hafner; Kant, I. (1952) *First introduction to the critique of judgement.* Indianapolis: Bobbs-Merrill.

10. Mill, J. S., (1978). *On liberty.* Indianapolis: Hackett.

11. Kant, I. An answer to the old question: "What is enlightenment?" In I. Kant, *Political writings* (2nd enlarged ed.) (H. Reiss, Ed.) (pp. 177-90). New York/Cambridge, UK: Cambridge University Press.

12. Ibid., p. 58.

13. Kant. I. Perpetual peace. In I. Kant, *Political writings* (2nd enlarged ed.) (H. Reiss, Ed.) (pp. 93-130). New York/Cambridge, UK: Cambridge University Press; and *Perpetual peace and other essays.* Indianapolis: Hackett, 1980.

14. Kant, I. (1960). *Education.* Ann Arbor: University of Michigan Press; Kant, I. (1974). *Logic.* Indianapolis: Bobbs-Merrill; Kant, I. (1991). What is enlightenment? In *Political writings* (2nd enlarged ed.) (H. Reiss, Ed.) (pp. 54-60). New York/Cambridge, UK: Cambridge University Press.

15. Kant, What is enlightenment?

16. Habermas, J. (1984-1985). *Theory of communicative action* (Vols. 1-2). Boston: Beacon Press; Habermas, J. (1988). *Philosophical discourse of modernity*. Cambridge: MIT Press. See also Ophis, A. (1988). The ideal speech situation: Neo-Kantian ethics in Habermas and Apel. In Y. Yovel (Ed.), *Kant's practical philosophy reconsidered* (pp. 213-235). Norwell, MA: Kluwer.

17. Beiser, F. C. (1992). *Enlightenment, revolution, and romanticism*. Cambridge, MA: Harvard University Press; Crowther, P. (1989). *The Kantian sublime*. New York: Oxford University Press; Deleuze, G. (1984). *Kant's critical philosophy*. Minneapolis: University of Minnesota Press; Dietze, G. (1985). *Liberalism proper and proper liberalism*. Baltimore: Johns Hopkins University Press; Feher, F. (1989). Practical reason in the revolution: Kant's dialogue with the French revolution. In F. Feher (Ed.), *The French revolution and modernity* (pp. 201-215). Berkeley: University of California Press; Habermas, J. (1988). *Structural transformation of the public sphere*. Cambridge: MIT Press; Howard, D. (1989). *Defining the political*. Minneapolis: University of Minnesota Press; Howard, D. (1985). *From Marx to Kant*. State University of New York Press; Howard, D. (1988). *The politics of critique*. Minneapolis: University of Minnesota Press; Kelly, G. A. (1969). *Idealism politics and history*. New York/Cambridge, UK: Cambridge University Press; Krieger, L. (1970). *Kings and philosophers 1689-1789*. New York: Norton; Krieger, L. (1957). *The German idea of freedom*. Boston: Beacon Press. Krieger, L. (1975). *An essay on the theory of enlightened despotism*. Chicago: University of Chicago Press; Luik, J. (1991). An old question raised again: Is Kant an enlightenment humanist? In D. Goicoechhea, J. Link, & T. Madigan, Eds., *The question of humanism* (pp. 117-137). Buffalo, NY: Prometheus; Makkreel, R. A. (1990). *Imagination and interpretation in Kant*. Chicago: University of Chicago Press; Nisbet, H. B. (1982). "Was ist Aufklarung?" The concept of enlightenment in eighteenth century Germany. *Journal of European Studies*, 77-95; O'Neill, O. (1989). *Constructions of reason*. New York/Cambridge, UK: Cambridge University Press; O'Neill, O. (1992). Vindicating reason. In P. Guyer (Ed.), *Cambridge companion to Kant* (pp. 280-308). New York/Cambridge, UK: Cambridge University Press, 1992; O'Neill, O. (1988). The public uses of reason. *Political Theory, 15*, 523-551 (reprinted in O'Neill, *Constructions of reason*, 28-51); Rundell, J. F. (1987). *Origins of modernity*. Madison; University of Wisconsin Press; Seebohm, T. (1988). Kant's theory of revolution. In R. Schurmann (Ed.), *The public realm* (pp. 60-82). Albany: State University of New York Press; Sullivan, R. J. (1989). *Immanuel Kant's moral theory*. New York/Cambridge, UK: Cambridge University Press, 1989; Williams, H. (1983). *Kant's political philosophy*. Cambridge, MA: Blackwell; Zammato, J. H. (1992). *The genesis of Kant's critique of judgment*. Chicago: University of Chicago Press.

18. Dietze, *Liberalism proper and proper liberalism*, p. 169.

19. Kant, *Political writings*, p. 188.

20. Derrida, J. (1992). Contest of the faculties. In R. Rand (Ed.), *Logomachia* (pp. 1-35). Lincoln: University of Nebraska Press; Derrida, J. (1983). The principle of reason: The university in the eye of its pupils. *Diacritics, 12*, 3-20; Fenves, P. (Ed.). (1992). *Raising the tone of philosophy*. Baltimore: Johns Hopkins University Press.

21. O' Neill, *Constructions of reason*, p. 48. See also Laursen, J. C. (1986). The subversive Kant: The vocabulary of "Public" and "Publicity". *Political Theory, 13*, 584-603.

22. Gay, *The enlightenment: Vol. 2*, pp. 517ff.

23. O'Neill, *Constructions of reason*, pp. 3-65.

24. Arendt, H. (1982). *Lectures on Kant's political philosophy*. Chicago: University of Chicago Press.

25. Beiner, R. (1983). *Political judgment*. Chicago: University of Chicago Press.

26. Caygill, H. (1989). Post-modernism and judgment. *Economy and Society, 16*, 1-20; Caygill, H. (1989). *The art of judgment*. Cambridge, MA: Blackwell.

27. Cohen, T., & Guyer, P. (Eds.). (1982). *Essays in Kant's aesthetics*. Chicago: University of Chicago Press.

28. Ingram, D. (1988). The postmodern Kantianism of Arendt and Lyotard. *Review of Metaphysics, 41*, 51-77.

29. Lyotard, J. F. (1989). *The differend*. Minneapolis: University of Minnesota Press.

30. Saner, H. (1982). *Kant's political philosophy*. Chicago: University of Chicago Press.

31. Lyotard, *The differend*; Carrol, D. (1987). *Paraesthetics*. New York: Routledge.

32. O'Neill, *Constructions of reason*, p. 25.

33. Goldmann, L. (1971). *Immanuel Kant*. New York: New Left Books; Howard, *Defining the political*; Williams, X. (1983). *Kant's political philosophy*. Cambridge, MA: Blackwell; Laski, H. J. (1936). *The rise of European liberalism*. Winchester, MA: Unwin Hyman; Marcuse, H. (1972). *Studies in critical theory*. Boston: Beacon Press.

34. Laursen, The subversive Kant, p. 593.

35. Rundell, J. F. (1987) *The origins of modernity*. Madison: University of Wisconsin Press; Chapter 1.

36. Gay, *The enlightenment: Vol. 2*, pp. 517-28; Riedel, M. (1981). Transcendental politics? Political legitimacy and the concept of civil society in Kant. *Social Research, 48*(3), 588-613.

37. Foucault, M. (1984). What is enlightenment? In P. Rabinow (Ed.), *The Foucault reader* (pp. 32-50). New York: Pantheon, p. 43.

38. Foucault, M. (1986). Kant on enlightenment and revolution. *Economy and Society, 14*, 93.

39. Foucault, M. (1978). Introduction. In G. Canguilhem, *On the normal and the pathological* (p. xii). Cambridge, MA: Reidel.

40. Rabinow, P. (Ed.). (1984). *The Foucault reader*. New York: Pantheon, p. 42.

41. Foucault, M. (1988). Critical theory/intellectual history. In M. Foucault, *Politics, philosophy, culture* (pp. 17-47). New York: Routledge 1988; Foucault, Kant on enlightenment and revolution; Rabinow, *The Foucault reader*.

42. Foucault, Introduction.

43. Rabinow, The Foucault Reader, 43ff.

44. Dreyfus, H., & Rabinow, P. (1986). What is maturity? Habermas and Foucault on "What is enlightenment?" In D. Hoy (Ed.). *Foucault: A critical reader* (pp. 109-21). Cambridge, MA: Blackwell; Flax, J. (1992). Is enlightenment eman-

cipatory? A feminist reading of "What is enlightenment?" In F. Barker, P. Hulme & M. Iverson (Eds.), *Postmodernism and the re-reading of modernity* (pp. 232-249). New York: Manchester University Press and St. Martins; Flynn, T. R. (1989). Foucault and the politics of postmodernity. *Nous*, *22*, 187-98; Gordon, C. (1986). Question, ethos, event: Foucault on Kant and enlightenment. *Economy and Society*, *15*, 98-115; Hiley, D. R. (1985). Foucault and the question of enlightenment. *Philosophy and Social Criticism*, *12*, 63-83; McHugh, P. (1989). Dialectics, subjectivity and Foucault's ethos of modernity. *Boundary*, *2*, 91-108; Norris, C. (1993). What is enlightenment? Foucault on Kant. In *The truth about postmodernism* (pp. 29-99). Cambridge, MA: Blackwell.

45. Jacques Derrida in discussion with Christopher Norris. In A. Papadakis, C. Cooke, & A. Beryamm (Eds.), *Deconstruction: Omnibus volume*. New York: Rizzoli, p. 75.

46. Rieff, P. (1979). *Freud: the mind of the moralist* (4th ed.). Chicago: University of Chicago Press; Freud, S. (1964). New introductory lectures on psychoanalysis. In S. Freud, *The complete introductory lectures on psychoanalysis* (pp. 622-46.) New York: Norton.

47. Nancy, J. L. (1990). Our probity. In L. Rickels (Ed.), *Looking after Nietzsche* (pp. 67-87). Albany: State University of New York Press.

48. Foucault, M. (1983). On the genealogy of ethics. In H. Dreyfus & P. Rabinow, *Michel Foucault: Beyond structuralism and hermeneutics* (rev. ed.) (pp. 229-253). Chicago: University of Chicago Press.

49. Megill, A. (1985). *Prophets of extremity*. Berkeley: University of California Press.

50. Calinescu, M. (1985). The end of man in twentieth-century thought. In S. Friedlander, G. Holton, L. Marx, & E. Skolnikoff (Eds.), *Vision of apocalypse*. (pp. 171-95). New York: Homes and Meier; Derrida, J. (1982). Of an apocalyptic tone recently adopted in philosophy. *Semia*, 63-97; Norris, C. (1986). On Derrida's "apocalyptic tone." *Southern Review*, 13-29; Norris, C. (1987). Derrida and Kant: The enlightenment tradition. In C. Norris, *Derrida* (pp. 142-72). Cambridge, MA: Harvard University Press; Watson, S. (1987). Kant and Derrida at the end of metaphysics. In J. Sallis (Ed.), *Deconstruction and philosophy* (pp. 71-86). Chicago: University of Chicago Press.

51. Bennington, G. (1988). *Writing the event*. New York: Columbia University Press; Bernstein, R. (1992). Serious play: The ethic-political horizons of Derrida's philosophy. In R. Bernstein, *The new constellation* (pp. 172-98). Cambridge: MIT Press; Carroll, D. (1989). *Paraesthetics*. New York: Routledge; Derrida, J. (1988). The politics of friendship. *Journal of Philosophy*, *85*, 632-644; Lyotard, J. F. Judiciousness in dispute, or Kant after Marx. (1989). In A. Benjamin (Ed.), *The Lyotard reader*. Cambridge, MA: Blackwell; Lyotard, J. F., & Thebaud, J. L. (1985). *Just gaming*. Minneapolis: University of Minnesota Press. Readings, B. (1990). *Introducing Lyotard*. New York: Routledge.

2

MODERNITY

Modernity[1] began at about the time of Francis Bacon in the late 16th century; even earlier, according to some writers.[2] It is characterized as the period of the "quarrel between the ancients and the moderns"[3] that manifested the struggle of science and the political philosophy of individualism against the wisdom of the ancients.

Modernity as a Philosophical Concept

Philosophers often believe that Descartes was the founder of philosophical modernity, but Bacon,[4] Hobbes,[5] and Machiavelli[6] also address the key issues of modernity: the nature of knowledge and modern methodology (Descartes); science as power (Bacon); political individualism, the newly emerging state and the science of human nature (Hobbes); and the nature of modern power politics (Machiavelli).

Bacon's[7] notion of knowledge as power, of putting nature on the rack, marks a significant point of departure from the ancients, for whom knowledge of nature consisted of passive understanding of a world that cannot be changed. For Bacon, knowledge is tantamount to control and prediction, so knowledge can increase only as humankind's power over nature does. Bacon's idea that knowledge exists to promote the relief of the human estate is the first step in the direction of technocracy, scientific utopianism, and social engineering; the reduction of the practical and moral to the technical; and thus, arguably, the beginning of modern instrumental or technological rationality.

Hobbes,[8] to some extent following Machiavelli, develops the canonical conception of human nature during much of modernity, with its attendant disciplines of the social and behavioral sciences. In tandem with this new conception of the individual, modern political ("possessive") individualism,[9] social contract theory, and modern liberal political theory all began with Hobbes.

Hobbes sought to model human behavior on the newly emerging science of physics. His materialism, the idea that human beings are complex physical systems, had profound effects on the social sciences. But Hobbes is also the founder of rational choice theory. He ascribes the causes of human behavior to pleasure and pain, believing that these stimuli must be tempered by reason. Rational self-interest is necessary because we live in a world of scarce resources in which all people have roughly equal powers and desires; to avoid a "war of all against all," the state of nature, human beings enter into a social contract. Exchange theory is born: Each party to the contract trades license for security. Freedom becomes rational self-interest, defined as a calculation of one's self-interest and the most cost-efficient ways of obtaining it. Reasoning becomes reckoning.

For Hobbes, human behavior is thus predictable and controllable. Self-development is defined as the maximization of personal utility, governed by rational choice. Much of modern economics and psychology, including the "law of effect," the "principle of rationality,"[10] and modern behavioristic conceptions of the self,[11] stem from Hobbes. Hobbes was also the first to address the problem of "social order," which is more recently debated in conflict versus consensual models of modern society in Parsons, Freud, and others.[12]

Modernity in the Age of Enlightenment

In the 18th century, Smith incorporated Hobbes's theories into *The Wealth of Nations*, but he gave Hobbes's egoism a moral coloring by developing the idea of "private vices, public virtues" from Mandeville and others.[13] Rational self-interest becomes a moral virtue. Society is understood as the net result of rational selfishness through the mechanism of the "invisible hand," or the unintended consequences of intentional action. The resulting model of "public choice," which Arrow has proven to be, at best, severely limited,[14] remains the basic model of social choice today.

Other thinkers developed more "altruistic" models of utilitarianism, but they accepted Hobbes's conception of human nature. Education (in more recent times, behavioral engineering) would convince people that it is in each person's enlightened self-interest to care about others and to take the general welfare into account when acting. Cost-benefit analysis was born when Bentham developed his calculus of pleasure and pain.[15]

The result was the development of the modern liberal theory of society, politics, and individual development. Society is a Newtonian machine; each person is an atom, whose behavior is governed by Hobbes's principles of human nature and whose interactions can be explained by the laws of psychology. Society is viewed as an aggregation of individuals that tends toward equilibrium if left to its own devices. Parsonian systems theory is the culmination of this theory.

Descartes was the architect of the modern idea that "method" is the road to knowledge and truth. He canonized Galileo's notions of objectivity and subjectivity for the modern world. One of the ramifications of this view is the idea of value freedom in the social sciences: Whatever can be known must be proven by a "rational, objective" method. Value claims cannot be so proven; therefore value judgments do not constitute knowledge or belong in the realm of science. This argument requires many refinements and embellishments. Distinctions between types of value judgments were made by later writers. The outcome is that either value judgments can be "naturalized," in which case ethics becomes a branch of applied science (cost-benefit analysis, utilitarianism, rational choice theory, the policy sciences), or value judgments are subjective and belong outside the sciences, even the social sciences. Strictly speaking, according to this view, interpretations, mentalistic and teleological vocabularies, are also subjective, or at least untestable, and they, too, have no place in science. This view leads to positivism and behaviorism, strict applications of the notion that the social and behavioral sciences are branches of physics.

For Descartes, the "objective" is essentially that part of the world that can be described in what he calls "nature's language," the language of mathematical physics. Nothing else is objective. Perceptions, values, interpretations, perspectives, and all other mental languages cannot describe objective reality. Although Descartes does not explicitly draw all of these conclusions, later thinkers draw out the implicit logic of his arguments largely because of his belief in the immaterial and immortal soul. Objective reality, Galileo's "primary qualities," causes our individual perceptions, which are subjective and vary from person to person. Only the quantifiable data of physical reality are objective. To discover the truths about this reality, we need a method, which must itself be rational and objective, where objective now means disinterested, not tainted by values, interpretations, perspectives, or psychological or other factors. Leibniz, in "Toward a Universal Characteristic,"[16] argues that someday all human problems will be solved by a mechanical algorithm, an idea of tremendous import until this century, when Godel demonstrated this goal to be impossible. Godel's results influenced the role of indeterminacy in Lyotard and Derrida. If the age-old dream of starting from self-evident axioms or irrefutable observations of phenomena and proving everything within a determinate system is impossible, then the question remains how determinate, provable, and systematic knowledge can be.

For Descartes, only rigorous methodological objectivity permits the acquisition of objective knowledge and truth. But to achieve this result, the human enquirer must become objective, and the human body and all subjective qualities must be set aside in the process. Objectivity requires a God's-eye view of the world and ourselves; we must develop a view from nowhere[17] to achieve objective knowledge. Descartes thinks that one can salvage religion, morality, and even social customs and traditions from total destruction, but his arguments reflect internal inconsistency, if not disingenuousness. Later writers have fewer qualms about eliminating customs and values that could not be reduced to science or scientific method. Despite Kant's valiant efforts to reconcile science, religion, morality, and a teleological conception of nature, attempts within modernity to unify human experience have failed. The dualisms of facts and values, the objective and subjective, science and the rest of culture, and reason and emotions have persisted. Perhaps postmodernists such as Derrida can do a better job than Hegel in overcoming or defusing these dualisms of modernity.

These philosophical themes are of the first importance for understanding modernity, and they play a continual role in the remainder of this book. As Chapter 1 argues, modern social science, especially sociology, is born out of a concern to understand and come to grips with modernity. We should expect to learn more about modernity by focusing on sociological theories about it. The next section discusses the social scientific characterization of modernity and the twists and turns it has taken since the 18th century.

Modernity as a Sociological/Historical Category

The sociological notion of modernity is based on the idea of traditional societies, societies with relatively small, homogeneous populations, without a sharp division of labor (structural and functional differentiation) or a market economy (capitalism) that are not industrialized, and where tradition, custom, and religion play the dominant role. By contrast, modern societies are highly industrialized, have a capitalist economy (market or otherwise), have highly specific social differentiation and large, heterogeneous populations, are increasingly dominated by science and technology, and are more or less secularized. *Modernization* is the name for the process whereby a society is transformed from traditional or premodern to modern.

Generally, modernity means the rise of industry, cities, market capitalism, the bourgeois family, growing secularization, democratization, and social legislation. The old order of church and king was transformed not just by the French and Industrial Revolutions, but also by the institutional and valuational changes that modernization brought about. Modernization created a different world. Societies were no longer small, homogeneous, kin-based communities (usually rural) where age-old traditions guided human life as always. The modern world is increasingly a society of strangers, of large populations and huge geographical areas, of plurality and heterogeneity in religion and culture, of urban blight and poverty. Modern societies as we know them began in the 19th century.

Although many changes occurred during the 19th and 20th centuries, especially the decline of the traditional family and church and the rise of voluntary associations and occupational groups, modernization primarily occurred during the aftermath of the French Revolution and the first Industrial Revolution in England. The scientific revolutions of the 17th century and the emergence of the modern bourgeois state, economy, and society mark the earliest beginnings of modernization. But it was not until the 19th century that modernity brought about (in social science terms) the age of the *Gesellschaft*, further endangering the *Gemeinschaft*.

Gesellschaft and Gemeinschaft

The distinction between Gesellschaft and Gemeinschaft, made famous by Tonnies[18] but found in various writers since Rousseau and Hegel, is highly problematic. The appearance of this dualism marks the rise of the characteristic modern attitudes of optimism and pessimism, ideology, nostalgic longing for premodernity, and socialist visions of utopia that have dominated most of the philosophy, literature, and social sciences within modernity.[19]

The notion that we need to return to some form of a Gemeinschaft, or premodern community, persists in modern thinking. Such as community is envisioned as the Golden Age of classical Athens favored by the romantics, Nietzsche, and Heidegger; or the Florence of the Renaissance favored by the 19th-century German historian Burkhardt. Hegel, Comte, Saint-Simon, Durkheim, and Parsons visualize modernity as a new type of Gemeinschaft that is both desirable and necessary.

The notion that all was wonderful in some real or imagined Gemeinschaft, or could be in a new one, and that things have been going downhill without one is little more than a nostalgic longing for something that never existed. The idea that modernity ruined heaven on earth and that we need to recover or at least emulate one of these Gemeinschafte to overcome modernity's alienation may better be addressed by psychoanalytic theory or deconstructionism than by serious historical or philosophical examination. In fact Freud does psychoanalyze this longing in

"The Uncanny," where the longing symbolizes a desire to return to the womb.[20] Postmodernists such as Derrida attack this nostalgia as both false and harmful. Even if there was ever such a Gemeinschaft, its feasibility and desirability in the modern world, with all the attendant complexities and diversities, is by no means obvious.

The notion of a Gesellschaft as a form of association between strangers also persists in discussions of modernity. But the evil ascribed to it by romantics and other modern writers including Marx) may be equally false and dangerous. The supposed evils of Gesellschaft are connected with the general outlook of the rural on the urban, because the rural is the locus of the Gemeinschaft in the modern world, while the modern city is the essence of the Gesellschaft. The model of Gemeinschaft based on primary group relations of solidarity (kith and kin) does and can exist in the modern world, as Hegel makes clear in his distinction between civil society and the state. Does Gemeinschaft promise to be a good model for modern society? Arguably, Hitler's notion of Das Volk in *Mein Kampf*,[21] with its clear implication that strangers are like a cancer that need to be eliminated for the vitality of the community, is the culmination of this ideal. Conversely, the modern Gemeinschafte that do exist—churches, families, professional groups—also have Gesellschaft-like properties, as anybody who writes a check to their church or synagogue will attest. The ideal types of Gemeinschaft and Gesellschaft should not be pushed too far as models of ideology and utopia, much less as models for modernity in general. At the same time, even though modern societies, for both good and ill, may be predominantly Gesellschafte, it is not unreasonable to think of some associations as better served by a Gemeinschaft model.

It is not a coincidence that most critics of modernity and the excesses of the Enlightenment, including Marx, modern conservatives,[22] most romantics and "neoidealists,"[23] Simmel, Weber, the young Lukacs, Tonnies, and Dilthey,[24] have shared a vision of some sort of Gemeinschaft. Both the left and the right have had a nostalgic longing for Gemeinschaft since the dawn of modern society, a longing that has been used as a standard for judging the modern world as corrupt, even rotten. What is it about the modern world of capitalism, democracy, science, and liberalism that both the left and right abhor?

It probably has something to do with alienation, with the notion that in the modern world the self is fragmented, as society is fragmented, into the spheres of art, science, morality, politics, and law. The world has become rationalized, disenchanted, complex, and ambivalent, and modern economic life is dehumanizing. Coupled with this is the recognition that the traditional family, moral values, the church—all the older sources of consolation—are gone or unavailing. In Nietzsche's terminology, "God is dead," the old tablets are in pieces, and there are no healthy cultural horizons to give meaning to life, death, toil, and suffering (or, for that matter, success and rewards). Like the priest in Brecht's *Galileo*,[25] critics of modernity believe that modern science and secularization, indeed everything in modernity, make life meaningless, give rise to massive alienation, and provide no sources of consolation.

Of course, others see the more positive aspects of modernity: the advances in modern medicine, the relative absence of back-breaking labor, the wealth of capitalism, universal education, science and technology, the elimination or at least diminution of various miseries and superstitions, the relative success of modern democracy.

The Categories of Modernity

The various responses to modernity within the social science traditions can be grouped into several broad categories.

   A. Modernity is uniformly good, and traditional societies are uniformly bad (e.g., Saint-Simon, Comte, positivists, Parsons).
   B. Modernity is uniformly bad, and traditional societies are good (e.g., Heidegger, the romantics, Tonnies, Simmel, Heidegger, the "reactionary modernists").[26]
   C. Modernity is ambivalent; critics draw uncertain conclusions concerning modernity and premodernity (e.g., Weber, Marx, Freud, Hegel, Nietzsche, Habermas, recent work by Baumann and Levine).[27]
   D. Modernity is different but potentially beneficial, and a new form of Gemeinschaft will emerge from modernity (e.g., Durkheim, Giddens).

E. The conflicts about modernity and traditional societies need to be overcome, and we should move away from the optimism and the pessimism, the ideology and the utopia, that go with the territory (e.g., the postmodernists).

Aestheticism stems from romanticism and is discussed in Chapter 3. (For another typology of modernity, see Stauth and Turner[28].)

The issue of modernity also finds expression in the title of Blumenberg's book, *The Legitimacy of the Modern Age*.[29] Is modernity "legitimate" or not? If modernity needs to be judged and validated, how is this to be done? Does the question allow anything other than a categorical response? Is it assumed that premodern or traditional societies are legitimate? What does that mean?

"Legitimacy" might suggest that human life and history clearly have meaning and purpose within traditional societies and the meaning of life is at issue in modern society. But surely modern societies have been legitimated by philosophies of history, from Bacon through Hegel and Comte to Parsons.[30] Perhaps the demand that modernity legitimate itself is a demand for a certain kind of philosophy of history: a theodicy, which invokes God's purpose. Even here, modernity has this justification, notably in Hegel. Perhaps the key idea is suggested by Habermas in *Legitimation Crisis*:[31] that people must feel or believe that the practices, institutions, and values of modernity are meaningful. The so-called crisis of modernity is that people feel this meaningfulness less and less often, so modern culture is not providing the sort of spiritual legitimacy that is necessary for the economic and political spheres of modern society to be accepted as legitimate.

Preoccupation with the demand for legitimacy is characteristic of many modern writers, including Weber, Durkheim, Parsons, and Habermas. Only the postmodernists, influenced by Nietzsche and Freud, abandon the demand for legitimacy. They reject the presumption that it is appropriate, indeed meaningful, to talk about legitimacy or illegitimacy. They reject the idea that we should somehow legitimate ourselves. In Blumenberg's terminology, postmodernists accept the idea that modernists want self-assertion without self-grounding. According to Lyotard, modernists have abandoned the demand for philosophical or religious or historical metanarratives. Writers such as Nietzsche, Freud, and Heidegger (who is an antimodernist) insist on a kind of self-grounding; this could be one reason why they are not postmodernists. The issue is whether postmodernists can abandon these requirements for the sake of a radical ethos of modernity. If not, what lessons should we draw from their failure to do so? If so, do they represent a different stance toward modernity, that of Olympian detachment, or a set of doctrines that denotes the "post" of postmodernity?

The remainder of this chapter discusses the categories of modernity described above. The crisis of legitimacy is discussed in the appropriate context.

Promodernists

The idealized version of a promodernity approach is that modernity is, on the whole, good or beneficial. The foremost proponents of this view are Comte, Saint-Simon, Parsons, and many positivists.

Promodernists believe that the Enlightenment is both unproblematic and is being realized in human history. Human societies are evolving from the mythical to the philosophical to the scientific. The main cause of human misery—ignorance in the form of religion, myth, custom, and tradition—is being gradually eliminated or at least rationalized or marginalized. Modern science and technology are proceeding, and human progress is being gradually realized. Modern societies, which are becoming more secularized and rationalized, are proceeding with the Baconian goal of relieving the human estate. The modern division of labor and the spheres of modernity, science, culture, and politics are moving forward so that all spheres of human life are becoming more rational and enlightened. In this view, objections to problems in modernity reflect a nostalgic yearning for some relatively primitive stage of social evolution, which is irretrievable. The modern social system is more or less self-correcting, so the problems that arise will be corrected by the operations of those very features of modern societies that constitute modernity. The development of specialization, expertise, and a morally neutral, reformist elite will mean further human progress.

Antimodernists

The extreme opposite view, antimodernity, criticizes those aspects of modernity that promodernists defend: industrialization, the division of labor, the fragmentation of life and culture, secularization, urbanization, the growing dominance of science and technology. One can find this attitude in the Romantics, both German and English (as well as in Thoreau and Emerson); in the attitudes and policies of the conservative reaction and Restoration period in Germany and France (D'Maistre);[32] in late 19th-century historicism and Weltanschauung philosophy (Dilthey); in the writings of some of the neo-Kantians who influenced Weber and Heidegger;[33] in the "romantic anti-capitalists"[34] (Simmel, early Lukacs); in the recently labeled "reactionary modernists" (Spengler, Junger, Speer); and in the first-generation Frankfurt school theorists (Benjamin, Horkheimer, and Adorno).[35] The negative stance toward modernity is given canonical expression by Tonnies in *Community and Society*, although later writers emphasize issues that are either absent from or not as pronounced in Tonnies; for example, instrumental rationality, modern bureaucracy and technology, and value pluralism.

Much of the antimodern literature is also premodern in its outlook; it embodies what has been called the sociology of nostalgia.[36] Modernity is measured against some notion, real or imagined, of a stage of society Tonnies characterizes as Gemeinschaft. But there is no evidence that such communities ever existed in quite the form imagined by modern writers such as Tonnies, nor do these writers address the dark side of such communities: slavery, superstition, violence, health and sanitation problems, intolerance for deviants, and rigidity and stagnation.

Although the problems of modernity should not be ignored, we need to ask why this nostalgic view of the past, with its accompanying view that the modern world is rotten to the core, has taken hold among a group of intelligent and historically astute writers whose political leanings range from reaction to anarchism and whose cultural proclivities range from elitist to democratic.

A number of explanations have been offered.

- The German mandarins and other cultural elites did not want the old order to die since they played an important role in it.[37]

- The romantic anticapitalists had religious motives for rejecting modernity.[38]
- Psychological[39] factors were in play: these writers, and people of like minds, could not cope with the complexities of modern life; the transformations that occurred during modernization, as well as the result, overwhelmed antimodern thinkers, whose only recourse was to some ideological (in Mannheim's sense) vision of a simpler, more tranquil society and way of life.

There is surely some truth to these explanations. But do they prove that the antimodernists have no case? One could argue that the polarities between tradition and modernity are "misplaced," as Gusfield does.[40] Perhaps the mutual exclusiveness of the dualism between traditional and modern societies is fallacious. Granting this point, and acknowledging the efforts to explain the sociology of nostalgia, can one make a case on behalf of this group? One could adopt the messianism of Benjamin[41] and argue that this nostalgia is really a wish for a form of utopia that has never been actualized but whose revolutionary potential exists and must be kept alive. However, this position is only a form of antimodernist pessimism.

Ambivalent About Modernity

It might be more helpful to consider the antimodernity arguments in the context of the writers who regard modernity as ambivalent. Some proponents in this group, notably Weber, incorporate many of the antimodern arguments. In addition, there seems to be more plausibility in the ambivalent stance than in the antimodernist stance.

There are two versions of the ambivalent view of modernity. The optimistic account holds that modernity gives us possibilities for development that did not exist before. Modernity allows us to continue to develop ourselves and our species in new and exciting ways. The dark side of modernity must either be balanced against these possibilities or be viewed as part of the inevitable tensions and dynamics of modern life, tensions that make modernity more fluid and more enabling than earlier stages of social development. This view is defended most forcefully by Baumann,[42] Berman,[43] Coser,[44] Gergen,[45] Giddens,[46] Hardison,[47] and Levine,[48] as well as by Bell, whose views are discussed in later chapters. Marx also belongs in this camp, since his analyses of modern societies, the advantages and limits of capitalism, and the prospects for the future unquestionably embody optimism. The possibilities for surpassing the shortcomings of capitalist society, for "humanizing nature and naturalizing humans," Marx's promethean ideal, make Marx a proponent of the ambivalent attitude.

The pessimistic version includes many antimodernists who either influenced or were influenced by Weber: Simmel, early Lukacs, and the first-generation Frankfurt theorists, especially Adorno, Horkheimer, and Benjamin; Freud;[49] and perhaps some of the so-called reactionary modernists, who wanted to deploy modern technology in the interests of premodernism.[50] This view defines modernity as the entwinement of Calvinism and capitalism, along with science and bureaucracy, governed by instrumental rationality. Though society has made advances through rationalization and calculation, the dark side of modernity threatens to overpower the advantages and imprison us in an "iron cage." The spiritual, ethical, and communal aspects of life are threatened by instrumental rationality, technology, bureaucracy, and "specialists without spirit."[51] Individuals must lead fragmented lives governed by conflicting values or at least must choose instrumental rationality to cope while abandoning the values of tradition and feelings. In this view, the question is open whether the dark side of modernity will win the day or whether the possibilities for human liberation and life enhancement will prevail.

For Nietzsche,[52] human life is always ambivalent; every moment of human greatness is intertwined with barbarism. Modernity, which culminates in nihilism and the decline of healthy culture, brings with it the possibility of overcoming nihilism and the creation of new values that are healthier than the values of Christianity, democracy, and socialism. Nietzsche agrees with Marx that there are positive benefits to the fact that in modernity, "all that is solid melts into air."[53]

For Weber,[54] modernity is an iron cage: A rationalized, secularized world that is irrational from the perspective of every other known civilization, including earlier societies of the West, and from the viewpoints of substantive rationality (affective, traditional, idealistic). Yet this very iron cage makes it possible for the Lutheran ideal of the calling or vocation to be subjectively infused into the life of the individual in terms of "life choices"; even the scientist and the politician in the modern world can have a vocation and be responsible for their individual fates by reconciling the ethics of conviction or ultimate ends with the ethics of responsibility or consequences. This may give breathing room for the free and rational self in the iron cage and may allow modern individuals to "meet the demands of the day" in a responsible way. For Weber, as for Freud and perhaps for Nietzsche, this may be the best that we can hope for in modernity, or at least the best the leading scientists, scholars, and philosophers can hope for. The masses must still "shut up and obey" because they are dangerous and incapable of self-governance.[55]

The ethos of the Enlightenment sometimes leads to elitism. Chapters 9 and 10 discusses whether the postmodernists, in carrying forward this ethos from Nietzsche, Weber, and Freud but without their optimism or the pessimism, can avoid the same result.

Certainly the Frankfurt school writers—Horkheimer, Adorno, Marcuse, Benjamin—do not avoid either pessimism or elitism in their analyses of the mass culture industry and their defense of high culture.[56] In a sense, they combine the arguments of Marx, Weber, and Nietzsche, but they reach even more pessimistic conclusions. Given the historical situation in Germany in the 1930s (most of them were Jewish), it is understandable that they approach antimodernists, except that they always held out some hope, no matter how faint, for modernity and the project of Enlightenment.

Habermas defends a version of ambivalence about modernity against the pessimistic version by developing a theory of "selective evolution" that explains why and to what extent Weber and the others are right about developments in modernity but wrong in their pessimistic judgments about modernity.[57] Part of his strategy is to attack the philosophy of consciousness that underlies the pessimistic and the optimistic versions of the ambivalence about modernity. In doing so, Habermas addresses the major themes about modernism taken up in Chapter 3: humanism and subjective consciousness.

Modernity Is Different

The view that modernity is different is most forcefully expressed by Durkheim, especially in *The Division of Labor in Society.*[58] Traditional societies exhibit "mechanical solidarity." Modern societies exhibit "organic solidarity." Following Hegel, Comte, Saint-Simon, and Spencer, Durkheim argues that modern societies will evolve into organic unities where civil society, the state, market economies, and rational individuals will be coordinated by professional groups to form something like Hegel's corporate state. Durkheim believes this society will be a version of the organic model of community that for Tonnies and others defines the traditional Gemeinschaft. Durkheim thus marks the beginnings of modern structural-functionalism and a systems view of society, which culminates in Parsons. For Durkheim, modern organic solidarity is qualitatively different from the (alleged) mechanical solidarity of traditional societies, but it is no less real or no less a genuine Gemeinschaft.

Unfortunately, Durkheim's optimism has not been realized to the extent he envisioned. Writers such as Bell argue that the newly emerging postindustrial society will be a Durkheimian community.[59] Even if this is true, it may turn out to be a dangerous idea.

Postmodernists

As for the postmodernists, Lyotard, Foucault, Derrida, and Baudrillard are discussed throughout this book. Suffice it to say that the writers from the above categories that have been most influential in the social sciences all presume some sort of contrast between the modern and the premodern. All take for granted the legitimacy of the need either to defend or to attack modernity. All share a desire to give comprehensive explanations of modernity and to treat its characteristic qualities in a unified theoretical way. And all exhibit some form of the optimism versus pessimism and good versus bad dualisms. Even those who are ambivalent about modernity support these dualisms, albeit in more nuanced ways. The postmodernists suggest that the only way out of the never-ending debates about the "legitimacy of the modern age" is to radicalize the idea that modernity is ambivalent by getting rid of all the assumptions, labels, and judgments that give rise to these dualisms and by applying the radical ethos of the Enlightenment to the sociological and historical lessons that modernists have drawn from the analysis of modern society.

Notes

1. Kosellnick, R. (1985). *Futures past*. Cambridge: MIT Press.

2. Blumenberg, H. (1983). *The legitimacy of the modern age*. Cambridge: MIT Press. See also Ingram, D. (1987). Blumenberg and the philosophical grounds of historiography. *History and Theory*, *27*, 1-15; Jay, M. (1988). Blumenberg and modernism: A reflection on the legitimacy of the modern age. In M. Jay, *Fin de siecle socialism* (pp. 149-64). New York: Routledge; Pippin, R. (1987). Blumenberg and the modernity problem. *Review of Metaphysics*, *40*, 535-57;

3. Jones, R. F. (1961). *Ancients and moderns*. Mineola, NY: Dover.

4. Whitney, C. (1986). *Francis Bacon and modernity*. New Haven, CT: Yale University Press.

5. Kraynak, R. P. (1991). *History and modernity in the thought of Thomas Hobbes*. Ithaca, NY: Cornell University Press.

6. Machiavelli, N. (1961). *The prince*. New York: Penguin.

7. Bacon, F. (1960). *Novum organon*. Indianapolis: Bobbs-Merrill; Bacon, F. (1980). *The great insaturation and the new Atlantis*. Arlington Heights, FL: Harlan.

8. Hobbes, T. (1986). *Leviathan*. New York: Macmillan.

9. McPherson, C. B. (1962). *The political theory of possessive individualism*. New York: Oxford University Press.

10. Homans, G. (1967). *The nature of the social science*. New York: Harcourt Brace and Company.

11. Taylor, C. (1989). *Sources of the self*. Cambridge, MA: Harvard University Press.

12. Collins, R. (1985). *Three sociological traditions*. New York: Oxford University Press; and Rhoads, J. (1991). *Critical issues in social theory*. University Park: Pennsylvania State University Press.

13. Smith, A. (1985). *The wealth of nations*. New York: Random House. See also Hirschman, A. (1976). *The passions and the interests*. Princeton, NJ: Princeton University Press; Pockock, J. (1976). *The Machiavellian moment*. Princeton, NJ: Princeton University Press; and Pockock, J. (1985). *Virtue, commerce and industry*. New York/Cambridge, UK: Cambridge University Press.

14. Arrow, K. (1963). *Social choice and individual values*. New Haven, CT: Yale University Press. For summaries of Arrow's argument, see Hardin, R. Rational choice theory. In T. Ball (Ed.). (1987). *Idioms of inquiry* (pp. 67-94). Albany: State University of New York Press.

15. Bentham, J. (1970). *Principles of morals and legislation.* New York: Free Press.
16. Leibniz, G. W. (1951). Toward a universal characteristic. In P. Wiener (Ed.), *Leibniz: Selections* (pp. 17-25). New York: Scribner.
17. Nagel, T. (1986). *The view from nowhere.* New York: Oxford University Press. See also Putnam, H. (1987). *The many faces of realism.* Peru, IL: Open Court; Putnam, H. (1990). *Realism with a human face.* Cambridge, MA: Harvard University Press, and Putnam, H. (1992). *Renewing philosophy.* Cambridge, MA: Harvard University Press; and Rorty, R. (1982). Introduction. In R. Rorty, *Consequences of pragmatism* (pp. xiii-xlvii). Minneapolis: University of Minnesota Press.
18. Tonnies, F. (1957). *Community and society.* New York: HarperCollins.
19. Koselleck, R. (1988). *Critique and crisis.* Cambridge: MIT Press; Mannheim, K. (1936). *Ideology and utopia.* New York: Harcourt Brace and Company; Megill, *Prophets of extremity*; Yack, B. (1985). *The longing for total revolution.* Princeton, NJ: Princeton University Press.
20. Freud, S. (1963). The uncanny. In S. Freud, *Studies in parapsychology* (pp. 122-61). New York: Norton.
21. Hitler, A. (1986). *Mein kampf.* Newport Beach, CA: Noontide Press; Mosse, G. L. (Ed.). (1981). *Nazi culture.* New York: Schocken.
On Heidegger, see Neske, G., & Kettering, E. (Eds.). (1990). *Martin Heidegger and national socialism.* New York: Paragon House; Rockmore, T., & Margolis, J. (Eds.). (1992). *The Heidegger case.* Philadelphia: Temple University Press; Wolin, R. (Ed.). (1991). *The Heidegger controversy.* New York: Columbia University Press.
22. Berlin, I. (1991). Joseph D'Maistre and origins of fascism. In I. Berlin, *Crooked timbre of humanity* (pp. 91-175). New York: Knopf. See also Nisbet, R. (1978). Conservatism. In T. Bottomore & R. Nisbet (Eds.), *A history of sociological analysis* (pp. 80-117). New York: Basic Books; and O'Sullivan, N. K. (1976). *Conservatism.* New York: St. Martin's.
23. Arato, A. (1974). The neo-idealist defense of subjectivity. *Telos, 16*, 108-61; and Lowy, M. (1984). Figures of romantic anti-capitalism. *New German Critique, 10*, 42-96.
24. Ringer, F. (1967). *Decline of the German mandarins.* Cambridge, MA: Harvard University Press.
25. Brecht, B. (1966). *Galileo.* New York: Grove.
26. Herf, J. (1984). *Reactionary modernism.* New York/Cambridge, UK: Cambridge University Press; and Zimmerman, M. E. (1989). *Heidegger's confrontation with modernity.* Bloomington: Indiana University Press.
27. Baumann, Z. (1991). *Modernity and ambivalence.* Ithaca, NY: Cornell University Press; and Levine, D. (1984). *The flight from ambiguity.* Chicago: University of Chicago Press.
28. Stauth, G., & Turner, B. (1988). *Nietzsche's dance.* Cambridge, MA: Blackwell, pp. 216-20.
29. Blumenberg, *Legitimacy of the modern age.*
30. Lowith, K. (1949). *Meaning in history.* Chicago: University of Chicago Press.
31. Habermas, J. (1975). *Legitimation crisis.* Boston: Beacon Press.
32. See note 22.

33. Arato, The neo-idealist defense of subjectivity; Barash, J. A. (1988). *Martin Heidegger and the problem of historical meaning*. Hingham, MA/The Hague, The Netherlands: Martinus Nijhoff; Gillespie, M. A. (1984). *Hegel, Heidegger and the ground of history*. Chicago: University of Chicago Press.

34. Lowy, M. *Figures of romantic anti-capitalism*.

35. Connerton, P. (1980). *The tragedy of enlightenment*. New York/Cambridge, UK: Cambridge University Press; Friedman, G. (1980). *The political philosophy of the Frankfurt school*. Ithaca, NY: Cornell University Press; and Herf, *Reactionary modernism*.

36. Stauth & Turner, *Nietzsche's dance*; Turner, B. (1986). Against nostalgia: Talcott Parsons and a sociology for the modern world. In J. Holton & B. Turner (Eds.), *Talcott Parsons on economy and society* (pp. 207-35). New York: Routledge.

37. Ringer, F. K. (1990). *Decline of the German mandarins*. Hanover, NH: University Press of New England.

38. Liebersohn, H. (1988). *Fate and utopia in German sociology: 1870-1923*. Cambridge: MIT Press.

39. Mitzman, A. (1971). *The iron cage*. New York: Grossett & Dunlap; Mitzman, A. (1973). *Sociology and estrangement*. New York: Knopf.

40. Gusfield, J. (1967). Tradition and modernity: Misplaced polarities in the study of social change. *American Journal of Sociology*, *72*, 351-62.

41. Wolin, R. (1982). *Walter Benjamin*. New York: Columbia University Press. See also Jay, M. (1984). *Marxism and totality*. Berkeley: University of California Press.

42. Bauman, Z. *Modernity and ambivalence*. Ithaca, NY: Cornell University Press.

43. Berman, M. (1982). *All that is solid melts into air*. New York: Simon & Schuster.

44. Coser, (1991). *In defense of modernity*. Stanford, CA: Stanford University Press.

45. Gergen, K. (1991). *The saturated self*. New York: Basic Books.

46. Giddens, A. (1989). *Consequences of modernity*. Stanford, CA: Stanford University Press; Giddens, A. (1991). *Modernity and self-identity*. Stanford, CA: Stanford University Press.

47. Hardison, O. B. (1984). *Entering the maze*. New York: Oxford University Press.

48. Levine, D. N. (1988). *Flight from ambiguity*. Chicago: University of Chicago Press.

49. Connerton, *Tragedy of enlightenment*; Friedman, *Political philosophy of the Frankfurt school*; Stauth & Turner, *Nietzsche's dance*.

50. Herf, J. (1986). *Reactionary modernism*. New York: Cambridge University Press.

51. Weber, M. (1976). *The protestant ethic and the spirit of capitalism*. New York: Macmillan, p. 182.

52. Ditwiler, B. (1990). *Friederich Nietzsche and the politics of aristocratic radicalism*. Chicago: University of Chicago Press; and Warren, M. (1989). *Nietzsche and political theory*. Cambridge: MIT Press.

53. On Marx, see Berman, *All that is solid*; Love, N. (1985). *Nietzsche, Marx and modernity*. New York: Columbia University Press.

54. Brubacker, R. (1983). *The limits of rationality*. Winchester, MA: Unwin Hyman; and Scaff, L. (1989). *Fleeing the iron cage*. Berkeley: University of California Press.

55. Beetham, D. (1984). *Max Weber's theory of modern politics*. Cambridge, UK: Polity; Freud, S. (1961). *The future of an illusion*. New York: Norton; Freud, S. (1962). *Civilization and its discontents*. New York: Norton; Weber, M. (1946). Politics as a vocation and Science as a vocation. In H. Gerth & C. W. Mills (Eds.), *From Max Weber* (pp. 77-128 and 129-58). New York: Oxford University Press. For an illustration of how elitism plays a role in critical theory, see Horkheimer, M. (1972). *Critical Theory*. New York: Seabury. For Nietzschean and Weberian influences on the Frankfurt school, see Friedman, *Political philosophy of the Frankfurt school*.

56. Held, D. (1990). *Introduction to critical theory*. Berkeley: University of California Press; Ingram, D. (1989). *Critical theory and philosophy*; New York: Paragon; Kellner, D. (1990). *Critical theory, Marxism and modernity*. Baltimore: Johns Hopkins University Press.

57. Habermas, J. (1989). *Theory of communicative action*. Boston: Beacon Press.

58. Durkheim, E. (1962). *The division of labor in society*. New York: Free Press. See also Durkheim, E. (1957/1992). *Professional ethics and civic morals*. New York: Routledge. For an interesting discussion on Durkheim and modernity, see Mestrovic, S. G. (1992). *Durkheim and postmodern culture*. New York: Aldine de Gruyter.

59. Bell, D. (1973). *The coming of post-industrial society*. New York: Basic Books; and Bell, D. (1978). *The cultural contradictions of capitalism*. New York: Basic Books.

3

MODERNISM

Just as there are a variety of views about modernity and a host of positions on it, the same diversity of views and positions exists about modernism. Narrowly defined, modernism (sometimes qualified by terms such as "late" or "high") refers to several movements and styles of literature, art, and architecture.[1] Broadly defined, modernism is the entire culture of modernity, including high modernism, which is complexly interrelated with modernity but not coextensive with it. The concern here is the broader cultural definition and its implications for the social sciences.

Cultural Modernism and Its Ambiguities

In an insightful paper titled "Modernity and Modernism, Postmodernity and Postmodernism,"[2] Schulte-Sasse observes that modernism should be seen as the "cultural precipitate" of modernity. This characterization is vague enough to leave room for maneuver, but it is not quite determinate enough to be helpful. Although Schulte-Sasse is aware of the ambivalence about modernism, echoing the ambivalence about modernity examined in Chapter 2, he is not as pointed in his articulation of this ambivalence as one would wish. Calinescu, in the best overall treatment of the subject, *Five Faces of Modernity*, talks about "two modernities," and says the following:

> It is impossible to say precisely when one can begin to speak of the existence of two distinct and bitterly conflicting modernities. What

is certain is that at some point during the first half of the 19th century an irreversible split occurred between modernity as a stage in the history of Western civilization—a product of scientific and technological progress, of the industrial revolution, of the sweeping economic and social changes brought about by capitalism—and modernity as an aesthetic concept. Since then, the relations between the two modernities have been irreducibly hostile, but not without allowing and even stimulating a variety of mutual influences in their rage for each other's destruction.

With regard to the first, bourgeois idea of modernity, we may say that it has by and large continued the outstanding traditions of earlier periods in the history of the modern idea. The doctrine of progress, the confidence in the beneficial possibilities of science and technology, the concern with time...the cult of reason, and the idea of freedom defined within the framework of an abstract humanism, but also the orientation toward pragmatism and the cult of action and success—all have been associated in various degrees with the battle for the modern and were kept alive and promoted as key values in the triumphant civilization established by the middle class.

By contrast, the other modernity, the one that was to bring into being the avant-gardes, was from its romantic beginnings inclined toward radical antibourgeois attitudes. It was disgusted with the middle class scale of values and expressed its disgust through the most diverse means, ranging from rebellion, anarchy, and apocalypticism to aristocratic self-exile. So, more than its positive aspirations...what defines cultural modernity is its outright rejection of bourgeois modernity, its consuming negative passion.[3]

This section elaborates on Calinescu's remarks (which show how disparate the uses of the terms "modernity" and "modernism" are). First, one needs to recall the division of modernity into spheres, science, politics and art. Modernism in the narrower definition may seem to be limited to the sphere of art. Certainly, the "art for art's sake" movement was so limited. But literary modernism is not always so confined; for example, there is a connection between politics and aesthetics in some literary works, and some avant-garde movements (surrealism, dadaism, cubism) reject the modern separation of spheres.

Second, modernism surely has something to do with what can be called "the philosophy of consciousness," "subjectivity," or "humanism." Third, as Calinescu,[4] Berman,[5] and others have made clear, Baudelaire's influential definition of modernism as a combination of the eternal and transitory appears paradoxical, because it combines a concern for the new and the transient with the eternal. Perhaps Baudelaire is echoing Nietzsche's idea that being and becoming are identical, so the present moment and the eternal are one. But the "experience of modernity," which defines modernism for Berman, Simmel,[6] and (in Berman's view) Marx, is likewise ambivalent. This combining of the fixed and transitory may provide a hint as to how to interpret the remarks of Schulte-Sasse and Calinescu.

Modernism denotes a type of experience and a type of culture that is ambivalent. This is partly due to the "ambivalence of modernity." It is also because modern ideas of subjectivity are ambivalent and because one finds manifestations of cultural and literary modernism that express two different attitudes toward modernity: The rebellious, antibourgeois attitudes alluded to by Calinescu and the promodernity inherent in other modernist literature. The ambivalent nature of modern subjectivity can be mapped onto the pro- and antimodernity aspects of modern culture, just as attitudes toward modernity are in Chapter 2.

A. Promodernity modernism (e.g., modern architecture).
B. Anti- (or pre-) modernity modernism (e.g., T. S. Eliot).
C. Cultural modernism that is ambivalent toward modernity (e.g., Baudelaire: modernism as the union of the new and the eternal).
D. Cultural modernism is different (e.g., Marx, James Joyce).
E. Postmodernist cultural modernism: modernist culture requires neither glorification nor condemnation, but ("reflexive") recontextualization (e.g., the postmodernist reflexive novels of Umberto Eco and Donald Bartheleme).

Modern Ideas of the Self

A typology of modern ideas about the self encompasses the following perspectives.

1. Rational choice models (egoism) support a promodernity culture in the spheres of science, architecture, literature, business, politics, and law.

2. The expressivist and romantic view of the self supports antimodernity culture: the literature and art of rebellion, but also fascism (as in Italian futurism).
3. The modern self is ambivalent. In this view, the first two perspectives embody the same view of the self as subject (humanism).

Postmodernists reject the first two perspectives. Calinescu does not emphasize that the promodernity, bourgeois doctrines he mentions are themselves bound up with a particular conception of modern subjectivity and modernist culture. The cultural ideals that grew out of Cartesian rationalism and that underlie the Enlightenment's faith in reason and science also underlie a particular idea of modern identity and self-development. Taylor charts the development of this idea in *Sources of the Self.*[7] The modern self creates or asserts itself, according to Blumenberg,[8] without recourse to God or tradition. This is the Faustian and Promethean self, which is creative in literature as well as science, engineering, and technology, and which fits into modernity and sees modernity as having a positive value for cultural creativity. Cultural writers such as Arnold, Howe, Spender, and Trilling sometimes fall into this camp.[9] In this view, modernity provides the conditions for "the new," for constant creativity, and for the experiences of modernity that for Berman are liberating. The growing relationship between science, technology, and modern art and architecture bears witness to the connections between a rationalistic, even utilitarian notion of the self and cultural movements that are promodernist. This is especially true of architecture, but even writers such as Williams are not immune to this affinity.[10] Many modern artists have tried to combine art with engineering in terms of style.

But this view of the creative self is often elitist and sometimes combines a distrust of democracy and the masses with some misgivings about science and instrumental rationality. Eventually a split develops between modernity and creative modernism, which culminates in Bell's *Cultural Contradictions of Capitalism* and the cultural neoconservatism of Trilling[11] and other Cold War liberals. Trilling and Bell blame what Lasch calls "the culture of narcissism"[12] for the antibourgeois attitudes that undermine modern society and its benefits. Here the promodern rationalists turn their attack on modernist culture.

At the other extreme, one finds the antimodernity ideas of the self beginning with the romantics, who take up the self-realization tradition of Aristotle and Hegel but disengage it from God and tradition. They see this self as endangered by bourgeois society and scientific modernity. From here it is but a short step to the adversary culture. The rebellious modernism that Calinescu identifies with antimodernity is no less a part of modernity. What needs to be explored is how both of these modernist positions grow out of modernity and, indeed, are equally part of it.

Taylor labels the promodernity idea of selfhood "utilitarianism," and the antimodernity view "expressivism."[13] He shows how both of these modern notions of the self embody what Sartre calls "the desire to be God." In the utilitarian view, which for Taylor leads to consumer culture, the paradigm of human action and self-development is action that "pays off." The expressivist view, on the other hand, is concerned about tuning into, or creating, the "true self," usually against both the bourgeois social self and the utilitarian egoistic self. (One important wrinkle here is the thesis that the expressive or romantic notion of the self actually underlies modern consumer culture.)[14] Taylor believes that both the utilitarian and the expressivist selves are expressions of the inherently ambivalent nature of modernism. These two notions of modern identity are rooted in, or variations on, common themes: humanism, the "man is God" motif, the idea of modern self-assertion, the death of God theme. The two selves epitomize a variety of modern attitudes about how one can give life meaning.

If these two modern views of self-identity only appear to be at odds, we must examine how they can be combined. Given the modern doctrine of spheres of culture, one can, for example, believe in the utilitarian model in the economic sphere and believe in the expressivist model in the aesthetic sphere. Weber and Bell maintain that this two-faced view of the self exists in modernity.

In practice, the tension and fragmentation created by this bifurcated existence and culture will either break down or produce extreme responses. One such response is withdrawal into the aesthetic or private sphere, as in Weber, some romantics,[15] and the existentialists. Another strategy, discussed in Chapter 4, is the attempt to keep human values from usurpation by science.[16] Still other responses involve the "plurality" of spheres, regarded by some as fragmentation and alienation, as does Weber. Yet not everyone agrees with Weber on this point. Bell claims to be a socialist in economics, a liberal in politics, and a conservative in culture.[17] Habermas seeks to preserve the three spheres of modernity yet harmonize them in more or less a Kantian fashion by invoking the expressivist function of (a rationalized) aesthetics as the means for doing so. But Bell and Habermas do not refute Weber's claim that modern self-identity is fragmented. They insist upon this point and try to put a happy face on it.

If there is no single successful strategy for resolving the tensions between modern society and modernist culture, what is to be done? Some writers try to make one of the spheres the consummate point of modern culture: aestheticism (Simmel, Lukacs, Adorno), moralism (Weber and Durkheim), or scientism (positivists). Perhaps these recommendations are a symptom of how modernism continues to be in conflict with modernity while being an essential part of it. In any case, the relations between art and politics do not receive any uniform response by postmodernists either.

Philosophical Views of the Modern Self

Descartes invented the idea of the modern self with his idea of subjective consciousness, but Hobbes and Sartre are paradigms of the utilitarian and the expressivist views of the modernist self. Indeed, it may not be a coincidence that they stand at the beginning and the end of the modern period. One could argue that Sartre's aesthetic, expressivist view of the self as totally subjective and self-created is either the dialectical outcome or the dark underbelly of Descartes's view. Yet this view is also similar to Hume's view about the self, which clearly is meant as a *reductio ad absurdum* of Descartes. This theory supports Foucault's point that the modern idea of the self may be incoherent. In any event, Hobbes and Descartes' modern idea of self-identity spawned the modernist expressivist view of identity in Sartre and aesthetic modernism. In both cases, subjective consciousness creates or defines the subject.

For Descartes and Bacon, and for modern utilitarians and rational choice theorists, the self is a rational subject who discovers what is true and good or who discovers what is true and invents what is good (positivism) or vice versa (German idealism), and who has the freedom to act, create, and rationally transform society and history. For Sartre and Kierkegaard, the self is not and should not be controlled by the idea of rationality or egoism, but by the expressivist attitudes of romanticism. So the modern self and the idea of self-creation and freedom can move in two directions: along the rationalist, promodernity line that stems from Descartes, Bacon, Hobbes, and Bentham or along the antimodernity line that stem from the romantics and German idealists. Antimodernity modernists reject the rationalist-utilitarian interpretation of self-development but not the basic concept of the self as subject that defines modernity in general. They negate but do not reject the modernist concept of the self.

Foucault makes this point in *The Order of Things*[18] by talking about the confusions and dangers in modern humanism, which are rooted in the "transcendental doublet," the view of the self as both empirical and transcendent, as both subject and object. Moreover, the modern self becomes subjugated by the disciplinary society,[19] so the humanist view of the self contributes to "normalization" in modern society.

For Habermas,[20] the "dialectic of enlightenment," and thus all extreme modernist cultural attitudes for and against modernity, is rooted in the philosophy of consciousness or subjectivity, which must be bypassed in favor of a theory of communicative action.

The idea of "subjective freedom" that defines both the modern self and the culture of modernism is ambiguous. In promodernism, freedom and reason must be interrelated; freedom is defined as rational self-determination. However, this formula leaves little room for choice because there usually is only one possible rational choice in any given instance (owing to assumptions about truth and objectivity). Freedom and reason in effect become separated by critics of rational choice theories. Freedom is pitted against reason in existentialism and other counter-Enlightenment movements.

At this point, we may well ask what other alternatives exist.

Some Alternatives to the Modern Self

One alternative to modern concepts of the self is suggested by the themes of structuralism and poststructuralism: the "end of man," the "death of the subject," or humanism as a bourgeois ideology (Althusser); in short, the idea that the self is constituted by social structures or by a matrix of social structures and human agency.[21]

One could interpret antihumanism along Heidegger's lines,[22] which would mean becoming a premodernist antimodernist in both the sociological and cultural meanings of these terms. Nevertheless, Heidegger's radical historicism and his view that the self is not a subject paved the way for postmodernist ideas.

One could adopt a sort of Hegelian view: Selfhood and self-realization require a Gemeinschaft; the self is social. This is Durkheim's view. But this form of social determinism has problems of its own, including well-known methodological problems as well as political worries about totalitarianism and collectivism, as Popper[23] would say. The Nazi example and Orwell and Huxley warn us about the dangers of viewing society as an organism and the self as a part of an organism. The various forms of behaviorism, materialism, cognitivism, and biological theories of human nature are variations on the modern idea of identity, and raise similar concerns. We may be at a stalemate: The concept of the self that dominates modernity seems problematic, but alternative ideas are either variants of this concept or are dubious or dangerous.

The Fragmentation of the Self

Adorno,[24] Marcuse,[25] Weber, and some radical critics of Freud, especially Deleuze and Guattari[26] and Lacan,[27] maintain that the self should not to be unified or normalized in modernity on pain of imprisonment in the iron cage. In this view, Freud's biological determinism and his idea of normality as adjustment to the reality principle[28] seem to neglect the social sources of the self and support American ego psychology. The so-called antipsychiatrists, such as Laing,[29] join many of the above writers in attacking this idea. As Laing once put it, anyone who is normal in an insane world is crazy. This leads to the "schizoanalysis" of

Anti-Oedipus by Deleuze and Guattari.[30] The modern schizo-
phrenic is the model of human liberation and gets closer to the
romantic true self. Weber and the Frankfurt theorists never approach this extreme. But they agree with Lacan that one should
avoid overcoming fragmentation and alienation within modernity at all costs, although they always hope for a Marxist form of
expressivism as a model for human selfhood in cultural and political conditions that are at best a utopian hope.

Elitism and Mass Culture

Modernity separates art, politics, and science into separate
spheres. With science and politics, the problem of value neutrality arises. With art and politics, several themes emerge: the art
for art's sake movement, which often involves withdrawal into
the private; the privatization of public values (as in Weber); and
the notion of Mann's "unpolitical man"[31] who divorces himself
from politics or wants high culture to stem its tide.[32] Connecting
politics and art is dangerous for many antimodernity modernists,[33] as well as for many promodernity advocates of modernist
culture. Some believe such a connection sucks the artist into
bourgeois society;[34] others fear it violates the Enlightenment
project and breeds irrationalism or political romanticism, turning politics into an aesthetic experience and leaving a power
vacuum for Machiavellian leaders. In Schmitt's view,[35] parliamen-
tary democracy is a version of political romanticism. Although
Habermas is a severe critic of Schmitt's conservative antimodern-
ism, he applies Schmitt's criticism of political romanticism to
postmodernism and the avant-garde.[36] (Chapter 8 shows Habermas
believes that postmodernists are conservative antimodernists.)

One important issue is how the attempt to aestheticize politics
leads to conservative, indeed fascist politics, as in Italian futurism, Ezra Pound, and T.S. Eliot, as well as to leftist messianic
utopianism, as in Bloch, Benjamin, Brecht, and Lukacs.[37] The
hypothesis formulated in Chapter 2 that the left and the right
have had the same criticism of modern society (that it destroys
community and produces alienation) since at least Hegel may
answer this question.

The Frankfurt theorists are not easy to discuss. Some of their
views of modernity and modernism come closer to those of some

postmodernists. For example, there's a closer affinity on these themes between Adorno and Lyotard than between Adorno and Habermas, even though Habermas is in many respects the direct successor of the Frankfurt theorists. Moreover, the Frankfurt school's "cultural Marxism" is complicated, by no means uniform, and not entirely defensible. The basic idea[38] is that modern mass culture turns high culture into an economic commodity—the culture of consumption and eliminates the critical role that high culture plays in society, including its revolutionary potential. (Arendt, a Heideggerian, shares this view.[39] Many of the Frankfurt theorists, for instance, Marcuse and Strauss, were students of Heidegger. The Frankfurt school combines features of both antimodernist and Marxist criticisms of modernity.) Thus, art and high culture become the locus of resistance, criticism, and revolution for Adorno, Benjamin, and Marcuse.[40]

Some accuse the Frankfurt theorists of being cultural elitists who distrusted the masses as Bell and other promodernist critics of "mass society" did 20 years later.[41] This charge raises all sorts of issues about the role of the intellectual in modern capitalist societies, especially if one gives up on the masses, as happened in Frankfurt, although this did not happen to the radical American cultural critics[42] during the 1930s. The various avant-garde movements, especially surrealism, may have been even more guilty of this oscillation between elitism and the glorification of the masses.[43] At least the Frankfurt theorists attempted to move beyond the strictures imposed by the three spheres and promote the idea that politics need not be irrational if infused with or guided by aesthetic and cultural criteria. This does not mean that these attempts were successful. They clearly were not, and the irrational mentality of Weimar and Hitler's Reich remains Habermas's main worry about postmodernism.

This is not to suggest that these matters are settled. This is far from being the case. It does suggest that the Frankfurt theorists had a metanarrative of modernity that holds that what goes on in one sphere has systematic interconnections with the other spheres, but that modernity is too corrupt to make a holistic life possible in the present. The hope for such an ideal is reasonable and necessary. A Marxist Gemeinschaft is the ideal of the Frankfurt theorists. But in the climate of fascism, any Gemeinschaft would be a disaster. Hence, Adorno developed the idea of "negative dialectics," the idea of resisting totality at all costs. Yet cultural modernism, whether pro- or antimodernity, does not escape from the confines of modernity, envision alternatives to make this escape, or question the assumptions about human history that writers such as Megill[44] see as sustaining the dialectic of modernity, between optimism and pessimism, aestheticism and rationalism, and the rest. Only the postmodernists take this step, according to Megill, and only Derrida takes it fully. This is the only way, Megill claims, of overcoming the dialectic of modernity.

The Sociological Discourse of Modernism

At this point it may be helpful to survey the sociological discourse of modernism, as distinguished from Habermas's philosophical discourse on modernity.[45] By examining the idea of modernity as divided into spheres of culture, it may be possible to clarify the relations between modernity and modernism. Following the earlier schemas, modernist attitudes about modernity can be identified by ideal types that take science, aesthetics, and morality and politics as the dominant sphere of modern culture.

A. Science
   1. Promodernity (e.g., Durkheim)
   2. Antimodernity (e.g., Speer)
   3. Ambivalent (e.g., Freud, Marx, Weber)
B. Aesthetics
   1. Promodernity (e.g., Dewey, modernist architecture)
   2. Antimodernity (e.g., Adorno, Eliot)
   3. Ambivalent (e.g., Marcuse)
C. Ethics and politics
   1. Promodernity (e.g., liberalism)
   2. Antimodernity (e.g., fascism)
   3. Ambivalent (e.g., Bell)

The main voices in the sociological discourse of modernism are Marx, Weber, Durkheim, Simmel, Freud, the Frankfurt school, and, more recently, Parsons, Bell, Giddens, and Habermas. The writings of postmodernists such as Foucault, Lyotard, and Baudrillard that bear on this sociological discourse are discussed in later chapters.

Science

Advocates of the scientific outlook are sometimes promodernists, such as Durkheim, and sometimes reactionary modernists, such as Speer,[46] Heidegger, and the Nazis.[47] Freud, Weber, and Marx exhibit ambivalence toward science and modernity.

Aesthetics

Those inhabiting the aesthetic realm can be divided along parallel lines. Many "technological utopians" seek to combine aesthetics and engineering to defend a promodernity cultural modernism. Rorty and Dewey can be placed in this camp. Antimodernity cultural modernism can be found in Adorno and Benjamin and in conservatives such as Eliot and Pound.[48] Simmel[49] and Marcuse[50] are ambivalent about modern culture and its effect on the individual.

Ethics and Politics

Those who define modernism as a culture by elevating the sphere of ethics, politics, and law exhibit similar views. Modern liberalism, in either Mill's individualistic version or Durkheim's corporate liberalism, is the most sanguine about modernity. Weber is clearly the most ambivalent in his writings on politics, science, and scholarship as vocations infused with a calling from the moral sphere of conscience.[51] Giddens is more upbeat in his ambivalence, as are Levine and Baumann, who have been more influenced by Simmel.[52] Bell and others use a defense of modernity against cultural modernism. Writers such as Lasch and Sennett sometimes defend cultural modernism against modernity.[53]

Other factors besides science, art, and politics bring out the ambivalent nature of cultural modernism vis-a-vis modernity. For example, the continuum that ranges from elitism to popular democracy supports both pro- and antimodernity modernism. The ascetic ideal analyzed by Nietzsche,[54] as well as the associated "will to truth," gives rise to pro, anti, and ambivalent positions on modernity. Thus Freud, Weber, Lasch, Sennett, Bell, and others make use of the ascetic ideal, some defending modernity against modernism, some doing the reverse, and some, notably Weber and Freud, being ambivalent. Narcissism can be embodied in egoism and expressivism, in both types of modernity and modernism, and in liberal, reactionary, and revolutionary culture and politics.

Is Modernism a Useful Concept?

These ambivalences may make the concept of modernism too indeterminate and empty to be of much use, as Anderson maintains.[55] Perhaps the two modern ideas of identity—rational choice egoism and romantic expressivism—are at the bottom of these difficulties, since they may be equally ambivalent and indeterminate. The cult of genius, the hero, or the world historical individual, whether the artist, the engineer, the scientist, or a charismatic political leader, fits both notions of identity, and pro, anti, and ambivalent positions taken by different cultural modernists. Perhaps these two modern versions of the self are variations on the same paradigm, as Heidegger maintains when he argues that Western culture from Plato to Nietzsche to "the age of the world as picture" (technological civilization) is a variation on subjectivism and nihilism. Perhaps there is nothing peculiarly modern in all this. As Nietzsche and Benjamin remark (following Thucydides and Machiavelli),[56] civilization and barbarism, good and evil, progress and regress are inseparable in human life.

What if we try to move beyond this view, beyond good and evil, beyond progress and regress, to the completed nihilism that Nietzsche postulates and to which, perhaps, postmodernists move us closer? Then the lessons of Nietzsche, Simmel, and Marx that the ambivalence of modernity is our "joyful wisdom" might gain acceptance "without regret or nostalgia."[57] Here is one possible dividing line between the modern and the postmodern.

This discussion suggests that cultural modernism and the ideas of the self that define modern culture reflect the same ambivalence about modernity seen in Chapter 2. Contrary to the "two cultures" thesis, neither science nor art nor ethics and politics is exclusively promodernist or antimodernist. Instead, modern culture is indeterminate about the relations between the spheres of modern life.

Similarly, neither rational egoism nor romantic expressionism represents the essence of the modern self. Their joint influence on consumer culture illustrates this point.

The complexity and ambiguity of cultural modernism and self-identity may convince us that the postmodernist concern to set aside these sorts of questions and issues is a wise one. The ramifications of this ambivalence in connection with the themes of antihumanism and the postmodernist idea of "resituating the self" are explored in Chapter 6.

Notes

1. Berman, *All that is solid*; Bradbury, M., & McFarlane, J. (Eds.). (1976). *Modernism: 1890-1930*. New York: Penguin; Calinescu, M. (1987). *Five faces of modernity*. Durham, NC: Duke University Press; Chefdor, M. (Ed.). (1986). *Modernism: Challenges and perspectives*. Champaign: University of Illinois Press; Gaggi, S. (1989). *Modern/postmodern*. Philadelphia: University of Pennsylvania Press; Howe, I. (Ed.). (1967). *The idea of the modern*. New York: Horizon. Karl, F. R. (1988). *Modern and modernism*. New York: Athaneum; Poggioli, R. (1968). *The theory of the avant-garde*. Cambridge, MA: Harvard University Press; Russell, C. (1985). *Poets, prophets and revolutionaries*. New York: Oxford University Press; Taylor, B. (Ed.). (1983). *Modernism and modernity: The Vancouver conference papers*. Halifax: Nova Scotia College of Art and Design; Taylor, B. (1987). *Modernism, postmodernism, realism*. Winchester: Winchester School of Art Press; Timms, E., & Collier, P. (Eds.). (1988). *Visions and blueprints*. New York: St. Martin's Press; Wilde, A. (1987). *Horizons of assent*. Philadelphia: University of Pennsylvania Press; Williams, R. (1988) *Politics of modernism*. New York: Verso. See also Calinescu, M., & Fokkema, D. W. (Eds.). (1987). *Exploring postmodernism*. Philadelphia: John Benjamins; Fokkema, D. W., & Bertens, H. (Eds.). (1986). *Approaching postmodernism*. Philadelphia: John Benjamins; Hardison, O. B. (1989). *Disappearing through the skylight*. New York: Viking; and Hardison, *Entering the maze*; See also the following journals; each issue is devoted to the topics of modernity and modernism: *Journal of Modern Literature*, 3(5), *New German Critique 33*, *Telos*, 62.

2. Schulte-Sasse, J. (1986). Modernity and modernism, postmodernity and postmodernism. *Culture Critique*, 5, 23-49. See also Burger, P. (1984). *Theory of the avant garde*. Minneapolis: University of Minnesota Press; Lunn, E. (1982). *Marxism and modernism*. Berkeley: University of California Press.

3. Calinescu, *Five faces of modernity*, p. 41.

4. Calinescu, *Five faces of modernity*.

5. Berman, *All that is solid*.

6. Simmel, G. (1971). The concept and tragedy of culture. In G. Simmel, *On individuality and social norms* (pp.375-95). Chicago: University of Chicago Press; Simmel, G. (1978). *Philosophy of money*. New York: Routledge. See also Frisby, D. (1981). *Sociological impressionism*. London: Heineman; Frisby, D. (1986). *Fragments of modernity*. Cambridge: MIT Press; Frisby, D. (1992). *Simmel and since*. New York: Routledge; Kaern, M., Phillips, B. T., & Cohen, R. S. (Eds.). (1990). *Georg Simmel and contemporary sociology* (*Boston studies in the philosophy of science: Vol. 119*) (especially pp. 39-74, 283-96, 341-56, 357-84). Boston: Reidel.

7. Taylor, *Sources of the self*.

8. Blumenberg, *The legitimacy of the modern age*.

9. Bell, D. (1976). Modernism mummified and Beyond modernism, beyond self. In D. Bell, *The winding passage*. New York: Basic Books; Bell, *Cultural contradictions of capitalism*; Howe, *Idea of the modern*; and Krupnick, M. (1986). *Lionel Trilling and the fate of literary criticism*. Madison: University of Wisconsin Press. See also Habermas, J. (1981). Modernity, an incomplete project. *New German Critique*, 7, 3-14.

10. Segal, H. P. (1985). *Technological utopianism in American culture*. Chicago: University of Chicago Press; Steinman, L. (1987). *Made in America*. New Haven, CT: Yale University Press; and Ticchi, C. (1987). *Shifting gears*. Chapel Hill: University of North Carolina Press.

11. Trilling, L. (1965). *Beyond culture*. New York: Viking, 1965; and Trilling, L. (1971). *Sincerity and authenticity*. Cambridge, MA: Harvard University Press. See also Krupnick, *Lionel Trilling and the fate of literary criticism*.

12. Lasch, C. (1978). *The culture of narcissism*. New York: Norton; and Lasch, C. (1984). *The minimal self*. New York: Norton. See also Hearn, F. (1985). *Freedom and reason in sociological thought*. Winchester, MA: Unwin Hyman; Sennett, R. (1977). *The fall of public man*. New York: Knopf; and Sennett, R. (1980). *Authority*. New York: Knopf.

13. Taylor, C. (1985). Legitimation crisis?. In C. Taylor, *Philosophical papers: Vol. 2* (pp. 248-89). New York/Cambridge, UK: Cambridge University Press.

14. Campbell, C. (1987). *The romantic ethic and the spirit of modern consumerism*. Cambridge, MA: Blackwell.

15. Schmitt, C. (1986). *Political romanticism*. Cambridge: MIT Press.

16. Proctor, R. (1991). *Value free science?*. Cambridge, MA: Harvard University Press.

17. Bell, *Cultural contradictions of capitalism*.

18. Foucault, M. (1973). *The order of things*. New York: Random House.

19. Foucault, M. (1980). Truth and power. In M. Foucault, *Power/Knowledge* (pp. 109-33). New York: Random House.

20. Habermas, J. (1987). *Philosophical discourse on modernity*. Cambridge: MIT Press and *Theory of communicative action*

21. Giddens, *Consequences of modernity* and *Modernity and self-identity*.

22. Ferry, L., & Renaut, A. (1990) *Heidegger and modernity*. Chicago: University of Chicago Press.

23. Popper, K. (1944). *The open society and its enemies* (2 Vols.). Princeton, NJ: Princeton University Press; and Popper, K. (1956). *The poverty of historicism.* New York: HarperCollins.

24. Adorno, T. (1973). *Negative dialectics.* New York: Seabury; Adorno, T. (1983). *Aesthetic theory.* New York: Routledge; and Adorno, T. (1991). *The culture industry.* New York: Routledge. See also Benjamin, A. (Ed.). (1990). *The problem of modernity.* New York: Routledge; Buck-Morss, S. (1977). *The origin of negative dialectics.* New York: Harvester Books; Held, *Introduction to critical theory;* Jay, M. (1988). *Adorno.* Cambridge, MA: Harvard University Press; and Rose, G. (1978). *The melancholy science.* New York: Columbia University Press.

25. Marcuse, H. (1969). *An essay on liberation.* Boston: Beacon Press; Marcuse, H. (1978). *The aesthetic dimension.* Boston: Beacon Press. See Held, *Introduction to critical theory* for discussion.

26. Deleuze, G., & Guattari, F. (1977). *Anti-Oedipus.* Minneapolis: University of Minnesota Press; Deleuze, G., & Guattari, F. (1987). *A thousand plateaus.* Minneapolis: University of Minnesota Press. See also Bogue, R. (1989). *Deleuze and Guattari.* New York: Routledge.

27. Rachjman, J. (1991). *Truth and eros.* New York: Routledge. See also Grosz, E. *Jacques Lacan: A feminist introduction.* New York: Routledge; Sarup, M. (1992). *Introductory guide to poststructuralism and postmodernism* (rev. ed.). Athens: University of Georgia Press; and Sarup, M. (1992). *Jacques Lacan.* Toronto: University of Toronto Press;

28. Freud, *Civilization and its discontents* and *Future of an illusion;* Sarup, *Introductory guide to poststructuralism and postmodernism.*

29. Laing, R. D. (1967). *The politics of experience.* New York: Pantheon.

30. Deleuze & Guattari, *Anti-Oedipus.*

31. Mann, T. (1983). *Reflections of an unpolitical Mann.* New York: Ungar. See also Bergmann, P. (1987). *Nietzsche: The last unpolitical German.* Bloomington: Indiana University Press.

32. Arnold, M. (1971). *Culture and anarchy.* Indianapolis: Bobbs-Merrill; Johnson, L. (1979). *The cultural critics.* New York: Routledge.

33. Chefdor, *Modernism: challenges and perspectives;* Grana, C. (1964). *Modernity and its discontents.* New York: HarperCollins; Russell, *Poets, prophets and revolutionaries;* Seigel, J. (1986). *Bohemian Paris.* New York: Viking; and Timms & Collier, *Visions and blueprints;* Williams, *Politics of modernism.*

34. In addition to the sources cited in note 33, see Gablik, S. (1984). *Has modernism failed?.* New York: Thames and Hudson.

35. Schmitt, *Political romanticism.*

36. Habermas, *Philosophical discourse on modernity.*

37. Timms & Collier, *Visions and blueprints.*

38. Held, *Introduction to critical theory.*

39. Arendt, H. (1959). Society and Culture. In N. Jacobs, (Ed.), *Culture for the millions?* (pp. 43-53). Boston: Beacon Press.

40. Held, *Introduction to critical theory.*

41. Brantlinger, P. (1983). *Bread and circuses.* Ithaca, NY: Cornell University Press; Bell, D. (1956). The theory of mass society. *Commentary,* 75-83; Kornhauser, W. (1959). *The politics of mass society.* New York: Free Press; and Wolfe, A. (1981). Sociology, liberalism, and the radical right. *New Left Review, 128,* 3-27.

42. Aaron, D. (1969). *Writers on the left*. New York: Avon Books; Abrahams, E. (1983). *The lyrical left*. Charlottesville: University of Virginia Press; Blake, C. (1990). *Beloved community*. Chapel Hill: University of North Carolina Press; Gilbert, J. (1968). *Writers and partisans*. Chichester, UK: Wiley; and Wald, A. (1987). *New York intellectuals*. Chapel Hill: University of North Carolina Press.

43. Timms & Collier, *Visions and blueprints*.

44. McGill, *Prophets of extremity*.

45. Habermas, *Philosophical discourse on modernity*. See also Pippin, R. (1991). *Modernism as a philosophical problem*. Cambridge, MA: Blackwell.

46. Herf, *Reactionary modernism*.

47. Ferry & Renaut, *Heidegger and modernity*.

48. Timms & Collier, *Visions and blueprints*.

49. See note 6 above.

50. See note 25 above.

51. Sayer, D. (1990). *Capitalism and modernity*. New York: Routledge. Weber, Science as a vocation and Politics as a vocation.

52. Levine, *Flight from ambiguity*; Baumann, *Modernity and ambivalence*; Giddens, *Consequences of modernity*.

53. Hearn, *Freedom and reason in sociological thought*.

54. Nietzsche, What is the meaning of ascetic ideals? See also Freud, S. (1908/1965), discussion of this essay in *Minutes of Vienna Psychoanalytic Society; Vol. 2* (pp. 30-33). New York: Hogart.

55. Anderson, P. (1984). Modernity and revolution. *New Left Review, 144*, 11-15, with response by Berman, 81-86. See also Nelson, C., and Grossberg, L. (Eds.). (1988). *Marxism and the interpretation of culture* (pp. 334-338). Champaign: University of Illinois Press; Berman. M. (1990). Why modernism still matters with responses. *Tikkun, 5* (reprinted in Lash, S., & Friedman, J. [Eds.]. [1991]. *Modernity and identity*. Cambridge, MA: Blackwell).

56. See Eden, R. (1984). *Political leadership and nihilism*. Tampa: Florida University Presses, for a stimulating discussion of these issues.

57. Hiley, D. R. (1984). Foucault and the analysis of power: Political engagement without liberal hope or comfort. *Praxis International, 3*, 192-207; Hiley, D. R. (1985). Foucault and the question of enlightenment. *Philosophy and Social Criticism, 12*, 62-83; Hiley, D. R. (1988). *Philosophy in question*. Chicago: University of Chicago Press.

4

REASON, METHODS, VALUES

Postmodernism is said to favor irrationalism and to have no norms for positive programs or critique. It appears to have very strange methods: deconstruction, archeology, genealogy. Its politics are questionable because of this lack of accepted values, methods, and loyalty to reason. Indeed, leading postmodernists seem to attack these ideas, along with much else in modernity. It is important to consider some of the characteristic modern approaches.[1] At the least, common assumptions about the ways in which social science knowledge is acquired and applied are at issue in these debates.

A Brief History of the Concept of Reason

The idea of "reason" is as old and contested as Western culture itself.[2] In the ancient world, reason was associated with necessity and the idea that the cosmos had a telos that was good and beautiful. "Man is a rational animal" captures this Greek functionalist view of reason. According to this perspective, the primary function of humans is reason or intelligence; the rational life is the most suited to the realization of our essence, and hence is the best life.

For Aristotle, there are three types of reason: theoretical, practical, and technical.[3] Theoretical reason is associated with the intellectual virtues, whose embodiment constitutes the highest form of human life. Practical reason is associated with the moral virtues—ethics and politics—which, unlike the physical world, are subject to human control. Practical reason helps us deliberate about ends and means and adjust them to each other. Morality is thus a type of prudence but also the basis for the polity. Practical reason cannot exhibit the exactitude of mathematics, for its objective, the attainment of human well-being, cannot be a rigorous theoretical science.

Technical reason is associated with productive knowledge. Here, reason is purely instrumental. To be a good carpenter, a person must take for granted the telos of the craft and learn to work with wood by mastering the techniques that are most conducive to this end.[4]

For Aristotle, these three types of reason and knowledge are all practices and not reducible to one another. That is, he does not believe that practical reason is a form of technology or an applied science. He does believe that the best life is that of the "pure" knower who seeks knowledge for its own sake.

Aristotle thus rejects the idea that politics can be scientific. Comte, Saint-Simon, and other Enlightenment figures are in this respect closer to Plato, for whom virtue is the application of theoretical knowledge.

For the Greeks, irrationality is connected to these ideas. For instance, one can have irrational desires, adopt means ill suited to one's ends, or choose goals that do not further human well-being or one's own well-being. Excess in general and hedonism in particular are the paradigms of irrationality for the Greeks. Moreover, what is irrational is unintelligible and thus not explainable; it is the "surd."[5] Indeed, even the contingent is irrational in this sense. Only what is necessary can be explained theoretically; reality is not contingent, and thus the world of experience and appearances is not fully real or rational. Finally, "weakness of will," intentionally doing what one knows to be wrong or bad for one (which Plato argues is merely a case of ignorance) is another form of irrationality for many ancients.

Reason in Modernity: Early History

The ideas of reason and rationality were transformed by Bacon, Machiavelli, Hobbes, and Descartes.[6] Bacon claims that the physical world can be transformed by humans: knowledge is power. Modern science will often reduce the theoretical to the practical and the practical to the technical, and subsume both under scientific knowledge and method. For Bacon, knowledge, especially science, is by definition technology. Science is placed in the service of traditional moral-religious ideas (the kingdom of heaven on earth). Science thus becomes utopian and seeks to replace Plato's philosopher-ruler with the scientist-technocrat.

For Galileo and Descartes, reason becomes the faculty that allows us to discover (often a priori) the fundamental absolutes of reality. Galileo's idea that mathematics is the language of nature is a form of Platonism. Method becomes the guarantor of truth,[7] whether one is a rationalist or an empiricist. For the rationalists, rationality is intelligibility. Rationality becomes reckoning for empiricists such as Hobbes. Moreover, Hobbes revitalizes ancient hedonism, which becomes a law of human nature: humans are selfish. Rational self-interest, however, is distinguished from crass hedonism. Eventually, modern liberalism, including utilitarianism, cost-benefit analysis, and market capitalism, assumes center stage as a standard of human rationality.

Values

"Values" is a modern idea. The Greeks had a functionalist idea of the good life; they talked about moral virtues (justice, moderation, courage, wisdom), and Aristotle has a well-developed notion of intrinsic and instrumental values and rational choice and action. But value as a general theoretical idea is a product of modern notions of the subjective and the objective, the idea of method as the road to truth, and the resulting split between facts and interpretations. The modern notion of value is also bound up with modern political individualism and the resulting conflicts between the individual and society and between prudence and morality, distinctly modern problems.

The history of values runs as follows.[8] If objective knowledge and truth exist, and if nature can be reduced to the language of mathematics, then the only reality is physical reality. (Descartes wants to preserve the irreducible reality of the mental, but this is a goal of those who resist the hegemony of modern science, not its defenders.) Thus, an objective account of the world must be guided by objective rules; that is, by a method. The method must be purged of all elements that prevent us from discovering objective truth. Because reality is universal and independent and truth is absolute, invariant, and independent, the most rational method will be purged of any factors that do not have these features. Because reason is absolute, invariant, and independent, while values, judgments, opinions, subjective states, interpretations, and emotions are not, these factors must be expunged or at least kept in abeyance. Moreover, because reality is physical, these factors are not themselves part of the objective world but are a result of individual reaction to that world. (The obvious fact that we and our brains or minds are part of the same objective world is overlooked or considered irrelevant, at least until 18th-century materialism.)

This is how distinctions between the objective and the subjective and between facts and values arose in modernity. Values are the subjective interpretation we put on the facts. Many modernists attempt to reduce values to facts, to consider values as just another type of natural fact. This view, sometimes called ethical naturalism, led to the idea, defended by Homans,[9] that social science discovers natural relations among social phenomena. Behaviorism, utilitarianism, and historicism are other attempts to reduce values to facts. However, for those who believe that these attempts failed, facts and values became an unbridgeable dualism: We cannot derive an "ought" from an "is." Values can still be rational and objective, but they must be rooted in something other than science and its method. This is the source of the modern distinction, canonized by Kant, among the spheres of modernity: science, aesthetics, and morality. For the reductionists, who believe that values can be reduced to facts, values become part of applied science and can be proved by science. This approach to values often reinforces the status quo by making values another type of "natural fact" that is objective.

Methods

The idea of method comes from the same (Greek) root as mathematics (measure). But method in the modern sense, which we owe to Descartes (rationalism) and to Bacon (empiricism) is something new. Descartes's "epistemological turn," Bacon's pragmatism, and Kant's "Copernican revolution in philosophy" define truth, knowledge, and objectivity as the result of an algorithmic, context-free method.

Objectivity, knowledge, truth, and method become intertwined by definition. Whatever falls outside this orbit becomes subjective and value laden. Even philosophers who develop a notion of rational, universal morality agree with this dogma.

Naturalism and Antinaturalism

There are two major positions concerning reason-methods-values configuration: the view that reason and method exclude values as subjective and the view that seeks to bring values within the scope of the configuration by constructing some sort of naturalistic account of values. Most notably, utilitarianism defines "good" and "bad" as "pleasure" and "pain"; "right" as whatever maximizes the pleasure; and "wrong" as whatever maximizes the pain. Kant believes that values are rational, universal, and absolute. Values can be discovered and justified by a method, but one very different from the scientific method. In this respect, Kant is an antinaturalist about values. This form of antinaturalism led to the 19th-century distinction between the natural and the human sciences, based partly on methodological claims. Kant formalizes these rational methods in ethics and models them on the logical consistency and generality in mathematics. This is the beginning of the modern distinction between "formal" and "substantive" rationality. Weber was influenced by the late 19th-century neo-Kantians.[10] But the price to pay is a heavy one: Science and values can have nothing to do with each other. This line of thought led to the modern controversy about values and methods in the social sciences.

The following list summarizes the ideal types of naturalism and antinaturalism concerning reason, methods, and values.

A. Naturalism type I: Science is objective, values are subjective (e.g., positivism).
B. Naturalism type II: Science is objective, values are objective (e.g., utilitarianism, behaviorism).

C. Antinaturalism type I: Science and values are not equal, but both are predominantly subjective (e.g., Weber).

D. Antinaturalism type II: Science and values are equal but are neither objective or subjective (e.g., Hegel, hermeneutics, neo-Kantianism).

Two important complexities emerge. The utilitarians believe ethical claims are objective because they are claims about pleasure and pain, which require empirical measurement to be valid. Value judgments are meaningful and have truth value. But behaviorism and some other forms of positivism[11] treat values as forms of behavior (responses) that can be explained scientifically but that make no claims and thus either are not cognitive or have no truth value. This view is called *emotivism*, or *noncognitivism* in the philosophical literature. Weber believes that value judgments are merely the expression of personal preferences, which can have no truth value. Their only justification is Luther's "Here I stand. I can do no other." This view is often called *decisionism* and resembles emotivism. Russell defends a view about values that blurs the distinctions, if any, between emotivism and decisionism. Some critics of postmodernism, notably Habermas, believe that postmodernists are also emotivists or decisionists about values. (Habermas' criticism of decisionism is discussed in Chapter 8.)

The second complexity that emerges from the ideal types concerns the idea that some methods and values are neither objective nor subjective, either because they belong to a third category or because they are partly objective and partly subjective. This complexity has important ramifications. The idea of a third category, besides the objective and the subjective, is rooted in German idealism. Hegel develops the idea of "objective spirit," which is not reducible to objectivity or subjectivity. Objective spirit is the realm of the social, the social world. A culture's language, symbols, practices, institutions, and values belong to its objective spirit. Objective spirit is not reducible to the psychological states of the individuals that make up the society or to the laws of physics. It is a unique type of reality that is as objective as rocks and trees. Durkheim's idea that social facts and social laws are not reducible to psychology or to physics is thus derived from Hegel. In this view, values are neither subjective nor objective, but cultural. Some neo-Kantians, for example, Rickert (Weber's mentor), use this idea of cultural value to distinguish the methods of the cultural sciences from those of the natural sciences.

The other major position concerning reason-methods-values configuration is to accept the view that objectivity and method together exclude values as subjective while reversing the significance of this assumption. In this view, values are more important because they are subjective. This is the view of Kierkegaard, Weber, and James, and it may also be Nietzsche's view.

A third view is to see science and values as equally subjective. In a sense this is also part of Weber's view and perhaps the view of some ethnomethodologists and phenomonologists.[12]

A fourth view, which stems from Hegel and is taken up by symbolic interactionists and hermeneutics following Dilthey and Gadamer,[13] is that science and values are neither objective nor subjective but intersubjective; that is, embodiments of cultural interpretations of nature and culture that interpenetrate each other everywhere and always. One could also interpret the neo-Kantians in this manner, as advocating a kind of objective idealism. One could read many of the German idealists as holding that values are more objective than science, or at least that values have a certain primacy over science, since nature is interpreted with cultural values and meanings that embody absolute consciousness.

Postmodernist views about methods and values are influenced by Hegel, Nietzsche, Weber, hermeneutics, phenomenology, and ethnomethodology. But postmodernism is more radically constructivist because it abandons the dualisms of facts and values, objectivity and subjectivity, descriptions and interpretations, and gives all methodologies a political coloration while contextualizing all claims, methods, and values.

Pro- and Anti-Enlightenment Views

Positions in the debates about naturalism and antinaturalism in the social sciences[14] can be mapped onto the list of ideal types concerning reason-methods-values.

A. Pro-Enlightenment type I: Science is rational. Morality is rationally applied science (e.g., utilitarianism, cost-benefit analysis).
B. Pro-Enlightenment type II: Science is rational. Morality is rational in the formal sense, as in mathematics, with consistency and universality of rules (e.g., Kant).
C. Anti-Enlightenment type I: Science is rational. Morality is historical and rational but particular, not universal (e.g., Dilthey) or particular but not rational (e.g., Nietzsche).
D. Anti-Enlightenment type II: Science and morality are both historically specific and both rational to the same degree, but in different ways (e.g., neo-Kantianism, Weber).

Naturalists, who argue that there is one method and subject matter to all the sciences, either reduce value judgments to some "naturalistic" variables or exclude them from science, thus paving the way for Weber's complex methodology and ideas of value neutrality and value relevance. Antinaturalists, who distinguish between the natural and the "human sciences," argue for different methods and different roles for values in the natural and social sciences. Giddens' "double hermeneutic"[15] is the view that both the natural and the cultural sciences are value laden, but the cultural sciences are doubly so because the subjects of the human sciences, human beings, are "self-interpreting animals," whereas billiard balls are not, even though physics is an interpretation of their behavior.

One wrinkle concerns the connections between objectivity and values. Marx and Weber try to define objectivity as connected to values, or at least to interests, either universal (Marx) or culturally specific (Weber). This is an important point, used by Weber and Habermas in very different ways. Their common point is that the demand that method be disinterested and that inquiry be objective too often leads to the view that objectivity requires one to be empty minded, as opposed to open minded.[16] But empty-mindedness cannot be connected with value freedom. If it is, then in practice value freedom can never be possible in either research or the policy sciences, for nothing significant could be done without some normative end in view. The idea of value freedom disguises this fact and makes it appear that decisions are technical or objective or that the ends are provable by science.

Starting with the pro-Enlightenment, promodernity views, one gets two approaches to the reason-method-values configuration. First is the attempt to rule out values as being incompatible with objectivity, method, and truth on the grounds that values are subjective, irrational, or noncognitive. Second are attempts to provide values with a rational foundation. Sometimes this takes the form of turning values (ethical as well as nonmoral) into a science or an applied science. Various forms of naturalism, most notably utilitarianism, rational choice theory, and behaviorism, take this route. In this view, science can "prove" goals, and ethics becomes the search for the best means for optimizing such goals. But this is hardly value neutral. When reason becomes instrumental, when values are allegedly "proven" by science, when value judgments are designed to optimize such results, the result is usually a defense of the status quo, hardly a value-free result. A clear example of this is the writing of Skinner, who argues that whoever survives in his newly designed culture will call it "good" simply because they have survived![17]

The second pro-Enlightenment, promodernity approach that seeks to give values a rational foundation stems from Kant. In this view, the idea of rational values does not involve construing ethics as an applied science. Instead, "rational" is construed on the model of rationality in the formal sciences: Universal, consistent rules make values rational. But here science and values can at best complement each other, or one can search for some type of formal science of values. It is no coincidence that Weber and the neo-Kantians took both of these routes at the beginning of this century.[18]

Counter-Enlightenment, antimodernity positions can actually take this latter view but can interpret values as either cultural values or personal values, which are either subjective or not. Many anti-Enlightenment, antimodernity approaches tend in the direction of some form of historicism, relativism, ideology, or sociology of knowledge, or even nihilistic approaches to values.[19]

Prefiguring Postmodernism

Two other points should be noted. First, there have been tremendous changes in the conceptions of science, knowledge, and rationality in the past 20 years that bring the connections between values and science into much closer contact than does positivism or antinaturalist views influenced by romanticism. This has profound ramifications for the ideas of reason, values, and methods.[20]

Second, many authors writing about the role of value judgments in science, including the natural sciences, approach a consensus that holds that all of science is infused with at least cognitive (nonmoral) values and that truth itself rests upon or is a value, as Nietzsche makes explicit in *The Gay Science* and *Beyond Good and Evil*. Recent work in the sociology of science[21] brings these points into focus for the natural sciences, and thus by implication for the social sciences. These developments call into question many of the assumptions and dualisms that accompany the debates about reason, methods, and values.

Combining these two developments borders on postmodernist themes about knowledge, science, interpretation, and methods. Many postmodernist themes on these topics are prefigured in the discussions of science, values, and reason inspired by Kuhn's historicist account of the physical sciences.[22] The ground was prepared for several key postmodernist themes about 20 years before postmodernism appeared upon the scene.

Relativism and the Sociology of Knowledge

Relativism has a long history. Historicism and ideology belong to modernity. All three became interrelated in various ways in the modern era. In its simplest form, relativism is the denial of absolute truth, truth with a capital T. The relativist does not say that relativism is the absolute truth, despite what many detractors maintain.[23] Relativism is based on Nietzsche's view that absolute truth is founded on "our longest lie," the belief in God. The deconstructionist's attack on "nostalgia" is directly rooted in Nietzsche's attack on absolute truth and reality and absolute knowledge.

Modern relativism, which has points of contact with the doctrines and methods of the sophists and ancient skeptics, began when Vico and Herder developed the view that each culture and each individual is a unique embodiment of what it is to be human.[24] Humanity as a general idea can only exist insofar as it is embodied; this is Hegel's "concrete universal," which plays such a large role in his attack on the Enlightenment. Different individuals and cultures may exhibit key similarities and may someday converge upon the same ideals, but even then these similarities cannot and should not be reduced to an abstract model, neglecting the particularities. The Enlightenment ideal of the "moral and epistemological unity of humankind"[25] does just that and thus destroys the concrete, the particular, the variable, the historical.

Here one can see precursors to postmodernism. The emphasis on particularity and difference; the suggestion that different people and cultures are just different, neither better nor worse than others; the refusal to be judgmental; and a reflexive awareness of difference are all basic themes of postmodernism.

One would think that the social sciences would be based on some loyalty to modern cultural relativism, not just because it promotes tolerance and diversity, but because the social sciences are supposed to be value free. One might expect cultural anthropology, given the connections between its own early history and European colonialism, and sociology, given the long history of social Darwinism and racism in Western culture, to adopt this stance. Yet the social sciences are often far removed from these ideals.

Several factors are relevant to understanding why the social sciences often do not take cultural diversity, much less relativism, seriously. First, the Enlightenment ideal of the moral and epistemological unity of humankind has dominated the social sciences. For many postmodernists, feminists, and postcolonialist writers, this ideal masks ethnocentrism, colonialism, sexism, racism, and other unattractive motives. Second, the idea that the social sciences are natural sciences, that culture is mainly composed of natural relations and laws between natural objects, tends to foster the Enlightenment idea that we should be approaching a universal civilization. This makes it possible to assume, if one is a naturalist, that people behave the same everywhere, so that one can find out what is happening in other cultures by using nothing but empirical methods, or that observed differences are insignificant. Or one can invoke the hypothesis that the "natives" or the "deviants" in our own society, are irrational.

If religious doctrines are factored in—for example, that Christianity is the one true religion—with the Enlightenment idea of evolutionary progress, modern capitalism, scientism, and the technological superiority of the West, it becomes possible to understand how many obstacles prevent the observation of cultural relativism in the social sciences.

The counter-Enlightenment traditions have tended to be conservative, religious, tradition-bound, and just as ethnocentric as the Enlightenment. From a global perspective, both schools of thought are engaged in a local skirmish about which Western tradition is more important, science or religion. It is little wonder that many postcolonialist scholars believe that postmodernism is just another Western ethnocentric outlook.

At the other extreme, cultural relativism often arises in reaction to this view. Cultural relativism may sometimes mask a romantic glorification of the primitive that also may do non-European cultures an injustice and be another form of Eurocentrism. These issues are offshoots of the controversies about modernity and postmodernity. In Chapters 6, 7, and 8 they are placed within the context of postmodernism's emphasis on difference.

The Age of Weltanschauung

A revival of relativism at the end of the 19th century was connected with the movements known as *Lebensphilosophie* (life philosophy)[26] and *Weltanschauungphilosophie* (the philosophy of worldviews). Partly under the influence of Nietzsche, these counter-Enlightenment trends were part of the effort, spearheaded by Dilthey, to reject the view that psychology is a natural science. To make his case, Dilthey appeals to several ideas. One idea is the concrete, lived experience, which is value laden, meaningful, and teleological and embodies specific cultural forms. According to Dilthey, we must understand human behavior through the use of descriptions, history, literature, biographies, and *Verstehen*, or subjective empathy.

Dilthey does not rule out the discovery of universal historical laws or trends, although Husserl and others[27] take him to be an extreme historical relativist. His doctrine of worldviews, which anticipates Jaspers and Mannheim, reinforces this interpretation. Different cultures, or a culture at different stages in its history, are guided by mythical, religious, or scientific worldviews. But none of these views is metaphysically privileged. This idea, that no doctrine or worldview is metaphysically privileged, is a key point of postmodernism.

For all intents and purposes, Dilthey started the famous *Methodenstreit*, the controversy about values and methods[28] made famous by Rickert, Weber, and Menger, by defending a sharp distinction between the natural sciences and the human or cultural sciences. The key issues in this argument center on the methodological differences between the natural and cultural sciences, the status of psychology as a natural or a cultural science, the role of values, and the gap between meaning and being and between the concrete and the universal.

This controversy had a tremendous effect on 20th-century developments in the social sciences. It also raised very real questions about whether determinate answers to such questions as "What is nature?" "What is history?" "What are values?" and "What is it to be human?" could be found. But no one until the postmodernists suggested that the answer to all of these questions must be "no."

Ideology and Nihilism

The concept of ideology originated in the wake of the French Revolution, reached peaks in the literature of Marxism and of Mannheim and the sociology of knowledge, then became celebrated in the end-of-ideology thesis of the 1960s.[29] The topic is having a revival due to the current political climate in the United States and elsewhere, as well as to important developments in the sociology of science, which in many respects updates the classical program of the sociology of knowledge.[30]

Ideology is often characterized as negative or critical, serving certain illegitimate or particular interests or classes at the expense of others. Sometimes it is a mask for class struggle and exploitation, unconscious motives, the will to power or hatred for life. This is why Marx, Nietzsche, and Freud have been called the "great unmaskers," "the masters of suspicion," who allegedly put forward a "hermeneutics of suspicion".[31] Others, notably Durkheim and Althusser, treat ideology as both positive and descriptive, as part of the social bond necessary for any society.

Ideology has usually been contrasted with truth and has been associated with power. One main point of contention between modernism and postmodernism concerns the validity of these points. For Enlightenment modernity, truth is universal, not tainted with interests, values, or power (at least the bad kind). Ideology substitutes causal explanations for explanations that talk about truth and rationality, and thus endangers the very idea of universal truth. The sociology of knowledge pushes the analysis of ideology to the point where it leads to relativism, or at least to the *relationalism* of Mannheim.[32] But the real danger here is not relativism, but the idea of the "free-floating intelligentsia" acting as "legislators and interpreters"[33] of culture while pretending to be detached and disinterested. (Chapter 8 shows how Habermas and the postmodernists debate this view of intellectuals.) Postmodernists may sometimes be guilty of the sort of Olympian detachment that Mannheim endorses.

One could argue that the movement to what Mannheim calls "total ideologies"[34] and to utopias and thence to the sociology of knowledge is the culmination of the Enlightenment in nihilism. In this view, the values of truth and reason are masks for nonrational, irrational, or politically motivated forces; that Enlightenment values are reduced to "might becomes right." Mannheim's final proposals for "man and society in an age of reconstruction" amount to a pragmatist, end-of-ideology thesis that paves the way for the dissolution of metanarratives, including the idea that knowledge is beneficial to society because truth enhances life. The result is what Lyotard calls the "mercantilization of knowledge," the idea of knowledge as a commodity whose validity is entirely a function of "performitivity," that is, economic and technological success.[35]

Does postmodernism support the mercantilization of knowledge? It seems to support the end-of-ideology thesis and the detached Olympian stance advocated by Mannheim, although even this is not clear. Does it endorse the view that all knowledge and values are ideological? That truth reduces to power? If so, is Rosen correct in claiming that postmodernism is the nihilistic culmination of the ethos of the Enlightenment? Or is the postmodernist idea of the specific, as opposed to the free-floating universal, intellectual of modernity, coupled with the emphasis on the intellectual as interpreter and not legislator, moving in a different direction?

To some extent, the hermeneutics of suspicion may be bound up with modern nihilism, the position that all values are either meaningless or indefensible, or, what can amount to the same thing (as in Weber), that all warring "gods and demons" are equally defensible. But the ethos of the Enlightenment is committed to carrying the will to truth all the way. If Mannheim's position lies at the end of that road, then Nietzsche's idea that knowledge that is not in the service of life needs to be forgotten is worthy of serious consideration. For when the will to truth serves the ascetic ideal, it does not serve life, but serves the idea that knowledge is more important than anything, including life. Do the postmodernists, in their zeal to unmask everything, serve life or promote nihilism?

Value Freedom in the Social Sciences

The claim that the social sciences are and ought to be value free or value neutral has a long history. This history is intertwined with the view that the social sciences cannot or should not be value free.

One must look to the history of philosophy to find the origins and nature of the thesis of value freedom. The so-called is-ought, fact-value or descriptive-prescriptive distinction underlies many versions of the value neutrality thesis. Hume[36] argues that logic can never allow us to derive an "ought" from an "is." That is, no statement of value can be logically derived from factual premises alone. This is true. But what does it prove? Hume assumes that only deductive justifications are possible. But if there are other ways of justifying assertions, then Hume's argument only shows that any attempt to justify value judgments by deductive syllogisms that contain solely factual premises will fail.

Hume has another argument that has an important bearing on value freedom. For Hume,[37] inductive or empirical reasoning is always circular, and hence invalid. Thus, deduction cannot increase empirical knowledge; empirical knowledge is based on habit, psychology, and custom and thus is not (for Hume) rational.[38]

However, Hume does not believe that value judgments are any more (or less) irrational than scientific judgments. In addition, Hume has a naturalistic view of values: Value judgments are rooted in universal human facts regarding sympathy. He shares this view with British moralists such as Smith and the writers of the Scottish Enlightenment.[39] So value judgments, though different from factual, are not inferior to them. Indeed, beliefs are derived from, are even a species of, feelings.

Hume can be seen as the first modern thinker to spell out the idea of value relevance: All our beliefs, scientific and otherwise, are rooted in, and colored by, human nature, including feelings and psychological mechanisms.[40] Custom is king, and habit and instincts serve this ruler as the only guides in life.

Kant, who wanted to refute Hume's skeptical conclusions, divides reason into three mutually independent but complementary spheres: science, morality, and art (pure reason, practical reason, and aesthetic judgment). Modernity is thus divided up into the same three cultural spheres. Weber uses this claim in defending his thesis of value neutrality. For Kant, each type of claim has its legitimate uses and limits. They are, moreover, complementary. Science leaves off where morality begins. The two do not conflict; they do not have any relations with each other because facts and values belong to different spheres.[41]

Kant also develops the idea that experience is always categorized and structured by built-in cognitive-interpretive principles of the human mind and that reality for us is always human reality.[42] This is supposed to limit knowledge to save religion and morality, but it does so at a cost: Moral judgments are not knowledge and can only be "proved" on pragmatic grounds and formal criteria of consistency. Furthermore, for Kant objectivity means "object of possible experience or knowledge," which implies the same result: Moral judgments are not objects of knowledge; only science yields knowledge (of objects of experience).

Writers after Kant, notably Hegel on the one hand and the positivists on the other, modify his views and those of Hume in ways that cannot be detailed here. Briefly, Hegel historicizes knowledge and the categories. The positivists render value judgments as either subjective or as natural facts reducible to science.

Several other developments deserve mention. The first is Nietzsche's view that the world is a Heraclitean flux that can only be understood as an aesthetic phenomenon. Nietzsche's *perspectivism* undermines traditional notions of objectivity and truth, and has a direct influence on Weber's thesis of value relevance, which is a version of Nietzsche's perspectivism. There are many perspectives, all are limited, and none is the complete or even partial objective truth, because objectivity in this sense does not exist, though objectivity does exist in the methodological sense of relative openness to evidence.

Second, the German idea of the *Geisteswissenschafte*, or human sciences, developed as an attack on positivism. Humanism was influenced by Romanticism and late 19th-century historicism. Dilthey rejects the "fact/value" distinction and argues that all knowledge of culture is both interpretive and inextricably value laden. In this view, all spheres of culture and life are interconnected in Hegelian fashion. This movement created a crisis in methodology, which culminates in Weber's writings on methodology.[43]

Writers such as Dilthey[44] seem to historicize all human knowledge and categories, and thus appear to defend historical and value relativism. His work had a major influence on the neo-Kantian movements that formed the immediate background for Weber. Windleband, Rickert, and other members of the Southwestern school[45] grapple with questions about nature and history, the natural sciences and the cultural sciences, the role of values in methodology, choice of perspective, and judgment. In addition, the question of whether economics is a positive science or a historical discipline played a major role in these developments.[46]

Weber, a student of Rickert, attempts to solve these controversies by reconciling the various positions on the methodological questions about the human sciences and combining naturalist and antinaturalist methods. His method of ideal types addresses the problems of Nietzsche's perspectivism, how to take one point of view and still achieve some kind of objective results. Contrary to Rickert, for Weber the values that we take our bearings from in research are not those of the individual, which are subjective, but those of the culture. The cultural significance of historical and social phenomena determines our research perspective. We can overcome the metaphysical gap between the ought and the is, between the world of repeatable, general laws and the unique individual, only in this way.[47]

Weber's views about value freedom involve transforming values into subjective preferences. Weber privatizes values in the interest of defending Luther's notion of the calling: Ultimate value judgments, including the (Kantian) values of liberalism and humanism, express a person's life choices in the iron cage. Science cannot and should not prove or disprove ultimate value judgments, as this would limit the individual's freedom and destroy the kind of ultimate values that Kant defends against scientific encroachment. The scholar must adopt a harsh ethic of responsibility and self-control and divide life in the same manner that modern culture is divided, into spheres of existence. One can save values only by privatizing them and by making value judgments matters of personal choice. In keeping with the thesis of value relevance, for research purposes one can take certain values as given without endorsing them. But value judgments, as terms of approval, disapproval, and appraisal, must be kept private and outside the realm of professional work. Moreover, cultural values, not personal values, guide value relevance. Cultural values determine what should be studied and how it should be approached because they embody judgments about social significance.

Weber's views[48] are most clearly evoked in two lectures, "Science as a Vocation" and "Politics as a Vocation."[49] Science, limited as it is, can only give us empirical knowledge; value judgments can never be proven or disproven, so they lie outside the realm of science, even though (contrary to Kant) science is ethically relevant to responsible individuals, who recognize the need to consider the consequences of their private judgments and values in the modern world of the iron cage.

Weber's position has had a profound effect; it is not clear that anybody has either refuted it or presented a viable alternative, although many have tried to do both. But do Weber's views and do those modern views about values, reason, and method surveyed here have any point of contact with the world order that postmodernism addresses? Weber may be surpassed because of his irrelevance to the postmodern scene. Or, Weberian motifs may be transformed into a postmodernist scholarly vocation, as Chapter 10 argues.

Notes

1. Brecht, A. (1959). *Political theory*. Princeton, NJ: Princeton University Press; Bruun, H. H. (1972). *Science, values and politics in Max Weber's methodology*. Copenhagen: University of Copenhagen Press; Crook, S. (1991). *Modernist radicalism and its aftermath*. New York: Routledge. Hearn, F. (1985). *Reason and freedom in sociological thought*. Winchester, MA: Unwin Hyman; MacRae, D. Jr. (1976). *The social function of social science*. New Haven, CT: Yale University Press; Proctor, *Value free science?*.

2. Blanshard, B. (1961). *Reason and goodness*. Allen and Unwin; Blanshard, B. (1962). *Reason and analysis*. Peru, IL: Open Court; Dearden R. F., Hirst, P. H., & Peters, R. S. (Eds.). (1972). *Reason*. New York: Routledge.

3. Bernstein, R. J. (1983). *Between relativism and objectivism*. University of Pennsylvania Press; Gadamer, H. G. (1989). *Truth and method*. New York: Continuum; Gadamer, H. G. (1981). *Reason in the age of science*. Cambridge: MIT Press; Habermas, J. (1973). *Theory and practice*. Boston: Beacon Press.

4. Habermas, J. (1976). A positivistically bisected rationalism. In T. Adorno (Ed.), *The positivist dispute in German sociology* (pp. 198-226). New York: HarperCollins; Habermas, *Theory and practice*.

5. Plato, Parmenides. In E. Hamilton & H. Cairns (Eds.), *The collected dialogues of Plato* (pp. 921-56). Princeton, NJ: Princeton University Press.

6. Spragens, T. A. (1981). *The irony of liberal reason*. Chicago: University of Chicago Press.

7. Gadamer, *Reason in the age of science*.

8. Hollinger, R. (1988). Introductions to Parts V and VI and From Weber to Habermas. In E. D. Klemke, R. Hollinger, & A. D. Kline (Eds.), *Introductory readings in the philosophy of science* (rev. ed.). (pp. 319-326, pp. 377-383, and pp. 416-427). Buffalo, NY: Prometheus. See also Lemke, D., Woodman, W. F., & Hollinger, R. (1991, April). *The concept of rationality in social theory: Its origins in Comte, Weber, and Durkheim.* Paper presented at the Midwest Annual Sociological Society Meeting, Des Moines, IA; and Lemke, D., Woodman, W. F., & Hollinger, R. (1992). *Scholars in the iron cage*. Paper presented at the annual Midwest Sociological Society Meeting, Kansas City, MO.

9. Homans, G. (1961). *The nature of social science*. New York: Harcourt Brace and Company.

10. Bergner, J. T. (1981). *The origin of formalism in social science*. Chicago: University of Chicago Press; Bruun, *Science, values and politics in Max Weber's methodology*; Bryant, C. G. A. (1985). *Positivism in social theory and research*. New York: St. Martin's Press; Oakes, G. (1988). *Weber and Rickert*. Cambridge:

MIT Press; Proctor, *Value free science?*; Turner, S., & Facor, R. (1982). *Max Weber and the dispute about reason and values*. New York: Routledge.

11. Proctor, *Value free science?*.

12. Ibid.; Spragens, *The irony of liberal reason*.

13. Dilthey, W. (1989). *Introduction to the Human Sciences (Selected Works: Vol. I)*, Princeton, NJ: Princeton University Press; Gadamer, *Truth and method*. See also Rickman, H. P. (Ed.). (1976). *Selected writings*. New York/Cambridge, UK: Cambridge University Press; Taylor, C. (1977). Interpretation and the sciences of man. In F. B. Dallmayr and T. A. McCarthy (Eds.), *Understanding and social inquiry* (pp. 101-32). Notre Dame: University of Notre Dame Press.

14. Rosenberg, A. (1988). *Philosophy of social science*. Boulder, CO: Westview; von Wright, G. H. (1971). *Explanation and understanding*. Ithaca, NY: Cornell University Press.

15. Giddens, A. (1976). *New rules of sociological method* New York: Basic Books.

16. This simple distinction is almost always missed in discussions of objectivity and values in the social sciences.

17. Skinner, B. F. (1969). *Beyond freedom and dignity*. New York: Knopf.

18. Proctor, *Value free science?*.

19. Ibid. See also Bryant, *Positivism in social theory and research*.

20. Lauden, L. (1977). *Progress and its problems*. Berkeley: University of California Press; Lauden, L. (Ed.). (1981). *Scientific revolutions*. New York: Oxford University Press; Lauden, L. (1984). *Science and values*. Berkeley: University of California Press; Brown, J. R. (Ed.). (1984). *Scientific rationality: The sociological turn*. Boston: Reidel.

21. Barnes, B. (1974). *Scientific knowledge and sociological theory*. New York: Routledge; Latour, B. (1987). *Science in action*. Cambridge, MA: Harvard University Press; Mulkay, M. (1979). *Science and the sociology of knowledge*. Sydney, Australia: Allen and Unwin; Sperber, I. (1990). *Fashions in science*. Minneapolis: University of Minnesota Press.

22. Kuhn, T. S. *The structure of scientific revolution* (rev. ed.). Chicago: University of Chicago Press.

23. Margolis, J. (1992). *The truth about relativism*. Cambridge, MA: Blackwell.

24. Berlin, I. (1976). *Vico and Herder*. London: Hogarth.

25. Hollis, M. (1979). The epistemological unity of mankind, and Horton, R. Reply to Hollis. In S. C. Brown (Ed.), *Philosophical disputes in the social sciences* (pp. 225-42). Atlantic Highlands, NJ: Humanities Press. See also Taylor, C. (1985). Rationality. In *Philosophy and the human sciences (Philosophical papers: Vol. 2)* (pp. 134-51). New York/Cambridge, UK: Cambridge University Press.

26. Lepenies, W. (1988). Between social science and poetry in Germany. *Poetics Today*, *9*, 112-143; Schnadelbach, H. (1984). *Philosophy in Germany*. New York/Cambridge, UK: Cambridge University Press.

27. Barash, *Martin Heidegger and the problem of historical meaning*; Husserl, E. (1981). The Dilthey-Husserl correspondence. In P. McCormick & F. Elliston (Eds.), *Husserl: Shorter works* (pp. 203-10). Notre Dame: University of Notre Dame Press; Mandelbaum, M. (1971). *History, man and reason*. Baltimore: Johns Hopkins University Press.

28. Bryant, *Positivism in social theory and research*; Proctor, *Value free science?*.

29. Berger, P., & Luckmann, T. (1967). *The social construction of reality*. Garden City: NY Doubleday; Eagleton, T. (1991). *Ideology*. New York: Verso; Mannheim, *Ideology and utopia*; Geuss, R. (1981). *The idea of a critical theory*. New York/Cambridge, UK: Cambridge University Press. Ricoeur, P. (1986). *Lectures on ideology and utopia*. New York: Columbia University Press; Thompson, J. (1991). *Ideology and modern culture*. Stanford, CA: Stanford University Press.

30. See works cited in notes 20 and 21 above.

31. Riceour, P. (1979). Psychoanalysis and the movement of contemporary culture. In P. Rabinow & W. M. Sullivan (Eds.), *Interpretive social science: A reader* (pp. 301-40). Berkeley: University of California Press.

32. Mannheim, *Ideology and utopia*.

33. Baumann, Z. (1988). *Legislators and interpreters*. Ithaca, NY: Cornell University Press.

34. Kettler, D., Meja, V., & Stolen, N. (1984). *Karl Mannheim* (Key Sociologists Series). New York: Metheun; Mannheim, *Ideology and utopia*.

35. Lyotard, J. F. (1984). *The postmodern condition*. Minneapolis: University of Minnesota Press.

36. Hume, D. (1975). *A treatise of human nature* (L. A. Selby-Bigge, Ed.). New York: Oxford University Press.

37. See also Hume, D. (1955). *An inquiry concerning human understanding* (C. W. Hendel, Ed.). New York: Library of Liberal Arts Press.

38. Hume, *Inquiry concerning human understanding* and *Treatise of human nature*.

39. Hume, D. (1975). Introduction. In D. Hume, *A treatise of human nature* (p. iii). New York: Oxford University Press; Hume, *Inquiry concerning human understanding*, pp. 72-90. Hume's reductionist model for explaining the belief in causal necessity, that its origin is psychological, is arguably a precursor of the concept of ideology.

40. See Hume, D. (1957). *An inquiry concerning the principles of morals* (C. W. Henderl, Ed.). Library of Liberal Arts Press. See also Schneider, L. (Ed.), (1967). *The Scottish moralists* (The heritage of sociology series). Chicago: University of Chicago Press.

41. Kant, I. (1965). *Critique of pure reason* (N. K. Smith, Trans). New York: St. Martin's Press.

42. Ibid., Preface and Introduction.

43. Bruun, *Science, values and politics in Max Weber's methodology*; Bryant, *Positivism in social theory and research*; Oakes, *Weber and Rickert*; Proctor, *Value free science?*.

44. See works cited in notes 12 and 27 above.

45. Aaron, R. (1964). *German sociology*. New York: Free Press; Kohnke, K. C. (1991). *The rise of neo-Kantianism*. New York/Cambridge, UK: Cambridge University Press; Liebersohn, *Fate and utopia in German sociology: 1870-1923*. Oakes, *Rickert and Weber*.

46. Bryant, *Positivism in social theory and research*.

47. Burger, T. (1976). *Max Weber's theory of concept formation*. Durham, NC: Duke University Press; Huff, T. (1984). *Max Weber and the methodology of*

the social sciences. New Brunswick, NJ: Transaction Publishing; Oakes, G. (Trans). (1986). *Heinrich Rickert, The limits of concept formation in natural science*. New York/Cambridge, UK: Cambridge University Press; Oakes, *Rickert and Weber*.

48. Albrow, M. (1991). *Max Weber's construction of social theory*. New York: St. Martin's Press; Glassman, R. M., & Murvar, V. (Eds.). (1984). *Max Weber's political sociology*. Westport, CT: Greenwood; Kasler, D. (1988). *Max Weber*. Chicago: University of Chicago Press; Proctor, *Value free science?*; Sadri, A. (1992). *Max Weber's sociology of intellectuals*. New York: Oxford University Press; Scaff, *Fleeing the iron cage*; Schroeder, R. (1992). *Max Weber and the sociology of culture* Newbury Park, CA: Sage; Turner, C. (1992). *Modernity and politics in the work of Max Weber*. New York: Routledge. See also Barnouw, D. (1988). *Weimar intellectuals and the threat of modernity*. Bloomington: Indiana University Press; Gluck, M. (1985). *George Lukacs and his generation: 1900-1918*. Cambridge, MA: Harvard University Press; Mommsen, W., & Osterhammel, J. (Eds.). (1987). *Max Weber and his contemporaries*. Winchester, MA: Unwin Hyman.

49. Weber, Science as a vocation and Politics as a vocation. See also Eden, *Political leadership and nihilism*; Goldman, H. (1987). *Max Weber and Thomas Mann*. Berkeley: University of California Press; Goldman, H. (1992). *Politics, Death, and the Devil*. Berkeley: University of California Press; Lassman, P., & Velody, I. with Martins, H. (Eds.). (1989). *Max Weber's "Science as a vocation."* Winchester, MA: Unwin Hyman.

5

FROM CRITICAL THEORY TO POSTSTRUCTURALISM

Critical theory is an attempt to revitalize Marx's humanism and his idea that modern society exploits and alienates individuals. As such, it embodies a narrative about human progress, a set of universal norms, and a utopian vision of society that grew out of the Enlightenment project. But the early critical theorists, influenced by Weber, Nietzsche, Heidegger, and Freud, had a pessimistic and skewed view of modernity, technological reason, and prospects for human emancipation. Indeed, they were convinced that the Enlightenment project was in deep trouble, so they had nothing to appeal to except hope for a far-off utopia combined with the "great refusal" against the status quo. Habermas later attempted to modify these aspects of early critical theory to eliminate its negative and pessimistic excesses.[1]

This chapter touches on the origins of Western, or "cultural," Marxism, including the influence of Nietzsche, Weber, and the romantic anticapitalists;[2] cultural Marxism and Freud; traditional and critical theory; the mass culture industry; the *Dialectic of Enlightenment*; negative dialectics (Adorno) and the great refusal (Marcuse); and aesthetics and politics.

Structuralism rejects the philosophy of the subject and the view of human agency and history that is central to critical theory and other modern versions of humanism. Growing out of the ideas of Comte, Durkheim, and Mauss, structuralism analyzes human behavior and societies in terms of the formal logical notions of structure, system, and binary opposition. The structuralists hold onto the ideas of objectivity and determinate representation that the poststructuralists call into question. Structuralism and post-structuralism provide a direct link to postmodernism.

Structuralism includes the work of Saussure in linguistics, Piaget in psychology, Levi-Strauss in anthropology, Althusser, and Lacan's version of Freud and psychoanalysis.[3] Durkheim and Mauss are the founders of structuralism, although its origins can be traced to Comte and Spencer. Structuralism can be combined with functionalism, the view that we explain social phenomena by the way they promote the maintenance of society, as it is by Durkheim and Parsons; or it can move in a less functionalist direction, as with Saussure, Levi-Strauss, Piaget, and Althusser, who emphasize the formal properties of languages and codes as keys to human behavior. Structuralism is also an outgrowth of the attempt to explain social and individual behavior as a system, as a biological organism, and as a mixture of the two, which can be traced to Comte, Spencer, Saint-Simon, Hegel, and Marx. Indeed, many structuralists argue that Marx and Freud were essentially structuralists *avant le lettre*.[4]

Critical Theory Versus Structuralism

Critical theorists discussed in this chapter include the members of the Frankfurt school that flourished in the 1930s and 1940s: Adorno, Fromm, Horkheimer, Lowenthal, Marcuse, and Pollock, with allies such as Benjamin.[5] These theorists defend humanism, philosophy, and history as the keys to understanding and changing modern societies. They are social realists; at the least, they reject methodological individualism.

The structuralists are antihumanists who want to distinguish sharply science from philosophy. They provide at best a truncated and marginalized notion of history, and thus none of the drama between alienation and redemption, utopia and anti-utopia that one finds in early critical theory. Structuralists gradually moved away from Durkheim's social realism to a type of constructivism that has points of contact with ethnomethodology, dramaturgy, and phenomenology. They place less emphasis on formal static features of social systems and the idea that social reality has a determinate objective existence to be represented correctly if one is to think validly and act properly. In phenomenology, ethnomethodology, dramaturgy, poststructuralism, and postmodernism, both the social world and the individual are always in a dynamic situation, always in the process of becoming that requires continual activity. The self and society are constructed by the actions of individuals without fixed rules or norms.

The questions "What is the self?" "What is society and the social?" and "What is community?" became more problematic as structuralism and then poststructuralism became more influential in the 1960s. At the same time, critical theory was revived and modified as Habermas came to grips with the traditions of cultural Marxism and romantic anticapitalism. As a result, critical theory and structuralism took on certain important similarities, such as the rejection of the philosophy of consciousness (or subjectivity), while becoming more antagonistic.

One instance of this growing antagonism is the issue of whether the ideas of objective reality and its determinate representation make any sense. Constructivism denies that it does, so that every claim becomes in principle indeterminate and undecidable. These two concepts play a pronounced role in poststructuralism and postmodernism, whereas critical theorists such as Habermas defend revised versions of the ideas of objectivity and determinate representation. Chapters 7, 8, and 9 show that differences between the Frankfurt school and structuralism took on added significance, especially regarding humanism, history, and the role of philosophy in social science.

Western Marxism and the Frankfurt School: Early Critical Theory

Western Marxism takes its point of departure from Lukacs' work *History and Class Consciousness*.[6] Lukacs began his career as a leading romantic anticapitalist, and he, Weber, Simmel, Mannheim, and others in this tradition mutually influenced each other.[7] Lukacs reacted to the crude materialism that was dominant among Marxists at the time. He makes a strong connection between Hegel and Marx by emphasizing themes of cultural alienation and objectification ("reification"), consciousness, class struggle, the importance of the proletariat, and the need for revolution, a new Gemeinschaft, and an intellectual vanguard to lead the struggle against the cultural forces of capitalist society. Lukacs' version of Marx was reinforced when Marx's 1844 Paris manuscripts were discovered in the 1930s.

Lukacs' emphasis on the connections between capitalism and modern culture paved the way for the Frankfurt school, which brought cultural Marxism to its fruition. Writing in Germany in the 1930s, these authors carried the pessimism of Weber to extremes, to the point of giving up on the idea of the proletariat. The uniformly repressive nature of modernity, centered as it was on science, technological rationality, and capitalism, became the focus of their work. In their view, the Enlightenment led to barbarism, instrumental reason led to Auschwitz, and the iron cage leads to the behemoth. Fascism is the culmination of capitalism, and alienation becomes a badge of honor. Adorno's concept of negative dialectics seeks to prevent the totalizing of the modern world order by means of a dialectical negation and great refusal. If the Hegelian whole were realized under Fascist rule, all would be lost. Writing on themes of alienation, negation, and hope, Adorno, Benjamin, and Marcuse in the 1960s emphasize the redemptive nature of art, thus revising themes from Romanticism and Nietzsche.

Critical Theory and Freud

Many of the Frankfurt school theorists came under the influence of Heidegger. At the same time, Freud became a major influence, thanks mainly to Marcuse and Fromm. A variety of attempts were made to wed Marx and Freud, despite Freud's own misgivings about Marxism.[8] Freud's ideas of illusion and repression were coupled with Marx's ideas of alienation and false consciousness. Freud's ideal of liberation and emancipation, based upon knowledge and the reality principle, were tied to Marx's version of the 18th-century Enlightenment. Freud's analysis of the "ego-ideal" was connected to Marx's doctrine of false consciousness to explain the influence of the Nazis on the masses. The Marxist concept of ideology was compared with Freud's analysis of the superego's role in the economy of human life.

But key differences were either ignored or pasted over. Freud refuses to buy into ideas of redemption or consolation, let alone utopianism (for example, he attacks some of the dogmas of the Enlightenment in the name of its ethos of probity and honesty). Freud insists that psychoanalysis is a value-neutral science and Marxism is a Weltanschauung (worldview), causing him to dispute the suggestion that psychoanalysis requires radical social transformation as part of its mission. Other themes that Freud stresses that are incompatible with Marxism include the biological basis for human violence and irrationality; the never-ending struggle between hedonism, conscience, and reality; the inevitability of labor; elitism and emphasis on the scientific outlook; misgivings about human rationality and its potential; the need for civilization to be the enemy of human beings and science the enemy of human happiness; and the positive, nonideological role of art as the healthiest form of sublimation (derived from Nietzsche).

Structuralists such as Lacan and poststructuralists such as Derrida, Lyotard, and Deleuze and Guattari all are critical of Marxism in many ways and respond to and appropriate Freud very differently than the Frankfurt theorists. But major themes of postmodernism are derived from Freud's insistence that there is no consolation to the harshness of life, that happiness is an illusion, that in basic ways individuals and societies have no history, that utopianism and pessimism are childish illusions, that understanding must be clinical, Olympian, and neutral.

Critical Theory Versus Traditional Theory

A key development in Frankfurt was Horkheimer's paper, "Traditional and Critical Theory."[9] Echoing Nietzsche, Marx, and Heidegger, Horkheimer argues that traditional theory is in the service of capitalism and instrumental reason. The idea of disinterested, neutral, objective theory, which arguably goes back to Plato, culminates in modern positivism, in the idea that science serves humanity by giving the state morally neutral, objective information and advice to improve the human condition. For

Horkheimer, as for Althusser, empiricism is a bourgeois ideology, and thus traditional theory is a business in the service of capitalism.

For the critical theorists of the 1930s, instrumental rationality dominates modernity. Science and technology are in the service of capitalism, which culminates in fascism. The masses in Germany, thanks to the mass culture industry and consumer culture, followed Hitler; the proletariat was no longer an audience for Marxist revolution. High culture and its critical, utopian role was being lost. At best, Gemeinschaft was impossible except as a hope. As things stood, the negative dialectics of resisting the totalizing efforts of the Fascist state, which also involved criticizing the masses, was the only available alternative. The Enlightenment emancipatory potential was at best hope for the indefinite future. All one could do in the present was to resist power and gesture toward the types of knowledge and values that could not be assimilated in the present. Horkheimer's programmatic statement, which announces many of the themes of *Eclipse of Reason* and *Dialectic of Enlightenment* (coauthored by Adorno),[10] was later developed by Habermas in a much fuller and more nuanced way.

Critical theory is rooted in the idea that knowledge is for human liberation and emancipation—for the uncovering of lies, repression, false consciousness, self-deception, and exploitation—and is aimed at the practical task of changing the world for the better.

The growing pessimism and negativism of the Frankfurt school theorists is understandable. But by the time Marcuse wrote *One Dimensional Man*[11] and his last works on aestheticism and redemption,[12] some postmodernists refuted, bypassed, or defused cultural pessimism. Other postmodernists have affinities with Adorno and are often fairly pessimistic as well. Foucault in particular carries forward the Enlightenment ethos of the Frankfurt school and Freud, but without the apocalyptic tones.

As Chapter 8 shows, Habermas and his followers reject the pessimism, the one-sided critique of science and technology, and the romanticism of the Frankfurt theorists to develop a more nuanced story about modernity and the potentials of Enlightenment emancipation.

In Lyotard's terms, the Frankfurt school theorists had a grand metanarrative of the rise, fall, and redemption of Western culture that hinges upon an Enlightenment philosophy of history according to Marx, a pessimistic story of its derailment influenced by Weber, and a Nietzschean genealogy mixed with aestheticism. The human subject or consciousness is the focal point of history, and individuals must be liberated and motivated to naturalize humanity and humanize nature (Marx's humanist recipe for communism). It is this philosophy of history that for Lyotard becomes incredulous in postmodernity But the structralists insist on this point in announcing "the death of man," just as Nietzsche does in announcing the death of God.

Antihumanism and Structuralism

The theme of the decentering of man as subject can be traced to Durkheim.[13] In this view, society is a unique reality that is not reducible to individual psychology. Society is a system governed by structural properties, by causal relations at the macrolevel. Social laws and social facts are objective and amenable to discovery by the use of natural science methods and techniques. Durkheim claims that if sociology is to be an objective empirical science, social functions can (and should) be ascertained independent of (and after) the discovery of social causes.

Durkheim mixes organic, functional, and structural models, as does Parsons. He emphasizes antihumanism, where humanism is construed as a methodological injunction to make the human agent the locus of society and history, the formal aspects of society as system ("social morphology"), and the idea that each social system is a unique species of social reality. Each individual is constituted by his or her place in the system and is determined by it. Mauss introduces the idea of symbolic exchange as the key to society, taking his point of departure from Durkheim's analysis of religion, the collective conscience, and organic solidarity.[14] The postmodernists Baudrillard and Derrida explicitly acknowledge the influence of Mauss.[15]

The French Hegelian-Marxists can be viewed as an intermediary between Durkheim and structuralism. Influential in France between the world wars, they reject the Cartesian heritage of the French tradition, as well as the heritage of Comte and Saint-Simon that leads to Durkheim. The French Hegelian-Marxists stress the ideas of desire, lack, and the struggle between master and slave that defines self-recognition, mutuality, and the social in Hegel's *Phenomenology*. This emphasis on desire, freedom, and struggle, which is taken up by Sartre in his version of humanism, accompanies a philosophy of history, a certain kind of pessimism, and a rejection of the ideals of French republicanism, even liberalism.[16]

Saussure

The death of man and the decentering of the subject that is a main characteristic of French structuralism, poststructuralism, and postmodernism has a political, even an ideological, root, but its theoretical agenda is taken from Saussure, the great Swiss linguist. For Saussure, language is a formal system or code whose connection to extralinguistic reality is arbitrary and conventional. Each term in the language system gets its meaning from its unique place in the whole—from its difference from all other possible positions in the system (which are all thus eternally present or at least always in play). Language (as opposed to speech) is this system of rules, together with the (noncausal) mechanisms by which transformations take place within the system. This amounts to a version of Hegelian dialectics without the subject; or, as in the case of Piaget and Levi-Strauss, Kantianism without the subject. The arbitrary differences in the system, the signifiers and the signs, as well as their connections within the system, are put to use in society by factors that have nothing to do with "natural" connections between language and the world. This is the Durkheimian notion that each social reality is a unique social species stripped of all vestiges of realism.

For Saussure, stable, determinate meanings grow out of the interplay of differences among the signs of the system. Identity is thus the product of difference; stability is the product of change. Language can be studied independently of history (synchronically), and historical or diachronic studies view a language system over different points in time. This is a very insubstantial conception of history that other structuralists and poststructuralists have been criticized for endorsing.

Levi-Strauss

Levi-Strauss takes Saussure's ideas about language systems and applies them to myths and practices and social systems. For Levi-Strauss, all social systems embody permutations and combinations of a universal binary code governed by dichotomies that express the main concerns of human life: life/death, male/female, hot/cold, wet/dry, raw/cooked, and, most basically, nature/culture. These codes and the human actions that articulate them must be studied scientifically, without recourse to the human subject or to the concerns that guide the Frankfurt theorists or the Hegelians and Marxists in France. To be sure, Levi-Strauss is not a political conservative. In "Race and History,"[17] he explicitly rejects the Western idea of progress and the Whiggish view that Western civilization is the high point of human history (as does Freud in *Civilization and Its Discontents*). Levi-Strauss emphasizes the primacy of ahistorical myth, society, and human life, at least in the humanist sense of the historical, as is evident from his criticism of Sartre.[18]

However, if Derrida is correct,[19] Levi-Strauss is a Rousseauian romantic, yearning for a glorious simple state where nature and culture are at one, a state that is alluded to in human myths. Indeed, Levi-Strauss demolishes the notion of the "savage" or "primitive" mind, and with it the ethnocentrism that had accompanied cultural anthropology since its beginnings during 19th-century colonialism. The modern mind is no different than the primitive mind in its logical, rational capacities, or sophistication. For Levi-Strauss primitive and modern societies, belief systems, and worldviews are merely variations of each other, different permutations and combinations of the same universal binary code.

This view has been used to develop radical claims in some recent postmodernist work in postcolonialism, ethnography, and cultural studies. It complements the emphasis of Lacan and Deleuze and Guattari on the positive aspects of pre-Oedipal desire and play, as well as Foucault's ethics of the care of the self, a form of life that seeks to avoid the technologies of the self of our modern disciplinary society. Recent work on ideas such as society without the state by radical cultural anthropologists may be nostalgic, but at least it moves away from the blatant ethnocentrism and racism that often accompany the idea of the primitive in modern cultural studies. These writers are indebted to Levi-Strauss for this outlook.

Western attitudes toward non-Western cultures have veered between extremes. Members of non-Western cultures were seen either as barbarians who needed Western Enlightenment or as noble savages who could teach Westerners how to live closer to nature and thus be happier. Both views are equally mistaken and equally ethnocentric. The task we face is to let others speak for themselves so that we can understand them as best we can. But the tendency for us to be judgmental or to feel guilty or superior will prevent this sort of communication. By the same token, although non-Westerners are understandably angry with the West, their emphasis on blame and guilt does not promote the kind of understanding that is needed in an increasingly globalized world.

This is also the case of women, people of color, and other marginalized groups within Western societies. The mutual antagonisms that constitute the cultural wars, debates about political correctness, free speech, and multiculturalism can only be defused if the name calling is set to one side and when genuine communication between different voices occurs. The postmodernist attempts to defend Nietzsche's view that resentment makes human beings "the sick animal" are worthy of attention in the contexts of postcolonialist, African American, radical feminist, and Latino literature.

Furthermore, the ideas that there are or have been "societies without a state," or societies where people were not subject to the constraints of post-Oedipal development or modern technologies of the self, are useful insofar as they can teach us that things have been different in some ways and could change again. The nostalgia for lost innocence or the romanticizing of women and people of color may prevent us from rising out of the quicksand of the never-ending pro- and antimodernity debates. Postmodernists need to get past these debates to a nonjudgmental, reflexive assessment of the limits and possibilities of today's world.

Developments in cultural anthropology and feminist studies on race, class, and gender promise worthwhile results. Attempts to use ethnographic techniques and interviewing to let others speak are valuable. The infusion in technology transfer projects of a greater awareness for others will help. The recognition that the medical and psychological practices of Asia and Africa are both beneficial and rationally grounded in experience is another step in the right direction. Whether progress will continue along these fronts may depend upon the willingness of people to avoid the excesses of tribalism in searching for ways to give the voices of all peoples a legitimate place in the conversation. If postmodernism teaches us to reject the nostalgia of Levi-Strauss and the Frankfurt theorists and pursue instead Levi-Strauss' idea that all cultures are embodiments of some common elements, we may be able to balance identity and differences without privileging any one society or worldview. This is easier said than done, but what goal is more suited to postmodern world conditions?

Althusser

Althusser carries the logic of antihumanism even further, being more radical politically than either Levi-Strauss or Saussure. Seeking to revitalize Marx's historical materialism, Althusser argues that the early Marx, the Marx of the 1844 Paris manuscripts and the basis of Western Marxism, is not the real Marx. Marx's early humanism and emphasis on philosophy are part of the same bourgeois ideology as empiricism. Following Bachelard, who taught Foucault[20] and anticipated Kuhn, Althusser claims an "epistemological break" or rupture—a paradigm shift in Kuhn's terms[21]—between early Marx and the Marx of *Grundrisse* and *das Capital*. Only the later Marx gives us a science; all else is ideology.

Althusser adds nuances to historical materialism. Following Freud, Althusser develops the idea of overdetermination, the claim that one event can have multiple (independent) causes to explain the relations between base and superstructure and between and among various cultural, economic, and theoretical practices.[22] According to Althusser, historical materialism encompasses various practices, including theoretical practices, namely ideology and science. Marxism is construed as dialectical materialism, which develops independently of experience, because experience is laden with bourgeois ideology. Each sphere of society becomes relatively autonomous from both the economic base, which explains everything only "in the last instance," and each other. Thus, many contradictions between base and superstructure and among social spheres will occur and must occur for revolutionary change to be possible.

For Althusser, not all ideology is bad or negative or even normative. Here he clearly follows Durkheim, not Marx.[23] Althusser also tries to develop a notion of structural causation, which is obscure, because the causes become internal to, indeed part of, the structures they affect.[24] Despite his Durkheimian view of ideology, Althusser clearly reserves the right to criticize some ideologies as being incompatible with Marx's science: empiricism, humanism, philosophy. He is especially against Hegel, another crucial difference from critical theory.[25] Moreover, he criticizes the various "ideological state apparatuses" and claims that only Marxism can be a true science of social reality.

Althusser's structural Marxism became the rage for a time, especially in Britain, in the guise of "language and materialism" studies and work on the dominant ideology thesis, which has points of contact with Gramsci's notion of cultural hegemony. All these tracks of historical materialism led to new developments in the sociology of knowledge debates and spurred arguments within English Marxism between the materialists and the historically oriented Marxist humanists such as Thompson.[26] The work of Braudel and the Annales school of history, with their emphasis on the *longue duree* and the world systems theory of Wallerstein are also important outgrowths of structuralism.[27]

But Althusser is too caught up in talk about science and ideology, in the belief that an objective, indeed, a priori, Marxist science of historical materialism exists. Aside from the greater nuances in his version of orthodox dialectical materialism and his interesting synthesis of Marxism and structuralism, Althusser offers nothing new. Indeed, he repeats the dangerous mistakes of Marxist orthodoxies, most notably in his espousal of a Leninist idea of the vanguard of the proletariat, the universal intellectual that will turn Marxism into a science of revolution and serve the party leaders. All these aspects of Althusser's analysis are rejected by postmodernists.

Lacan

Lacan in some ways is the most radical and original of the structuralists. By rejecting Freud's idea that normality means adjustment to reality via a unification of the id and superego by the ego or "reality principle," Lacan tries to undermine American ego-psychiatry, which takes normality to be adjustment to the status quo. Lacan rejects the idea of a unified self as a dangerous illusion. Following Nietzsche and Bataille, Lacan wants to take individuals to the pre-Oedipal play of desires so that people can continually create themselves without giving themselves a fixed unity. The idea of the self as a multiplicity of transitory selves in healthy tension is carried to extremes in the radical antipsychiatry of Laing and the "schizoanalysis" of Deleuze and Guattari in *Anti-Oedipus: Capitalism and Schizophrenia;*[28] only the pre-Oedipal play of desires can form the basis for resistance to capitalist society, which is the real source of our psychological makeup (contrary to Freud's biologism).

Lacan's most insightful move is to interpret Freud's unconscious as a language and then interpret language along Saussurian lines, as the arbitrary free play of signs (differences and identities) without end or unity. Freud's two main psychic mechanisms, condensation and displacement, are glossed by Lacan as the metaphoric and metonymical uses of language without any natural meaning but rather structured by social norms, which a person, to avoid becoming a unified self, must continually transgress. Lacan agrees with Althusser that the humanist self or subject is both theoretically indefensible and politically dangerous, a theme explored by Foucault and Lyotard in connection with their discussions of Freud[29] and in the debate between Derrida and Foucault about madness and reason.[30]

Lacan gives Freud's doctrines about the unconscious a linguistic gloss while rejecting Freud's biologism and his notion of normality as adjustment to the status quo. Lacan emphasizes "desire" as a lack (a theme derived from French Hegelianism, Bataille, and Sartre). The self is not independent of language; rather, linguistic customs define and constrain the self in objectionable ideological ways. The subject is split off from its own drives, and its desires represent a lack that results from its domination by culture.

One difficulty with Lacan, as Deleuze and Guattari argue, is his view that desire is a lack, which gives rise to what Nietzsche terms slave morality, resentment, and vengeance against the past. Instead of affirming one's desires, one has a negative, reactive outlook on life, owing to the permanent "lack" that can be yearned for but never recaptured. Yet, insofar as Lacan moved psychoanalysis away from a model of objective science toward a closer contact with literature and language, he was a positive influence on some poststructuralists and postmodernists. In particular, the movement away from the structuralist emphasis on objectivity and on determinate representation and totality in structuralism provides a direct link to postmodernism.

In summary,[31] the structuralists put forth a rigid, objectivist notion of human behavior (allegedly the result of social and structural forces), a totalizing binary view of social codes, a nostalgic sense of lack or loss, and the idea that we are forever alienated from an objective, natural order and thus condemned to a reactive outlook on life. Postmodernism rejects all of this; in doing so, it may break the optimism versus pessimism cycle of modernity.

Notes

1. On the topic of critical theory, refer to Held, *Introduction to critical theory*; Ingram, *Critical theory and philosophy*; Jay, M. (1973). *The dialectical imagination*. Boston: Little, Brown; Jay, *Marxism and totality*; Kellner, *Critical theory, Marxism and modernism*.

2. Lowy, Figures of romantic anti-capitalism; Arato, The neo-idealist defense of subjectivity.

3. Callinicos, A. (1982). *Is there a future for Marxism?*. New York: St. Martin's Press; Caws, P. (1988). *Structuralism*. Atlantic Highlands, NJ: Humanities Press; Clarke, S. (1981). *The foundations of structuralism*. New York: Harvester Books; de George, R., & de George, F. (Eds.). (1972). *The structuralists: From Marx to Levi-Strauss*. Landover Hills, MD: Anchor Publishing; Ehrmann, J. (Ed.). (1970). *Structuralism*. Landover Hills, MD: Anchor Publishing; Fekete, J. (Ed.). (1984). *The structural allegory*. Minneapolis: University of Minnesota Press; Giddens, A. (1987). Structuralism, post-structuralism and the production of culture. In A. Giddens & J. Turner (Eds.), *Social theory today* (pp. 195-224). Stanford, CA: Stanford University Press; Glucksmann, M. (1974). *Structuralist analysis in contemporary social thought*. New York: Routledge; Harland, R. (1987). *Superstructuralism*. New York: Metheun; Kearney, R. (1986). *Modern movements in European philosophy*. Manchester, UK: Manchester University Press; Kurzweil, E. (Ed.). (1980) *The age of structuralism*. New York: Columbia University Press; Lane, M. (Ed.). (1973). *Introduction to structuralism*. New York: HarperCollins; Merquior, J. G. (1986). *From Prague to Paris*. New York: Verso; Petit, P. (1977). *The concept of structuralism*. Berkeley: University of

California Press; Robey, D. (Ed.). (1977). *Structuralism*. New York: Oxford University Press; Seung, T. K. (1982). *Structuralism and hermeneutics*. New York: Columbia University Press; Sturrock, J. (Ed.) (1979). *Structuralism and since*. New York: Oxford University Press; Sturrock, J. (1986). *Structuralism*. New York: Oxford University Press.

4. de George, *Structuralists*.

5. Held, *Introduction to critical theory*.

6. Lukacs, G. (1971). *History and class consciousness*. Cambridge: MIT Press.

7. Congdon, L. (1991). *Exile and social thought*. Princeton, NJ: Princeton University Press; Gluck, *George Lukacs and his generation*.

8. Freud, *New introductory lectures on psychoanalysis* and *Civilization and its discontents*.

9. Horkheimer, M. (1972). *Critical theory*. New York: Seabury.

10. Horkheimer, M. (1974). *The eclipse of reason*. New York: Seabury; Horkheimer, M., & Adorno, T. (1972). *Dialectic of the enlightenment*. New York: Seabury.

11. Marcuse, H. (1964). *One dimensional man*. Boston: Beacon Press.

12. Marcuse, *Essay on liberation* and *Aesthetic dimension*.

13. Durkheim, E. (1957). *The rules of sociological method*. New York: Free Press.

14. Ibid. and Durkheim, *Division of labor in society*.

15. Mauss, M. (1967). *The gift*. New York: Norton. See also Derrida, J. (1992). Given time: The time of the king. *Critical Inquiry, 18*, 161-87; Pefanis, J. (1991). *Heterology and the postmodern*. Durham, NC: Duke University Press.

16. Butler, J. (1988). *Subjects of desire*. New York: Columbia University Press; Poster, M. (1975). *Existential Marxism in postwar France*. Princeton, NJ: Princeton University Press.

17. Levi-Strauss, C. (1976). Race and history. In *Structural anthropology II* (pp. 323-63). Chicago: University of Chicago Press.

18. Levi-Strauss, C. (1972). History. In de George, *Structuralists* (pp. 219-37).

19. Derrida, J. (1970). Structure, sign and play in the discourse of the human sciences. In R. Mackey & E. Donato (Eds.), *The language of criticism and the sciences of man* (pp. 247-65). Baltimore: Johns Hopkins University Press; Mackey, R., & Donato, E. (1970). Discussion. In *The language of criticism and the sciences of man* (p. 265).

20. Gutting, G. (1989). *Michel Foucault's archeology of scientific reason*. New York/Cambridge, UK: Cambridge University Press; Lecourt, D. (1975). *Marxism and epistemology*. New York: New Left Books; Tiles, M. (1984). *Bachelard, science and objectivity*. New York/Cambridge, UK: Cambridge University Press.

21. Kuhn, T. (1962). *The structure of scientific reason* (2nd ed.). Chicago: University of Chicago Press.

22. Benton, T. (1984). *The rise and fall of structural Marxism*. New York: St. Martin's.

23. Durkheim, *Division of labor in society*.

24. Bhaskar, R. (1985). *The possibility of naturalism*. Atlantic Highlands, NJ: Humanities Press; Keat, R., & Urry, J. (1982). *Social theory as science*. New York: Routledge.

25. Gouldner, A. (1980). *The two marxisms*. New York: Seabury; and Jay, *Marxism and totality*.

26. Abercrombie, N. (1980). *The dominant ideology thesis*. Sydney, Australia: Allen and Unwin; Abercrombie, N. (1980). *Class, structure and knowledge*. New York: New York University Press; Anderson, P. (1976). *Considerations of Western Marxism*. New York: Verso; Anderson, P. (1980). *Arguments within English Marxism*. New York: Verso; Anderson, P. (1984). *In the tracks of historical materialism*. New York: Verso; Clarke S., Seidler, V. J., McDonnell, K., & Robins, K. (1980) *One dimensional Marxism*. New York: Schocken; Eagleton, T. (1983). *Literary theory*. Minneapolis: University of Minnesota Press; Eagleton, T. (1984). *The function of criticism*. New York: Verso; Eagleton, *Ideology*; Thompson, E. P. (1978). *The poverty of theory*. New York: Monthly Review Press; Williams, R. (1980). *Problems in materialism and culture*. New York: Verso; Williams, R. (1981). *The sociology of culture*. New York: Schocken; Williams, R. (1987). *Marxism and literature*. New York: Oxford University Press.

27. Braudel, F. (1980). *On History*. Chicago: University of Chicago Press; Clark, S. (1985). The annales historians. In Q. Skinner (Ed.), *The return of grand theory in the social sciences* (pp. 177-98). New York/Cambridge, UK: Cambridge University Press (This volume contains good introductory essays on Lacan, Saussure, Althusser, and Levi-Strauss); Wallerstein, I. (1988). World systems analysis. In A. Giddens & B. Turner (Eds.), *Social theory today* (pp. 309-25). Stanford, CA: Stanford University Press. See also Kearney, *Modern movements in European philosophy*; Holdcroft, D. (1991). *Saussure: Signs, system, and arbitrariness*. New York/Cambridge, UK: Cambridge University Press; Sarup, *Jacques Lacan*.

28. Deleuze & Guattari, *Anti-Oedipus* and *A thousand plateaus*. See also Bogue, *Deleuze and Guattari*.

29. Foucault, M. (1980-1988). *A history of sexuality* (3 Vols.). New York: Random House and *Order of things*; Lyotard, J. F. (1977). Jewish Oedipus. *Genre, 10*(3), 395-411; Lyotard, *The differend*.

30. Boyne, R. (1990). *Foucault and Derrida*. Winchester, MA: Unwin Hyman; D'Amico, R. (1984). Text and context: Derrida and Foucault on Descartes. In Fekete, *Structural allegory* (pp. 164-83); Derrida, J. (1978). The cogito and the history of madness. In J. Derrida, *Writing and difference* (pp. 31-63). Chicago: University of Chicago Press; Foucault, M. (1973). *Madness and civilization*. New York: Random House; Said, E. (1980). The problem of textuality: Two exemplary positions. In M. Philipson & P. J. Guden (Eds.), *Aesthetics today* (rev. ed.) (pp. 87-135) New York: New American Library.

31. For a good discussion, see Soper, K. (1986). *Humanism and antihumanism*. Peru, IL: Open Court.

6

POSTMODERNISM, IDENTITY, AND THE SELF

This chapter focuses on some key aspects of postmodernism: deconstructionism, antihumanism and the self, textuality and indeterminacy, otherness, logocentrism, difference, and some recent movements within the social sciences to "resituate" the self in the spirit of postmodernism. Works on postmodernism from a literary or aesthetic point of view[1] are not discussed. Works that deal with postmodernism from a philosophical or historical-philosophical point of view[2] are subsidiary, although philosophers such as Nietzsche and Heidegger are discussed in the appropriate places. Finally, unlike many recent books,[3] this chapter does not focus on key writers or summarize their writings, although Lyotard, Derrida, Foucault, Baudrillard, Deleuze and Guattari, and (in criticism of postmodernism) Habermas are discussed. Instead, this chapter and the next one focus on the following themes and issues.

- Textuality, indeterminacy, representation, deconstruction, and the subject
- The self and identity: antihumanism, the body, desiring machines, postmodernism, and psychology
- The end of the social and the masses
- Post-Fordism, postindustrial society, globalization, and late capitalism
- Knowledge and power
- Plurality, otherness, community, and dialogue
- Legitimation problems; postmodernism and nihilism
- The end of history, new social movements, post-Marxism, feminism

The first two themes, regarding plurality, otherness, community, and dialogue, are discussed in this chapter and in Chapter 7. The other topics are the subject of Chapter 7.

Textuality and Deconstruction

Chapter 5 rehearses Derrida's arguments against structuralism. Saussure and Levi-Strauss, in Derrida's view,[4] retain the notion of a determinate relation between signifier and signified, the idea of determinate meaning and reference. Levi-Strauss exhibits a Rousseauian nostalgia for some lost state of nature that our myths allude to and long for. Naturalists in the social sciences attempt to discover natural relations and laws about natural objects. So Levi-Strauss is not alone in yearning for the "natural." Marx, Nietzsche, and Freud, as well as Heidegger and other antimodernists, take this quest for the natural seriously. For Derrida, there are no lost origins, no natural guideposts, no determinate meanings—only the infinite play of signifiers in texts. This is the gist of poststructuralism, including deconstructionism. At the close of "Structure, Sign and Play in the Discourse of the Human Sciences,"[5] Derrida maintains that this nostalgia for lost origins is the saddened, negative, nostalgic, guilty, Rousseauian side of the thinking. The other side of this is the Nietzschean affirmation, that is, the joyous affirmation of the play of the world and the innocence of becoming, the affirmation of a world of signs without fault, without truth, and without origin. This affirmation then determines the noncenter otherwise than as a loss of center. Derrida articulates two general types of interpretation:

> There are thus two interpretations of interpretation, of structure, of sign, of play. The one seeks to decipher, dreams of deciphering a truth or an origin which escapes play and the order of the sign, and which lives the necessity of interpretation as an exile. The other, which is no longer turned toward the origin, affirms play and tries to pass beyond man and humanism, the name of man being the name of that being who, throughout the history of metaphysics—in other words, throughout his entire history—has dreamed of full presence, the reassuring foundation, the origin and end of play.

> The second interpretation of interpretation, to which Nietzsche pointed the way, does not seek...the "inspiration of a new humanism"....There are more than enough indications today to suggest we might perceive of these two interpretations of interpretation—which are absolutely irreconcilable even if we live them simultaneously and reconcile them in an obscure economy—sharing the field which we call, in such a problematic fashion, the social sciences.[6]

Derrida concludes by claiming that, despite the utter incompatibility of these two types of interpretations, we are (largely for historical reasons but also because of their pervasive role in our culture) unable to choose between them. We must first find their "common ground" and "the *differance* of this irreducible difference." Derrida compares his alternative, type II interpretation, with type I interpretation in terms of the contrasts between play and history, play and presence, and the relations of priority among play, presence, absence, and being. Derrida claims that in his Nietzschean interpretation, being and presence are to be understood in light of play and absence, thus suggesting that, in the view he opposes (the dominant view of Western culture, which Levi-Strauss represents) absence and play are defined in terms of being and presence.[7]

Interpretation

Derrida alludes to hermeneutics, a mainstay of the antinaturalist approach to the human sciences. Behind hermeneutics is the view that human life is essentially historical and that human societies and behavior must be read like a text. Translation, understanding, empathy, dialogue, participant observation, "thick description,"[8] intentions, rhetoric, social construction, ethnomethodology, phenomenology, symbolic interactionism, and many writings of Freud and Lacan are all influenced by this idea.

Several questions surround interpretation: Is there a correct or true reading of a text? How do we judge rival interpretations? Does the idea of a final or complete interpretation make sense, or is it a dangerous idea? Does the "interpretive turn" preclude or downplay the material forces that influence interpretation and dialogue? How could such forces be interpreted as texts?

Is there anything outside the text we can appeal to? Derrida's notorious remark "There is nothing outside the text" is not a version of linguistic idealism; he defines "text" and "writing" so that all human life is textual in a broad sense, and writing denotes the rejection of the idea that a sign (e.g., a phoneme) is the name for or representation of some immediate presence or being. In this sense of writing, even speech, stripped of the idea of presence, counts as writing, or "arche-writing," which always indicates the primacy of absence of the self-identical presence. This echoes Heidegger's view that language is the house of being.[9]

Type I interpreters, whom Derrida attacks (Levi-Strauss, Saussure, and Gadamer) believe that a text speaks to us. An interpretation comes closer to grasping what the text is saying through the "fusion of horizons,"[10] in which the subject matter, not the speaker, is the focus of the dialogue or the interpretation. Interpretation may thus, at least in principle, be seen as a method or vehicle for arriving at a determinate goal of truth, meaning, reference, or understanding.

For Derrida, all writing is interpretation of interpretation, with no hope of getting to an origin, closure, determinate reading, or hearing of the text or its author, who becomes irrelevant; the author vanishes.

In Derrida's view, there are only texts and never-ending interpretations of previous writings or interpretations. The idea of hearing the voice in the text or blending it with one's own is a dangerous illusion that Derrida calls "the metaphysics of presence."[11]

A Commentary on Hermeneutics

Here it is helpful to ask what the significance of this discussion is to the social sciences. Type I interpretations aspire to get it right; that is, something really was said or really happened: Plato said that certain types of art should be banished from his ideal republic. The Nazis really exterminated 6 million Jews. Millions of people were unemployed in the United States in 1993. Type II interpretations demean the validity of the idea inherent in type I interpretations of "getting it right."

Two questions arise here. What role does interpretation play in these examples? What does it mean to say that an interpretation is the right one? The easiest case is Plato's remark. His claim may require interpretation because the original Greek is unclear or ambiguous. His concept of a poet may differ from ours or be a mystery to us. If these are not concerns, the main problem is that we may have to interpret Plato's remark within the context of the entire *Republic*. But then the question about interpretation can be raised about this text. If we do not know whether we have the correct interpretation of the entire *Republic*, we cannot be sure that we are interpreting his remark about the poets correctly. How do we know that we have the right interpretation of the entire dialogue? We cannot ask Plato. Can we discover his intentions, and would they settle the question? Many jurists, including Judge Robert Bork, believe that we must interpret the U.S. Constitution by figuring out the intentions of the men who wrote it. For example, if there were no intentions about banning automobiles inside buildings, then the Constitution does not cover that issue. How can we discover the intentions of other people without invoking the very idea of interpretation that intentions were supposed to settle?

Here we begin to move in a circle. Even if we knew Plato's explicit intent about poets, we would require interpretation. Or would we? Type I interpreters would say that at some point we hear or see some remark or event with obvious meaning. This is what Derrida means by the metaphysics of presence. Something natural, for instance, some bare fact or voice is seen or heard: the totally natural, the word of God, the voice of Plato or James Madison, the call of being. According to Derrida, type I interpretation claims that one test of the correct interpretation is that it is confirmed by voice or sight or the presence of God, nature, or another being.

Hermeneutics of type I may ultimately rest upon this assumption. Let us return to the circular argument above. According to hermeneutics, interpretation involves a "hermeneutic circle." To interpret Plato's remark about poets, we must interpret the *Republic*. But to interpret the book, we must give each sentence of the book an interpretation. The interpretation of each sentence is governed by, and a partial confirmation of, the interpretation of the book. Here we have a part-whole relation. The parts are interpreted in light of the interpretation of the whole, but the whole must be used to interpret each part. A text is like an organism, where parts and wholes are integrally related. It appears that there is no solution to the problem of circularity, because there is nothing else to appeal to except the text. How does the idea of the correct interpretation work?

Many social scientists and philosophers reject hermeneutics for these reasons. Social scientists raise the obvious question: How can hermeneutics be scientific if it is based upon circular reasoning? Where is the empirical content or confirmation procedures for testing an interpretation? Hermeneutics is tied to the anti-Enlightenment conception of the *Geisteswissenschaft* (human sciences). The defenders of hermeneutics claim that understanding culture and human behavior involves treating them as texts, not as billiard balls. Fair enough. But Gadamer argues that some interpretations are correct, or at least better than others. How does he defend this view?

A correct interpretation lets the text speak to us. Plato has something to say to us. But an interpretation of Plato, or of another person or culture, is a dialogue. Our own horizons or worldview must be fused with Plato's in dialogue so that we can talk to each other. Everybody who talks to Plato has a different horizon, and thus interprets him differently. Thus, there can never be a final interpretation, even though some interpretations are better or more correct. However, some advocates of type I interpretations (Judge Bork, Christian fundamentalists) believe that the correct interpretation can be discovered.

How does such a view work in the social sciences? Psychology, history, economics, cultural anthropology, and sociology all involve work that requires interpretation. Would type I interpretation help? Take the view of the 19th-century German historian Ranke, famous for his remark that historians must tell us how things really happened. Would a historian, cultural anthropologist, sociologist, or psychoanalyst be able to utilize Ranke's version of type I hermeneutics? Many historians have tried. Freud tried very hard. The techniques of psychoanalysis presuppose a correct interpretation of the dreams and suppressed unconscious in patients. Freud's interpretation of the origins of civilization in Totem and Taboo rests upon his claim that the primal scene occurred. Weber argues that the ethos of modern capitalism resulted from the Calvinist doctrine of predestination. Cultural anthropologists claim that other people have false beliefs and worldviews. Marxist sociologists believe that poverty and homelessness are caused by capitalism.

Type I hermeneutics face obvious difficulties. But difficulties do not add up to impossibility, unless something, for example, the metaphysics of presence, underlies the difficulties and can be shown to make type I interpretation impossible.

There are certain difficulties in rejecting type I hermeneutics. For example, debates about the Nazi Holocaust deny that the Holocaust ever took place, or was not as extensive as we think, or was not the fault of Hitler. There is plenty of evidence that the Holocaust occurred. But what about the war in the Persian Gulf? Do we really know what happened? Has the evidence been hidden or destroyed? There are many historical examples, including President Kennedy's assassination and the Vietnam War. But in these cases, the problem is partly due to the lack of evidence or its general unavailability. An Orwellian nightmare would be the result if there is no answer to the question of which interpretation is better. (Gadamer often appeals to the idea of internal consistency and comprehensiveness to distinguish better from worse narratives.) The real problem with type I interpretations appears in situations where an interpretation is required and where two or more interpretations claim to be the right one. In such situations the temptation to appeal to incontrovertible evidence is very strong, even if this idea is an illusion. Are type I interpretations theoretically impossible?

Type II interpretation rests upon a rejection of the assumptions of type I interpretations. There is no meaning to the idea of a correct, let alone the correct, interpretation, although there are better and worse interpretations. According to Derrida, the idea of a or the correct interpretation presupposes a number of conditions that are unrealizable, namely, that a text or an event is objective and determinate because it refers to objective reality or has a determinate meaning or the author or actor had determinate intentions that can be objectively discovered. Derrida denies these assumptions. This is where poststructuralism gets its teeth.

Derrida radicalizes Saussure's views about language. Everything is a text without determinate meaning. Writing and reading texts—that is, everything—amounts to comments upon comments. (Derrida's model for a text may be the Talmud, and his idea of interpretation, like Freud's, may stem from cabalism, a medieval Jewish mystical theory of interpretation.) What is the value of Derrida's argument for the social sciences?

If everything is a text, and if reading, writing, and interpreting are comments upon comments (or interpretations of interpretations), the social scientist becomes an interpreter of other interpretations. Cultural anthropologists and feminist scholars who use ethnographic techniques are interpreting the interpretations of other people. Historians who tell us a story about the Holocaust are interpreting texts that are themselves interpretations.

What about qualitative research techniques, such as interviewing? Here a complexity arises. Speaking and hearing are, for Derrida, bound with the metaphysics of presence. Writing and reading therefore have a kind of priority over speaking and listening. This may be a problem for interviewing techniques. In any case, because interviews can be transcribed, they can and must be interpreted.

Naturalists in the social sciences find this view outrageous. What about antinaturalists? What about people who are being interviewed or telling their story? They assume that at least some of their stories are not just comments upon comments but accounts of the way things really are or were. What is the point of viewing all human activities as comments upon comments? What can social scientists learn about human behavior from adopting this idea? What happens to empirical research, another type of comment upon comment? How can anything ever get settled in the social sciences? How can policy scientists justify their proposals and policies? What aspirations do the social scientists have? Will the distinction between sociology and literary criticism vanish or boil down to the fact that literary critics read James Joyce and sociologists read James Coleman? Will collapsing the distinctions between literature and history or anthropology allow the voices of others to make a significant difference into our understanding of real events?

The answers to these questions are not clear. If cultural anthropology is essentially literature, and if cultures are texts that are invented by the dialogues between contemporary anthropologists and members of other cultures, what becomes of the idea that certain historical events and cultural differences are important to understand?

Many scholars who take Derrida seriously and who employ deconstructive techniques or poststructuralist ideas about interpretation are mainly interested in having others tell their stories, in having their voices heard. If the approaches of poststructuralism are adopted, will social science become ethnography and narration or interpretation? Will social science contribute to the affirmative play of difference and plurality, without nostalgia, regret or judgment? Would this be a bad thing?

Derrida's belief that some interpretations are better than others, or that some are bad and need to be rejected or reinterpreted, must be given some credence. Aside from the obvious points that some readings are not as comprehensive or internally consistent as others and that some people are better readers than others (more insightful, more careful), how does Derrida rule out an interpretation as bad or incorrect?

Being, Presence, and Absence

According to Derrida, who follows Nietzsche,[12] Western culture is dominated by the ideas of being, presence, and self-identity. Being is present and speech and listening, rather than writing, can allow us to see or hear the presence that is always already there. Truth is whatever captures this presence. Nietzsche attacks this view.[13] The belief in such a presence, which underlies Western philosophy and science, is the belief in God, "our longest lie."[14] The idea of self-identity, which Hegel and the German idealists make so much of, gives rise to the ideas of pure knowledge, pure goodness, pure being, and pure selfhood, which Nietzsche undermines when he asks:

> What in us really wants "truth". . . .Suppose we want truth; why not rather untruth? and uncertainty? even ignorance? How could anything originate out of its opposite? For example, truth out of error? or the will to truth out of the will to deception? or selfless deeds out of selfishness? . . .Such origins are impossible; whoever dreams of them is a fool, indeed, worse; the things of the highest value must have another, peculiar origin–they cannot be derived from this transitory, seductive, deceptive, paltry world, from this turmoil of delusion and lust. Rather from the lap of Being, the intransitory, the hidden god, the "thing in itself"–there must be their basis, and nowhere else.[15]

This view rests on "the fundamental faith of the metaphysicians the faith in opposite values." Nietzsche continues:

> One may doubt, first, whether there are any opposites at all, and secondly whether these popular valuations and opposite values on which the metaphysicians put their seal, are not perhaps merely foreground estimates, only provisional perspectives, perhaps even from some nook, perhaps from below, frog perspectives, as it were, to borrow an expression painters use. For all the value that the true, the truthful, the selfless may deserve, it would still be possible that a higher and more fundamental value for life might have to be described to deception, selfishness and lust. It might even be possible that what constitutes the value of these good and revered things is precisely that they are insidiously related, tied to, and involved with these wicked, seemingly opposite things; maybe even one with them in essence.
>
> [Consequently] untruth may be a condition of life. [Any philosophy that recognizes this] would by that token alone place its self beyond good and evil.
>
> [Truth thus might turn out to be] a mobile army of metaphors, metonyms, and anthropomorphisms—in short, a sum of human relations, which have been enhanced, transposed, and embellished rhetorically and poetically;..and obligatory to a people: truths are illusions about which one has forgotten what they are; metaphors which are worn out and without sensuous power;...We still do not know where the urge for truth comes from; for as yet we have heard only of the obligation imposed by society that it should exist: to be truthful means using the customary metaphors—in moral terms, the obligation to lie according to a fixed convention, to lie herd-like in a style obligatory for all. . . .[16]

Truth, Knowledge, and Reality:
Nietzschean Themes

For Nietzsche and Derrida, truth, knowledge, and reality are neither objective nor subjective. More important, the idea that language could capture the eternally present being, if only we use the "right" language, is a dangerous myth. Writers such as Heidegger and Levi-Strauss define absence as a lack of being. But for Nietzsche and Derrida, it is the other way around: Presence or self-identity is defined by the difference from what may be absent. Truth is a matter of conventions that falsify and dissimulate to promote human survival. Writing (interpretation), without origins or end, not speaking or voice, shapes our world, a world of play, presence, absence, and difference.

Nietzschean Affirmation and Play

The idea of play as connected with being, presence, and absence can be found in the Romantics, notably Schiller's *Letters on the Aesthetic Education of Man*.[17] But it is Nietzsche's ideas about play that more directly influenced Derrida. Nietzsche wants to overcome "the spirit of gravity," of seriousness, that is associated with the ascetic ideal, especially the will to truth, to overcome the spirit of revenge: the vengeance against time and the "it was" that is the hallmark of the resentment of modern culture, with its reactive, negative, herdlike conventions.[18] This is what Derrida sees in Levi-Strauss's nostalgia. For Nietzsche, to live affirmatively is to laugh and dance.

For Nietzsche, the affirmation of life is connected with art, with the ability, which Nietzsche sees in the Greeks,[19] to view life as an aesthetic phenomenon and science as a species of art. It is the tragic pessimism of the Greeks, not the theoretical optimism of philosophy and science, that allows us to affirm life. The will to truth leads to world-weariness, the pessimism of weakness, and ultimately to nihilism, the loss of the will to live and create.[20] Only knowledge in the service of life, which takes perspective and becoming seriously, which moves beyond good and evil, can overcome nihilism (by completing it). Only the philosophers of the future, the strong, affirmative *Ubermenschen*, can pave the way to a new set of horizons, a new place for values that affirm life by way of self-differentiation.

Derrida is one such philosopher who wants to move past nihilism by experimenting with styles of writing that do not embody the metaphysics of presence or traditional genre distinctions (such as philosophy versus literature or psychology versus novels). These distinctions make nihilism more of a problem by preserving the traditional values and assumptions that embody it: humanism, scientism, Marxism, the idea of progress and regress. New styles of reading, writing, and interpretation may help achieve this result. Any defensible formulation of a textualist or type II interpretation of the social sciences must assess this suggestion. Stauth and Turner discuss other Nietzschean approaches to the social sciences in *Nietzsche's Dance*.[21]

The Noncenter as Otherwise Than a Loss of Center

Nietzsche is often accused of being a nihilist. His death of God speech from *The Gay Science* speaks of the loss of our horizon and our center. Yeats' "Second Coming" captures this reading of Nietzsche: "The center will not hold; mere anarchy is loosed upon the world."[22] But this ignores Nietzsche's distinction between passive/incomplete and active/complete nihilism and his view that theoretical optimism, not tragic pessimism, looses anarchy upon the world.

Our cultural center, which is only one (possible) center, may be gone; God is dead. But there are (and always have been) other centers. And we can create others. But the idea of the center has no meaning, except for us. Therefore, the idea of our being without the center also has no meaning. The nostalgia exhibited by Levi-Strauss and Heidegger is a longing for a lost center that is taken to be the absolute, fixed center. Derrida and other postmodernists feel no nostalgia or regret for the loss of that center. Their idea that there is no center means there is no absolute center but rather many centers; this is what the affirmative play of life is all about. This denial of the center is not negative but is the affirmation of life—of difference, of play, of becoming, of perspective—that Nietzsche envisions. As Rorty puts it, such a postphilosophical culture is one whose center is nowhere and circumference is everywhere.[23]

Another possibility is that our center is not gone but must be resituated, that is, looked at with Olympian detachment, at least in our more reflexive moments. This is one interpretation of postmodernism, the idea of reflexively taking our culture to be radically contingent and therefore optional. This does not imply that we must stop living or make a conscious effort to examine or abandon everything in our culture. It means that at some level we are aware of the fact that our ways of life are radically contingent and alterable. Perhaps this explains why Derrida talks as if he is not denying that there is a center but rather is situating it. He also asserts that his denial of center is not an affirmation and that he is sanguine about the noncenter. Derrida's Nietzschean effort to be reflexive about the center is compatible with these remarks. The center (and the subject) as metaphysical, as the center of being and presence, is rejected without nostalgia and regret, but is kept as a "function," as a formal placeholder of some sort. If we cannot escape the metaphysics of presence, we can at least denude or demystify it by taking an Olympian stance to it in reflexive moments, just as the Nietzschean Ubermenschen take a similar stance toward their own values in reflexive moments.

Difference

Derrida agrees with Nietzsche and Heidegger that Western culture oscillates between polar opposites that produce optimism and pessimism, ideology and utopia, in never-ending variation. This is the common ground that Derrida thinks produces the various differences and negations within Western culture. In Kuhn's language, all of Western culture since Plato has consisted of one paradigm with many variations. This is especially true for modern culture, as discussed in Chapters 2 and 3. Thus, for example, nature and male dominate culture and female; but writers who give culture or the female superiority become caught in the grip of what they oppose. The dualisms of modern culture, pro- versus anti-Enlightenment, pro- versus antimodernity and modernism, naturalism versus antinaturalism, exhibit the same problem.

Beyond Structuralism,
Beyond Heidegger, Beyond Nostalgia

Derrida's strategy for dealing with this never-ending spiral begins with the radicalization of Saussure. Derrida agrees with structuralists that identity and being are defined by difference, presence, and absence. He agrees with Saussure's view that all the elements of a system are ever present, even when they appear to be absent; we must bring them back into focus in order to define sameness and difference, presence and being, existence and negation. Reality within a system is arbitrary and relational. Derrida adds the idea of indeterminacy to undercut the remnants of the metaphysics of presence in Saussure's discussion.

For Derrida, the search for the self-identical, pure presence of being, whose lack or absence is negative, cannot be coherently stated, let alone reached. The self-identical being or presence of pure being (nature, truth, goodness) can be defined only by reference to the very absences or negations, the "traces" of otherness, that it seeks to displace or dominate. Presence is thus dependent on what is absent. For this reason, the search for this pure being (in whatever form) must be constantly deferred and can never be realized; the search for pure origins or being is a will-o'-the wisp, since the attempt to name or denote it results in naming or denoting other elements in the system of signifiers. Derrida's term "differance" indicates this dual "deferment" and "difference."

We are now in a position to discuss some of Derrida's characteristic topics: logocentrism, phallocentrism, hierarchy, the other, the other side of reason, deconstruction, indeterminacy, undecidability, and antihumanism (the ends of man).

Logocentrism

Derrida,[24] following Heidegger, believes that Western thought is dominated by the metaphysics of presence. In this view, pure (self-identical) being can be named and then represented in language. Philosophy and science can discover and express the objective truth about things.

Logocentrism manifests itself in a number of ways. First, it rests upon certain dualisms: identity and difference, being and negation, nature and culture, and male and female. These dualisms in turn engender a normative hierarchy: identity is privileged over difference, being over negation, presence over absence, nature over culture, male over female (phallocentrism). Reason is privileged over its "other" (madness, for instance), the self is privileged over its other, and so forth.

Whatever is other—difference, absence, madness, the female—becomes marginalized and devalued. The consequences of this are perhaps most obvious in the cases of male/female, reason/madness, and nature/culture, but the overall effects are much more pervasive. This hierarchy of binary opposition, this either/or metanarrative, leads to what Heidegger calls "the Europeanization of the Earth."[25]

Heidegger, perhaps following hints from Weber in *The Protestant Ethic*, believes that the categories and hierarchies of Western thought played a role in the European conquest of the planet. (Some writers[26] resist the idea that the West is the high point in world history.) The ideas of racism, sexism, colonialism, and so forth are all, in this view, outgrowths of what Derrida calls logocentrism, both without and within Western societies. Some of the theories and practices of the social and behavioral sciences, especially ideas of normality, primitive society, and rationality, are included in this view. Logocentric thought (metaphysics, science, ethics, the social and behavioral sciences, psychiatry) is thus violent: It violates the other and forces it into its privileged modes.

Deconstruction

As one commentator puts it, deconstructionism and antihumanism set out to

> destroy... nothing less than the ethno-centrism and self-referentiality of the West: the "mythology of the white man" who takes his own logos for the universal form of reason, who transforms his own consciousness into a universal form of appropriation, who makes everything and everyone the "same" as himself, and who makes himself the master of all things (and all beings). . . .[Deconstruction] demonstrates that the white man's logos cannot master all being; that his consciousness cannot appropriate all that is; that everything is not the same as himself. It shows him that he has these illusions only because he moves in a closed circle of repetitive texts which refer only to each other and represent only themselves. It shows him that there are everywhere and always in each of his texts and in every one of his writings unfilled gaps, spaces which escape his mastery and which elude appropriation by consciousness or domination by reason, just as there is always something "outside" the West's logic and tissue of texts which escapes their comprehension.[27]

These are strong words, but Nietzsche, Weber, Heidegger, and Derrida endorse them.

What, then, does deconstruction amount to? It does not merely reverse the hierarchies. This strategy of reversal would leave everything as it is. We cannot escape logocentrism until we invent other forms of writing (James Joyce's novels are, for Derrida, a paradigm of such writing). Rather, deconstruction tries to show that what is privileged, what is present, depends on the absent other that it seeks to dominate and erase. Derrida says that every opposition must introduce a " 'supplement' to produce a sense of the very thing that the supplement defers (presence). Yet this supplement. . . partakes of and transgresses both sides of the 'opposition.' " This practice rests on "differance" and will "undo the closure of the 'logocentric' opposition of texts," and produce spaces that "escape from inclusion in the philosophical (binary) opposition, and which nonetheless inhabit it, resist and disorganize it, but without ever constituting a third term."[28]

The supplement is a surplus, the measure of presence, yet it can neither replace nor escape the binary opposition and hierarchies. Deconstruction thus transgresses from within the margins, without escaping logocentrism. At best, we can look forward to a continual effort to make every manifestation of logocentrism implode, at least until we find ways of resituating concepts within contexts that permit a different kind of writing.

This procedure of deconstruction opens up the infinite other, the other side of reason. As Kearney puts it:

> By redirecting our attention to the shifting "margins" and limits which determine...logocentric procedures of exclusion and division, Derrida contrives to dismantle our preconceived notions of *identity* and expose us to the challenge of hitherto suppressed or concealed "otherness"–the *other* side of experience, which has been ignored in order to preserve the illusion of truth as a perfectly self-contained and self-sufficient presence....For Derrida, there is nothing that has been thought that cannot be rethought.[29]

There are no determinate, fixed, bounded, decidable answers to these questions, no axiomatic system of natural signs that cannot be rethought or resituated. This is not nihilism, but a more rigorous application of the Socratic quest, a more rigorous application of the ethos of the Enlightenment.

By the same token, *humanism,* the thesis that "man" has a goal or purpose that can reach closure, is not a metaphysical claim; or if it is, it implies that man has come to an end or conclusion. Indeed, Derrida, echoing Nietzsche, Heidegger, and Skinner, claims "there never has been a subject" while denying that anybody, including Foucault, Lacan, or Althusser, has ever wanted to eliminate the need to talk about the individual. We need to rethink the role of the subject in law, psychology, ethics, and other spheres within a discussion of freedom, autobiography, friendship, and community.[30] One way of resituating the subject is to talk about the ends of man, as Derrida and Foucault do.[31] Their aim is to move away from the idea of man or the subject as a "transcendental signified," the subject of experience or its object, the locus and creator of the world, and refocus on the idea that the individual is a "who" and not a "what."[32]

Antihumanism

The humanist tradition, which goes back at least to the Renaissance, is connected with a number of developments—modern individualism, free market capitalism, and liberalism—and many of their values: autonomy, privacy, the rule of law.[33] Connected with this ideology is the theory of human nature that began with Hobbes and culminated in rational choice theory. Underlying this worldview is the epistemology of Cartesianism, with its distinctions between subjectivity and objectivity and facts and values and its view of the self as subject. Even romanticism and existentialism develop variations on this theme, albeit in negative and reactive form.

In the humanist view, the self is an Aristotelian substance or subject, with certain defining properties such as rationality. Nietzsche criticizes this view because, despite efforts by Hegel, it cannot make room for human finitude and self-constitution. Despite the romantics (or perhaps because of them) this view cannot move away from the nostalgia associated with various forms of expressivism. The idea of the self as subject also is associated with various myths, such as that of free will, which separates the doer from the deed done and is thus connected for

Nietzsche with the reactive, negative, slave mentality of the weak.[34] For Nietzsche, self-constitution or self-creation, the attempt to see one's life as a work of art, allows strong individuals to recreate themselves continually in healthy ways, without being bogged down by the past.

Heidegger's notion of authenticity in *Being and Time*[35] stresses the idea that the individual is a who, not a what. The authentic individual resolves to be a unique self by making his or her future the unifying dimension of life's journey. One projects one's own possibilities, and in so doing interprets the entire world. (Sartre takes up this idea in his version of existentialism.) For Nietzsche, Heidegger, and Sartre, style is the hallmark of authentic individuals.

Heidegger later came to believe that humanism lies at the center of the will to dominate that defines Western culture. Philosophy from Plato to Nietzsche is subjectivist; reality is defined in terms of what humans can understand or control. Pragmatism and technological civilization are the culmination of the Western tradition. Genuine humanism rejects this subjectivist idea of reality and values. Genuine humanism means a return to the Greek idea of belonging to the earth, of living simply and serving as the caretaker of the earth.[36]

The antihumanism of Foucault and Derrida is tremendously influenced by Heidegger. Foucault's view that the self becomes a subjugated subject and his attack on the self as both subject and object motivate his desire to move from technologies of the self to the ancient idea of the care of the self (the art of living).[37]

Derrida's discussion of the ends of man sharply distinguishes between Nietzsche and Heidegger, because Nietzsche wants to move beyond humanism, whereas Heidegger wants to return to some "original" understanding of it, making Nietzsche a postmodernist and Heidegger a premodernist. Derrida's conclusion helps defuse the charge, pressed most forcefully by Habermas,[38] that postmodernists are young conservatives. For Derrida and Foucault, humanism is a temporary and contingent historical episode that needs to be overcome, not defended. But they do not reject everything about the humanist tradition or yearn for a return to a nostalgic past, although such ideas as individual freedom and self-development get resituated in very different ways.

Habermas, Humanism,
and the Philosophy of Consciousness

Habermas[39] also rejects one of the metaphysical theses of humanism, the philosophy of consciousness, which began with Descartes and pervades the decisionism of Weber and the cultural pessimism that the Frankfurt theorists inherited from him. For Habermas, the self and moral identity must be reconstructed, just as they need to be resituated for Foucault and Derrida.

An acceptable idea of self-constitution must avoid the philosophy of consciousness and the philosophy of the subject; on this Habermas and the postmodernists agree. Then the issues become joined. Habermas[40] advocates dialogue and a decentered idea of self-identity heavily influenced by Piaget, Kohlberg, Mead, and Dewey. A decentered, nonegoistic, rational, and unified self embedded in a dialogue community is part of Habermas's reconstruction of Enlightenment humanism.

Some postmodernists, following Bakhtin,[41] have developed a dialogue model of the self that is pluralistic in much the same way but without the Enlightenment doctrines that Habermas uses. Lyotard[42] shows that dialogue, pluralism, and community can avoid both the philosophy of consciousness and Habermas' Enlightenment alternative of a unified self grounded in humanism.[43]

Postmodernism and Self-Identity

For Derrida and Foucault, the idea of a unified self, even if self-constructed, misses the point that identity is a function of differance. Lacan offers, in opposition to Weber and Freud, a self without unity. Foucault, Lyotard, and Derrida agree with Lacan's movement away from a unified self. Echoing themes from Nietzsche, via Nehemas,[44] and from Freud via Rorty, who ascribes the Nietzschean multiple self view to Freud,[45] they define the self as multiple, not fixed, and always under construction with no overall blueprint. The various multiplicities that constitute the self at a given time are involved in play and dance with each other.

In Nietzsche's view, the multiple self is a tension between the Dionysian excess of desire and the Appollonian principle of order. Lacan, Bataille, and Deleuze and Guattari carry the Dionysian excess to extremes. The emphasis on the Dionysian, on the body, on sexuality and desires, on play, on difference seems to glorify the very fragmentation of the self that modernists pinpoint as a source of alienation. Indeed, many writers think it smacks of nihilism, romanticism (and thus, perhaps, consumerism), role theory, and dramaturgy, and thus exhibits lack of seriousness. To Lasch[46] this view affords a minimal notion of the self that supports either rational egoism, which aggravates economic individualism and prevents community, or romanticism or narcissism, which supports childish self-indulgence. To Bell,[47] this view undermines the capitalist work ethic and amounts to a dangerous kind of nihilism, irrationalism, and aestheticism. Deleuze and Guattari emphasize schizoanalysis and the affirmation of multiple desires *ad infinitum*. By rejecting the Oedipus complex and Freud's biologism and his reality principle, some postmodernist ideas of identity explicitly abandon the need for repression and sublimation. Modern identity, according to Deleuze and Guattari, places too much emphasis on the Apollonian, on order, and thus the modern self is, in effect, paranoid. Fascism is the culmination of this self[48] because fascism is the highest stage of capitalism, and the Protestant work ethic is the essence of the Apollonian order that produces paranoid behavior, the restricted economy that Weber and Bataille see as part of the iron cage.[49]

Critics insist that this new approach to the self abandons the humanist philosophy of history and values, giving grounds for hope, critique, and progress, resting as it does on the assumption that human agency is the locus of history and Enlightenment emancipation.[50] Even for Foucault,[51] and in recent works by Giddens,[52] Gergen,[53] and Bauman,[54] the modern self is not entirely trapped in an iron cage, but has enabling possibilities, not just constraints. To abandon the idea of self altogether, to give up any Apollonian constraints on the play of desires, can only do harm.

Some of these Dionysian writers, especially Bataille, seem to think that a definition of the self based on desires would move us closer to a "primitive," allegedly better society. But one can see Bataille as following Weber in maintaining that modern capitalist culture is totally irrational, so that the attempt to move away from it, while dangerous, is really no more irrational and violent, perhaps less so. Others, notably Foucault and Deleuze and Guattari, have no such aspirations. Instead, they hope we can discover or invent counterpractices that avoid disciplining the body and subjugating the self as modernity often requires. As Campbell make clear in *The Romantic Ethic and the Spirit of Modern Consumerism,*[55] the various technologies of the self, the various theories, practices, and institutions of modern society, sustain modern identity in two narcissistic forms: rational egoism and romantic expressivism. The therapeutic or "psychological man" view of Rieff, Sennett, Lasch, and the asceticism of the capitalist work ethic generate narcissism.

Perhaps Bataille's idea of a general economy of the self provides an alternative. What if a heterogenous "general economy" of life that moves away from the commodification of everything is less violent and irrational, even in its schizoid forms, than the repressive, ascetic, and paranoid restrictive economy of modern life fostered by the capitalist work ethic? Can a general economy of affirmation and giving, an idea of the self as a desiring machine, a "body without organs,"[56] do any worse? Perhaps it can do better. Minimally, the modern social and behavioral sciences, which reinforce and rationalize the egoist and expressivist forms of modern identity,[57] must either be set aside or radically transformed.

Other writers sympathetic to this point but not totally committed to postmodernism have attempted to develop more situated accounts of identity and selfhood for modern society. Giddens,[58] Touraine,[59] and Foucault's analysis of power as a microphenomenon, with its attendant ambivalence vis-a-vis enablement and coercion, take into account the relations between agency and structure in situating the modern self. (Chapter 8 discusses the need to rethink the idea of social structure.) Although some writers, some influenced by Habermas, want to continue to talk about human nature[60] and advocate an Enlightenment humanist approach to psychology and the self, it seems likely that the relevant disciplines, including social psychology,[61] will work out some modified conceptions of the self rather than follow the advice of some postmodernists to leave the field altogether.

Implications for the Social Sciences

Attempts to resituate or redefine the self in postmodernism have obvious implications for the development of psychology. If Derrida and Foucault are correct, we must abandon the basic assumptions of modern psychology and the technologies of the self that grow out of these assumptions.

First, we cannot assume that human nature is governed by natural universal laws that are deterministic. Psychology, including behaviorism, materialism, cognitive psychology, rational choice theory, sociobiology, and physiological psychology, must abandon its Newtonian model. Measurement, prediction, and control—that is, the disciplinary society that Foucault analyzes in his discussions of prisons, sexual practices, clinics, and asylums—grow out of these assumptions and reinforce them.

Second, some versions of the antinaturalst view hold that human behavior is determined by social forces, the patterns of culture, history, or objective spirit. These views also require modification.

Third, the idea that social structure plays a role in molding individuals will require further analysis of social structure. Chapter 7 discusses the serious questions postmodernism raises about this concept, which also needs to be reconstituted.

Fourth, approaches to psychology that have been called humanistic will require a radical transformation of the antihumanist arguments.

Purged of these ideas, humanistic psychology, ethnomethodology, and other forms of constructivism and antipsychiatry might promote a new postmodernist rethinking of the individual. In addition, feminists, African Americans, and other minority scholars; postmodern anthropologists; novelists; and others could make important contributions to a postmodern psychology. Given the central place of psychological assumptions in the social and behavioral sciences, this would be a major step forward. Certain methods—for example, ethnography, Sartre's existential psychoanalysis (which helps people understand their basic life choices), dramaturgy, and the Nietzchean goal of creating multiple selves in healthy tension—as well as such movements as standpoint epistemology in feminism may all prove helpful. Foucault's ideas about the care of the self may provide alternatives to the technologies for disciplining selves that continue to dominate our culture. One result may be a greater awareness of how power is both constraining and enabling, and thus an appreciation of a greater range of human possibilities for self-constitution and control. Understanding the processes and mechanisms whereby individuals are both constrained and enabled to act and create themselves (which require attention to Foucault's views about power) will provide a social, political, and economic dimension to society that is less judgmental and more honest than one often finds today. There will have to be changes in sociology, history, economics, politics and the applied disciplines and practices of medicine, psychiatry, behavioral engineering, and so forth. Prospects for postmodernist developments in these fields are discussed in Chapter 7.

Notes

1. Appignanesi, L. (Ed.) (1988). *Postmodernism* (ICA Documents). New York: Columbia University Press; Art, Literature and Politics [Special issue]. (1985). *Thesis Eleven, 12*; Behler, E. (1990) *Irony and the discourse of modernity*. Seattle: University of Washington Press; Berman, R. A. (1990). *Modern culture and critical theory*. Madison: University of Wisconsin Press; The crisis in knowledge: Poststructuralism, postmodernism, postmodernity [10th anniversary issue]. (1986). *Art Papers, 10*(1); Collins, J. (1989). *Uncommon cultures*. New York: Routledge; Debates in Contemporary Culture [Special issue]. (1984-85). *Telos, 62*, Fokkema & Bertens, *Approaching postmodernism*; Foster, H. (Ed.). (1983). *The anti-aesthetic*. Seattle, WA: Bay Press; Gavin, H. (Ed.). (1980). Romanticism, modernism, postmodernism. *Bucknell Review* Supplement; Hassan, I. (1987). *The postmodern turn*. Columbus: Ohio State University Press; Hebdige, D. (1988). *Hiding in the light*; Hoesterey, I. (Ed.). (1991). *Zeitgeist in Babel*. Bloomington: Indiana University Press; Huyssen, A. (1986). *After the great divide*. Bloomington: Indiana University Press; Jencks, A. (1986). What is postmodernism. *Art and Design, 2*, 6-48; Kaplan, A. E. (Ed.). (1988). *Postmodernism and its discontents*. New York: Verso; Kroker, A., & Cook, D. (1986). *The postmodern scene*. New York: St. Martin's Press; Milner, A. (1992). *Contemporary cultural theory*. Sydney, Australia: Allen and Unwin; Modernism [Special issue]. (1986). *New German Critique, 22*; Modernity and postmodernity [Special issue]. (1984). *New German Critique, 13*; Modernity and modernism, postmodernity and postmodernism [Special issue]. (1986). *Culture Critique, 5*; Newman, C. (1985). *The post-modern aura*. Evanston, IL: Northwestern University Press;

Silverman, H. (Ed.). (1990). *Postmodernism—Philosophy and the arts*. New York: Routledge.

2. Cahoone, L. E. (1988). *The dilemma of modernity*. Albany: State University of New York Press; Habermas, *Philosophical discourse of modernity*; Lachterman, D. R. (1990). *The ethics of geometry: A genealogy of modernity*. New York: Routledge. Lawson, H. (1985). *Reflexivity*. Peru, IL: Open Court; McGowan, J. (1991). *Postmodernism and its critics* Ithaca, NY: Cornell University Press; Pippin, *Modernism as a philosophical problem*.

3. Best, S., & Kellner, D. (1991). *Postmodern theory*. New York: Guilford; Connor, S. (1991). *Postmodern culture*. Cambridge, MA: Blackwell; Kolb, D. (1986). *The critique of pure modernity: Hegel, Heidegger and after*. Chicago: University of Chicago Press; Vattimo, G. (1988) *The end of modernity*. Baltimore: Johns Hopkins University Press.

4. Derrida, Structure, sign and play in the discourse of the human sciences (Reprinted in Derrida, J. (1973). *Writing and difference*. Chicago: University of Chicago Press); Derrida, J. (1973). *Speech and phenomena*. Evanston, IL: Northwestern University Press; Derrida, J. (1977). *Positions*. Chicago: University of Chicago Press; Derrida, J. (1977). *Of grammatology*. Baltimore: Johns Hopkins University Press;

5. Derrida, Structure, sign and play in the discourse of the human sciences, pp. 292-93.

6. Ibid.

7. Derrida, Structure, sign and play in the discourse of the human sciences, p. 292. See also Mackey & Donato, Discussion.

8. Geertz, C. (1973). *The interpretation of cultures*. New York: Basic Books.

9. Heidegger, M. (1978). Letter on humanism. In M. Heidegger, *Basic writings*. New York: HarperCollins.

10. Gadamer, *Truth and method*.

11. Derrida, J. (1984). Interview with Richard Kearney. In *Dialogues with contemporary continental thinkers* (pp. 105-126). Manchester, UK: Manchester University Press, 1984 and in *French philosophers in conversation* (pp. 92-108). (1991). New York: Routledge. See also Kearney, *Modern movements in European philosophy*, pp. 113-133; Sarup, *Introductory guide to poststructuralism and postmodernism*.

12. Nietzsche, F. (1969). *Beyond good and evil* (W. Kaufmann, Trans.). New York: Random House; Nietzsche, F. (1974). *The gay science* (W. Kaufmann, Trans.). New York: Random House. See also Lawson, H., & Appignanesi, L. (Eds.). (1989). *Dismantling truth: Reality in the post-modern world* (ICA Documents). New York: St. Martin's Press.

13. Nietzsche, F. (1979). On truth and lies in a nonmoral sense. In D. Breazeled (Ed.), *Philosophy and truth: Selections from Nietzsche's early notebooks in the 1870s* (pp. 79-100). Atlantic Highlands, NJ: Humanities Press. In this essay, which is very influential on Derrida, truth is defined as a series of metaphors, conventions, and metonymies whose origins have been forgotten. See also Nietzsche. *Gay science* and *Beyond good and evil*.

14. Nietzsche, *Gay science*, p. 283.

15. Nietzsche, *Beyond good and evil*, p. 8.

16. Nietzsche, On truth and lies in a nonmoral sense, p. 95.

17. Schiller, F. (1978). *Letters on the aesthetic education of man*. New York: Oxford University Press.

18. Nietzsche, F. (1954). *Thus spoke Zarathustra* (W. Kaufmann, Trans.). New York: Random House.

19. Nietzsche, *Birth of tragedy*.

20. Ibid., and Nietzsche, F. (1980). *The advantages and disadvantages of history for life* (P. Preuss, Trans.). Indianapolis: Hackett.

21. Stauth & Turner, Nietzsche's dance. Nietzsche, *Gay science*, passage reprinted in W. Kaufmann (Ed. and trans.). (1976). *Viking portable Nietzsche* (p. 95-6). New York: Random House.

22. Yeats, *Second coming*. In The poems of W. B. Yeats: A New Edition, (Ed.) R. J. Finneran. Copyright © 1924 by Macmillian Publishing Company, renewed 1952 by Bertha Georgie Yeats. Reprinted with permission of Macmillian Publishing Company.

23. Rorty, R. (1976). Professionalized philosophy and transcendentalist culture. *The Georgia Review*, *30*(4), 757-769; reprinted in R. Rorty. *Consequences of pragmatism* (pp. 60-71). Minneapolis: University of Minnesota Press. See also Introduction to *Consequences of pragmatism*.

24. See the interview with Derrida cited in note 11.

For a good introduction to Derrida, see Ryan, M. (1982). *Marxism and deconstruction* (Chapter 1). Baltimore: Johns Hopkins University Press.

25. Heidegger, M. (1966). *Discourse on thinking*. New York: HarperCollins; Heidegger, M. (1977). On Nietzsche's word: "God is dead" and The question concerning technology. In M. Heidegger, *The question concerning technology and other essays* (pp. 3-36 and 53-113). New York: HarperCollins.

26. Heidegger, *Discourse on thinking*, The question concerning technology, and On Nietzsche's word: "God is dead"; Levi-Strauss, Race and history.

27. Bannett, E. T. (1989). *Structuralism and the logic of dissent* (p. 222). Champaign: University of Illinois Press.

28. Derrida, *Positions*, p. 36. See also Young, R. (Ed.). (1981). *Untying the text*. New York: Routledge.

29. Kearney, *Modern movements in European philosophy*, p. 120.

30. Derrida, J. (1986). The ends of man. In K. Baynes, J. Bohman, & T. McCarthy (Eds.), *After philosophy*. Cambridge: MIT Press; Derrida, J. (1988). The politics of friendship. *Journal of Philosophy*. 632-644; Derrida, J. (1991). Eating well, or the calculation of the subject: An interview. In E. Cadava, P. Connor, & J. Luc-Nancy (Eds.), *Who comes after the subject?* (pp. 96-120). New York: Routledge.

31. Derrida, Ends of man; Foucault, *Order of things*. See also Soper, *Humanism and anti-humanism*.

For spirited criticism, see Ferry, L., & Renaut, A. (1985). *French philosophy of the sixties: An essay on antihumanism*. Amherst: University of Massachusetts Press; and McCarthy, T. (1992). *Ideals and illusions*. Cambridge: MIT Press.

32. Cadava, Connor, & Luc-Nancy, *Who comes after the subject?*; Kavale, S. (Ed.). (1992). *Psychology and postmodernism*. Newbury Park, CA: Sage.

33. Brinton, C. (1963). *The shaping of modern thought*. Englewood Cliffs, NJ: Prentice Hall; Merquior, J. (1991). *Liberalism old and new*. New York: Twayne Publishers.

34. Deleuze, G. (1983). *Nietzsche and philosophy*. New York: Columbia University Press.

35. Heidegger, M. (1962). *Being and time*. New York: HarperCollins. See also Kellner, D. (1968). *Heidegger's concept of authenticity*. Unpublished doctoral dissertation, Columbia University, New York.

36. Heidegger, *Word of Nietzsche: "God is dead,"* Question concerning technology, and *Discourse on thinking*.

37. Foucault, M. (1980). Truth and subjectivity. In *Howison lectures*. Unpublished manuscript; Foucault, M. (1989). An aesthetics of existence. In *Philosophy, politics, culture* (pp. 47-56) New York: Routledge; Foucault, M. Care of the self. In *History of sexuality*, Vol. 3; Foucault, On the genealogy of ethics. For recent essays on Foucault's care of the self, see Armstrong, T. J. (Ed.). (1992). *Michel Foucault: Philosopher, especially* pp. 215-283 and pp. 334-346. New York: Routledge; Rajchman, *Truth and eros*.

38. Habermas, J. (1982). Entwinement of myth and enlightenment. *New German Critique, 8*, 13-30; *Theory of communicative action*; *Philosophical discourse on modernity*; and Modernity: An incomplete project.

39. Habermas, *Theory of communicative action* and *Philosophical discourse on modernity*. See also Bernstein, R. (Ed.). (1985). *Habermas and modernity*, especially the essays by M. Jay (pp. 145-159) and J. Whitebook (pp. 160-80), with Habermas' response (pp. 197-219). Cambridge: MIT Press. See also Whitebook, J. (1985). Saving the subject: Modernity and the problem of the autonomous individual. *Telos, 27*, 79-102.

40. Habermas, *Theory of communicative action* and *Philosophical discourse on modernity*.

41. Bakhtin, M. M. (1981). *The dialogic imagination*. Austin: University of Texas Press; Carroll, D. (19XX). Narrative, heterogeneity and the question of the political: Bahktin and Lyotard. In M. Krieger (Ed.), *The aims of representation* (pp. 69-105). New York: Columbia University Press.

42. Lyotard, J. F. (1992). Sensus communis. In Cadava, Connor, & Luc-Nancy, *Who comes after the subject?*; Lyotard, *The differend*; Lyotard & Thebaud, *Just gaming*. See also Deleuze, G., & Parnet, C. (1987). *Dialogues*. New York: Columbia University Press; Derrida, J. (1988). Afterward: Toward an ethic of discussion. In J. Derrida, *Limited, Inc.* (pp. 111-160). Evanston, IL: Northwestern University Press.

43. Cascardi, A. (1992). *The subject of modernity*. New York/Cambridge, UK: Cambridge University Press. Evans, F. (1992). *Psychology and nihilism*. Albany: State University of New York Press.

44. Nehemas, A. (1985). *Nietzsche: Life as literature* (p. 175ff). Cambridge, MA: Harvard University Press; See also Blondel, E. (1992). *Nietzsche, the body and culture*. Stanford, CA: Stanford University Press; Thiele, L. P. (1990). *Friedrich Nietzsche and the politics of the soul*. Princeton, NJ: Princeton University Press.

45. Rorty, R. (1989). *Contingency, irony, and solidarity*. New York/Cambridge, UK: Cambridge University Press; Rorty, R. (1991). Freud and moral reflection. In *Essays on Heidegger and others* (*Philosophical papers: Vol. 2*) (pp. 143-64). New York/Cambridge, UK: Cambridge University Press.

46. Lasch, *Minimal self* and *Culture of narcissism*; Sennett, *Fall of public man* and Authority.

47. Bell, *Cultural contradictions of capitalism*.

48. Bogue, R., & Massumi, B. (1992). *A user's guide to capitalism and schizophrenia*. Cambridge: MIT Press; Deleuze & Guattari, *Anti-Oedipus*. See also Featherstone, M., Hepworth, M., & Turner, B. S. (Eds.). (1992). *The body: Social processes and cultural theory*. Newbury Park, CA: Sage.

49. Bataille, G. (1988). *The accursed share: Vol. 1*. Cambridge, MA: Zone Books/MIT Press (pp. 115-142); Derrida, J. (1978). From restricted to general economy: A Hegelianism without reserve. In *Writing and difference* (pp. 251-77). Chicago: University of Chicago Press.

For good discussions of Bataille, see Habermas, *Philosophical discourse on modernity*; and Nehemas, A. (1989). The attraction of repulsion. *New Republic*, 75, 31-36;

50. Callinicos, A. (1989). *Making history*. Ithaca, NY: Cornell University Press.

51. Foucault, Care of the self.

52. Giddens, *Modernity and self-identity*; Lash, S., & Friedman, J. (Eds.). (1992). *Modernity and identity*. Cambridge, MA: Blackwell.

53. Gergen, *Saturated self*. See also Levine, G. (Ed.). (1992). *Constructions of the self*. New Brunswick, NJ: Rutgers University Press.

54. Bauman, Z. (1991). *Ambivalence of modernity*. Ithaca, NY: Cornell University Press; Bauman, Z. (1992). *Intimations of modernity*. New York: Routledge.

55. Campbell, *The romantic ethic and the spirit of modern consumerism*.

56. Deleuze & Guattari, *Anti-Oedipus*; see also Hardt, M. (1993). *Gilles Deleuze: An apprenticeship in philosophy*. Minneapolis: University of Minnesota Press.

57. Taylor, C. (1993). *The ethics of authenticity*. Cambridge, MA: Harvard University Press; and *Sources of the self*, (1989). 507ff.

58. Giddens, A. (1987). *Social theory and modern society*. Stanford, CA: Stanford University Press; Giddens, A. (1984). *The constitution of society*. New York/Cambridge, UK: Cambridge University Press; Giddens, A. *Modernity and self-identity* and *Consequences of modernity*; Lash & Friedman, *Modernity and identity*; Smith, P. (1988). *Discerning the subject*. Minneapolis: University of Minnesota Press. See also Bryant, C. A., & Jary, D. (Eds.). (1991). *Gidden's theory of structuration*. New York: Routledge; Clark, J., Modgill, C., & Modgill, S. (Eds.) (1990). *Anthony Giddens: Consensus and controversy*. New York: Falmer Press; Cohen, I. J. (1989). *Structuration theory*. New York: St. Martin's Press; Held, D., & Thompson, J. (Eds.). (1989) *Social theory of modern societies: Anthony Giddens and his critics*. New York/Cambridge, UK: Cambridge University Press.

59. Touraine, A. (1988). *The return of the actor*. Minneapolis: University of Minnesota Press.

60. Smith, *Discerning the subject*.

61. Elliott, A. (1992). *Social theory and psychoanalysis in transition*. Cambridge, MA: Blackwell; Kvale, *Psychology and postmodernism*; Parker, I., & Shotter, J. (Eds.). (1990). *Deconstructing social psychology*. New York: Routledge.

7

POSTMODERNISM
AND SOCIETY

Postmodernist discussions of the social, the community, the political, history, and postindustrial society are often attempts to resituate these ideas, to develop practices more in tune with the realities of the present, and to support the call for the social sciences to move beyond the categories, methods, assumptions, and attitudes of modernity. Can postmodernism develop a genuinely integrated analysis of conditions as we move from late modernity to postmodernity? This chapter examines the charge that postmodernists glorify postindustrial society and the issue of creating a social science of postmodernity, rather than a postmodernist sociology that abandons classic social science categories and methods.

Chapter 6 discussed how postmodern writers call into question the idea of the self that has dominated modernity since Hobbes and Descartes. This antihumanism takes a variety of turns, ranging from the Nietzsche-inspired "visions of excess" to Foucault's care of the self to the various attempts to reconstitute and/or resituate the concept of identity in friendship, freedom, and responsibility. Giving up theoretical and political humanism does not lead to wholesale skepticism or a rejection of all values, even all humanist values. The postmodernist approaches to questions about the self are as wide ranging and ambivalent as those of the modernists.

For instance, as Featherstone points out,[1] the idea of multiple selves that are always in tension and conflict can become a version of aestheticism and self-affirmation and can also become the "ideal self" of consumer culture. Presumably this is a culture postmodernists should deplore, at least if they have the courage of their convictions, and make the values of freedom and probity that underlie their radicalized ethos of the Enlightenment more explicit. Critics of postmodernism argue that it is precisely because postmodernism and consumer culture are in tandem that postmodernism is the ideology of late capitalism, whether intentionally or not. Featherstone's point is that the Nietzschean idea that self affirmation is defined by differentiation from others embodies the same kind of ambivalence about self-identity and self-affirmation within postmodernist texts as does the modern idea of self-identity under modernity. In this respect, postmodernism does not move away from the problems about modern identity recounted in earlier chapters.

More generally, postmodernism may recapitulate the same ambivalences that were previously analyzed in terms of the various idealized stances toward modernity and modernism. Is postmodernism radical or conservative?[2] Is it nihilistic, or does it undermine or complete nihilism? Does it describe the cultural precipitates of late capitalism or endorse them?[3] Is postmodernism a radical departure from modernism, a completion of its more radical elements, or a neoconservative search for a nostalgic past? Does postmodernism abandon the elitism of modernist intellectuals and blur the distinction between high and popular culture? Does this advance the cause of late capitalism and consumer society or the cause of new social movements? Does the recent concern for community and solidarity weaken the influence of the global market mentality of late capitalism or reinforce it? What does all this tell us about postmodernism and its connection to Bell's end-of-ideology thesis and Fukuyama's end-of-history thesis? Why, for example, do Fukuyama and Baudrillard both proclaim "the end of history"? Do they mean the same thing? Do they mean anything?

Furthermore, is not the postmodernist version of the political, either in its search for autonomy or community or in its analysis of change and power, little more than the usual liberal meliorism, or, in effect, a variation on the neoconservatism of Bell and Bellah, as O'Neill argues in a recent issue of *Theory Culture and Society*?[4] If the answer to these questions is not "both/and,"

it is at least undecidable and most assuredly not a clear "either/
or." This is postmodern reflexivity with a vengeance.[5]

Similar conundrums might be made of postmodern ideas of
community, society, the political, and history, although here matters become more complex and more controversial.[6]

Postmodernist Social Science
Versus the Social Sciences of Postmodernity

Despite many significant differences, Featherstone, Bauman,
and Kellner emphasize the ambivalent nature of postmodernism.
For Bauman, and he is not alone,[7] sociology is part and parcel of
modernity. It is born in modernity, its mission is to theorize about
modernity, and much of its empirical research and practice has
either been in the service of the modern state or in the service
of critical stances to that state. That is, sociology either helps
legitimate the state and mold its members or stands in the vanguard of critique and change.

But the postmodern society is one in which the need to
legitimize the state or criticize it is not the focus of sociology or
the intellectual. The new world order of multinational corporations, media, and culture is dominated by the market. There is
thus no need for the traditional activities of social scientists,
because the need to explain modernity and legitimize it or to
develop ways of radically altering it are now futile. Rather than
developing a postmodernist sociology that pretends that business can continue as usual, that modernity exists to be theorized
about and acted on, sociologists should make postmodern society the object of their study. Instead of a postmodernist sociology, Bauman advocates a sociology of postmodernism. Bauman
draws a distinction between an approach to sociology that takes
as its focus the insights about society, methods, modern society,
and so forth that postmodernist writers afford, versus an approach
to sociology that focuses on promoting understanding of postmodern conditions such as globalization, the information society, the post-Fordist mode of production, the growing disparity
between rich and poor and the erosion of the traditional middle

class, the culture wars, and so on. Moreover, Bauman believes that sociologists must become interpreters and not legislators; their mission is to help us understand postmodern conditions rather than to support or criticize them. (Bauman's beliefs about a sociology of postmodernism can be generalized to the other social and behavioral sciences. The expression "social sciences of postmodernity" is used to denote this more general idea.)

It is not clear whether Bauman thinks these two approaches to sociology are mutually exclusive. I believe they are not, and that the sociology of postmodernity should take priority. Sociology will either disappear in its present form or become irrelevant if it does not pay attention to conditions of postmodernity. However, not everything in modern sociology needs to be set aside or resituated; sociology simply needs to become more systematically reflexive and historical.

Bauman is correct to assert that the aspirations of modernity, for instance, autonomy and solidarity, are still of concern. But with the state out of the picture or at least in a different role, the focus becomes the ways in which the new market and the multinationals alternate between the seduction of the affluent and the repression of the poor, the two new classes. According to Bauman, these two means of social control will interpenetrate each other so that, in the absence of both democracy and the state's need for legitimation in a postindustrial world, it is necessary for social scientists and other intellectuals to find a new public vocation. More specifically, it is necessary for sociologists of postmodernity to comprehend these new forms of control if autonomy and solidarity (or their postmodern surrogates) are to have any concrete use under conditions of postmodernity.

Bauman provides the most penetrating analysis of postmodernity and the agenda for social scientists who are not bent on joining the new corporate university or, alternatively, using outmoded categories and strategies for launching criticisms of it.

Kellner shows that, although Baudrillard, Lyotard, Jameson, and Foucault (for all their differences) illustrate Bauman's points in vivid and insightful ways, they do not give us enough of a sociology of postmodernism, nor have they avoided the political problems or ambivalence of postmodernism uncovered by Bauman. In fairness, it is not clear that anybody, including the many postmodern sociologists or sociologists of modernity or their critics, has done much better.[8] Rather than belabor this point, let us turn to some of the basic issues about society and its study raised by postmodernists.

Postmodernism and Society

Some writers tend to abandon the idea of society as a unity or as a macrolevel phenomenon, although these same writers, notably Baudrillard and Foucault, refuse to be labeled postmodernists. Others, such as Castoriadis,[9] Giddens,[10] and Unger,[11] develop accounts of society at the macrolevel (for example, structuration theory) that attempt to combine a theory of agency with a theory of social structure but with a decidedly late modern twist. They emphasize the constructivist aspect of the social, what Castoriadis calls the "institution" of society, Giddens calls the "constitution" of society, and Unger calls "plasticity." Even advocates of globalization[12] and international sociology[13] move away from the concept of unity that characterizes modernity and often amounts to ethnocentrism.

Postmodernists generally want to move away from the idea of society as a totality, for this smacks of totalitarianism.[14] Foucault says that he only wants to talk about society as a whole when it comes time to destroy it.[15] The words of Adorno and Marcuse echo in the need for some sort of "great refusal" of totality, including Marxist versions of it, for a variety of reasons: It is dangerous, it rests too much on modernist metanarratives of progress, apocalypse, or teleological or linear philosophies of history.

In the case of Foucault, the resistance to totality is partly based on an analysis of power and knowledge as power. In the case of Baudrillard, the very existence of society and "the social" becomes an issue. In the case of Lyotard, the fragmentation of language games and modern knowledge engenders various crises of legitimacy, crises that for Habermas require a kind of totality to resolve.[16] For Derrida, totality means the exclusion or marginalization of the other. For Deleuze and Guattari, who advocate a molecular (as opposed to both an atomistic and a macro-) analysis,[17] totality and unity mean paranoia and fascism. For many (but by no means all) feminists and members of other newer social movements (including some third-world postcolonialist writers), plurality, difference, and otherness require a rejection of any idea of totality. Post-Marxists such as Laclau and Mouffe similarly argue that traditional Marxism boils down to totalitarianism.[18]

Postmodernism and the Political

Postmodernist politics[19] thus rejects totality in analyzing, criticizing, and transgressing the present. The emphasis is on heterogeneity, plurality, tension, makeshift consensus, transgression, and excess. Lyotard[20] advocates dissensus coupled with a purely formal and aesthetic (Kantian) idea of justice as a sign and not a concept. In other words, community and unity are ideals without any content or guidelines; they are more of a hope than a specific ideal. In politics, difference and particularity (fragmentation?), not unity and consensus, is the preferred model. Lyotard develops a microlevel version of negative dialectics based on ideas from Kant and Wittgenstein; his language games, which preserve the spheres of modernity, are designed to prevent totality and totalitarianism. In these respects postmodernism differs both from liberal meliorism and Marxism and socialism, as well as from the varieties of modern conservatism; it perhaps comes closest to modern libertarianism without the uncritical endorsement of capitalism and rational egoism. Miller's recent book, *The Passion of Michel Foucault*,[21] reports that Foucault read the works of Hayek extensively; Hayek's emphasis on indeterminacy as an argument against totalitarianism may explain a lot about Foucault. This similarity to Hayek led Habermas and some of his followers to accuse postmodernist politics of being akin to that of neoconservatives such as Bell.[22] But recent efforts by postmodernists to work toward a conception of community[23] have often been accomplished in tandem with efforts to resituate or reconstitute the self in ways that vitiate Habermas's analysis.

Foucault on Power

Foucault[24] rejects both the traditional Marxist view of power and its view of the relations among truth, ideology, and power.[25] In Foucault's analysis, power is not a macrolevel, centralized, unitary force, nor is it entirely negative or constraining. Power is microscopic and invades everything, including our bodies.

This is one form of the subjugation of the modern self: biopower/ politics.[26] At the same time, power is both enabling and constraining, so that politics amounts to the transgression of limits and the possibilities for action. This is a never-ending task, without a telos or ultimate goal. Every society is dangerous; power is always everywhere, and everything is political.

Foucault rejects the Marxist view that power is connected to ideology, so that truth (in the form of a Marxist or other Enlightenment metanarrative) can cut the link with enslaving power and connect it to revolutionary liberating power. Following Nietzsche, Foucault argues that knowledge and power are always intertwined in specific ways. Various systems of discourse, and disciplines such as psychiatry, medicine, psychoanalysis, law, and penology, define certain concepts, such as normality, rationality, insanity, and madness, in tandem with practices and institutions (asylums,[27] prisons,[28] hospitals,[29] or sexual codes[30]) that together form a disciplinary society in which a historically contingent and specific set of knowledge/power relations becomes hegemonic and thus dangerous. It is only by constantly transgressing the limits of these power relations by practicing the Enlightenment ethos that totalitarianism can be prevented and we can enjoy the sort of freedom that Weber and Foucault[31] see as the best we can hope for in late modernity.

Baudrillard on the Social

Baudrillard carries the work of Kafka, Orwell, and McLuhan to their logical conclusions. If "the social" ever existed as an object of representation, study, or collective action, it no longer does, or else it has been transformed into an object for manipulation.[32] Ours is an age in which the distinction between reality and illusion has disappeared. Rather, what is real is itself a simulacrum; the medium is not only the message, but the hyperreal becomes the real. In an age when images, media, information, consumerism, and commodity fetishism have become everything, the social no longer has the sort of reality ascribed to it by theorists of modernity.[33] As a result, the masses, as either the Marxist revolutionary subject or the capitalist object of manipulation, disappear or "implode." The "shadow of the silent majority" is a sign that the masses have tuned out and dropped out. For

Baudrillard,[34] this means that, like the "proles" in Orwell's *1984*, the masses are free. He holds out the hope that things as they exist will self-destruct. In *Fatal Strategies*,[35] Baudrillard's idea is to speed up the lunacy of the excesses of consumerism and seduction so that the system will destroy itself. This kind of ironic cynicism may be another variation on Weber, Foucault, and Derrida.

Lyotard on Knowledge and Justice

Lyotard, who develops a richer and more positive conception of politics, justice, and community[36] than most postmodernists,[37] can also be seen as a kind of Weberian,[38] although Kant is the more direct influence. For Lyotard, freedom from totalitarian regimes of the left, the right, and the modern republicanism that Kant defends[39] requires the preservation of the distinct spheres of politics, art, and science. Making use of Wittgenstein's notion of language games,[40] Lyotard develops a "politics of the sentence,"[41] of the differend, which relies on Kant's ideas of imagination and judgment. We can at best have only an image or idea of justice (as of beauty), which is a sign for Lyotard[42] (and for Foucault)[43] of a concern for justice and community. But it is a sign without content, and a sign that proceeds negatively. Lyotard emphasizes the differences between aesthetic, political, and scientific phrases and sentences to avoid a totalitarian unity and destruction of the other. For Lyotard, a community based on consensus and unity would be totalitarian precisely because it would ignore differences. Like Bahktin, to whom he has been compared,[44] Lyotard wants community and agreement to be based upon, even constituted by, difference, particularity, heterogeneity, indeed, fragmentation.

What does this amount to? The agreement to disagree? A French version of Feyerabend's democratic relativism?[45] An extreme version of a kind of American pluralism, as construed by libertarians? A Weberian war of gods and demons, where justice means the avoidance of totalitarianism and nothing else? It may be too early to say what form Lyotard's community might take, not only because Lyotard, Nancy, and others are still working toward a postmodernist understanding of self and community,[46] but also because we are still in the grip of modernity's ideas and practices of the self, society, community, and the political.[47]

At the end of *The Postmodern Condition*, Lyotard claims that the computerization of society, the mercantilization of knowledge in the absence of metanarratives of legitimacy, makes "performativity" (pragmatic success) the only justification for knowledge, science, and politics. He declares that the computerization of society has the following ambivalent political implications:

> It could become the "dream" instrument for controlling and regulating the market system, extended to include knowledge itself and governed exclusively by the performativity principle. In that case, it would inevitably involve the use of terror. But it could also aid groups discussing metaprescriptives by supplying them with the information they usually lack for making knowledgeable decisions. The line to follow for computerization to take the second of these two paths is, in principle, quite simple: give the public free access to the memory and data banks. Language games would then be games of perfect information at any given moment. But they would also be non zero-sum games, and by virtue of that fact discussion would never risk fixating in a position of minimax equilibrium because it had exhausted its stakes. For the stakes would be knowledge (or information, if you will), and the reserve of knowledge—language's reserve of possible utterances—is inexhaustible. This sketches the outline of a politics that would respect both the desire for justice and the desire for the unknown.[48]

In Lyotard's view, contemporary science has no unity. It is thus possible to preserve the desire for the unknown and for difference in science. He uses Kant's term "paralogy" to name any procedure that keeps discontinuity in science alive. Strategies that involve challenging questions, assumptions, and results or proposing alternatives would achieve this result. In politics, promoting the desire for the unknown and the different means continual dialogue, questioning, and challenging claims to unity, totality, and closure. In the social sciences, Lyotard's strategy would mean challenging grand theories of the style of Parsons and all forms of reductionism.

Here Lyotard's similarities to Feyerabend come to mind. For Feyerabend, knowledge is an ocean of mutual incompatible alternatives that is constantly changing. Science consists of continual revolutions, at both the micro- and macrolevels.[49] This is Feyerabend's revolutionary "politics of the sentence" for science. Our body of knowledge is always changing and always consists of a shifting body of incompatible ingredients. Perhaps this is Lyotard's view, too. For both writers, freedom and the desire for the unknown can be served in this model.

Similarly, in the political sphere, Feyerabend argues for *democratic relativism,* where plurality, a kind of political occan of alternatives, is the only type of society that avoids stagnation and totalitarianism. Lyotard's extension of the strategy of paralogy from science to ethics and politics serves the same goal. It is not stretching the point to see Feyerabend and Lyotard not as anarchists,[50] but as defending a skeptical, radical democratic conception of politics.

How does politics construed in this way differ from the libertarianism of Popper and Hayek, who hold similar views about plurality, indeterminacy, and totalitarianism?[51] How does this differ from liberalism and American pluralism? Mill is often accused of turning democracy into a debating society where anarchy rules and either nothing gets done or nothing lasts for long.[52] How does this differ from the so-called neoliberalism of writers such as Reich,[53] who want the market to do everything?

Does this differ from Rawls, whose original position Lyotard's "micropolitical revolutions forever" may be radicalizing?[54] The ambivalence in Lyotard, in terms of how our computerized society might develop, reflects the ambivalence of postmodernity. To tackle these issues, we need to turn our attention to postindustrial society and its relations to postmodernism.

Postindustrial Society and Postmodernism

The main issue regarding postindustrial society is the charge by Marxists such as Callinicos,[55] Frankel,[56] Harvey,[57] Lash and Urry,[58] and (to a much lesser extent) Jameson[59] that postmodernism endorses, glorifies, and aggravates the trends in postindustrial society associated with late capitalism. The capitalism of multinational corporations, characterized by a post-Fordist method of production, is itself ambiguous. It may, in some readings, be compatible with a "post-Fordist" socialism.[60] For others, post-Fordism goes with the renewed emphasis on the market to solve all social problems, as in the neoliberalism of Reich and company,[61] and its accompanying emphasis on managerial elitism, end-of-ideology politics, and the Protestant work ethic. One aspect of this version of corporatism suitably is the wave of repression, drug testing, genetic screening, speech codes and the politicization of the private in the name of corporate efficiency.[62]

Some Marxists argue that Baudrillard's analysis of society in terms of commodification, consumption, media, and hyperreality and Lyotard's notion that the computer age gives rise to the mercantilization of knowledge describe the essence of the postindustrial information society. Generally, the postmodernists move away from Marxism and theories of totality and revolution. According to this Marxist reading, postmodernism becomes the ideology of postindustrial society.

This leftist thesis is echoed by Habermas's charge that the postmodernists are young conservatives, which is examined in Chapter 8. But it is worth recalling Foster's distinction between conservative and radical versions of postmodernism,[63] because some writers think there are parallel versions of postindustrialism. This may add plausibility to the hypothesis that postmodernism is as ambivalent as modernism because it does not completely transcend it.

It may help to have a more specific idea of the postindustrial society. Some features of postindustrial society, as defined by Bell follow.[64]

- Economics is based on a service economy.
- Society will give pre-eminence to a professional and technical elite and will be based on a reinvigorated meritocracy.
- Society will be based on the axial principle: the centrality of theoretical knowledge as the source of innovation and policy formulation.
- Control of technology and technology assessment will be based on future orientation.
- Decisions will be made by experts; an "intellectual technocracy" will emerge.
- Politics will be served by the idea of privitization—that the market takes care of everything.

- A new Durkheimian Gemeinschaft will eliminate modernism and narcissism, resulting in a culture tied to the Protestant work ethic.
- A new round in the two-cultures debate[65] will take place between marginalized humanist intellectuals and the new knowledge elites; there will be an increasing division and opposition between "the technical intelligentsia who are committed to functional rationality and technocratic modes of operation and the literary intellectuals who have become increasingly apocalyptic, hedonistic, and nihilistic."[66]

It is also important to note that Lyotard rejects the emphasis on theoretical knowledge, and talks about its mercantilization, which is dominated by pragmatic, utilitarian success. Lyotard's reading of modern science and knowledge is the one that is being actualized, especially at American research universities. Science and knowledge are now "real estate" or, more euphemistically, intellectual property.[67]

Not all postmodernists are apocalyptic, hedonistic, and nihilistic. Derrida goes out of his way to chastise the "apocalyptic tone in recent philosophy,"[68] and Baudrillard, who is arguably more nihilistic and hedonistic, argues that postindustrial society breeds these two phenomena. His strategy is to speed them up in the hopes that postindustrial society will implode.[69]

Marxism Versus Postmodernism

What is the evidence used to support the leftist charge that postmodernists glorify, support, and aggravate the postindustrial, late capitalist world order?

1. Postmodernism refuses to provide any metanarratives or universal standards, thus accepting the fragmentation of postindustrial society.

2. Postindustrial society subverts traditional cultural-geographic boundaries in the interests of post-Fordist "flexibility" for the multinationals.[70] Postmodernists glorify fragmentation and localization.

3. Multinational capitalism has postmodernism as its cultural dimension, just as industrial capitalism had modernism as its cultural dimension (Eagleton,[71] Jameson,[72] and Mandel[73]).

4. Information, commodification, commodity culture, and consumerism are dominant features of postindustrial society. Baudrillard and Lyotard not only admit this, they take it as a given that cannot be overthrown but only constantly transgressed. They are thus the heirs to Weber, for whom the iron cage is a fate we must accommodate ourselves to, even though we need to escape its effects by going private and underground.[74]

5. At the close of *The Coming of Post-Industrial Society*, Bell says the following:

> For most of human history, *reality was nature*, and in poetry and imagination men sought to relate the self to the natural world. Then *reality became technics*, tools and things made by men. . . . Now *reality is primarily the social world*–neither nature nor things . . . . Inevitably, a post-industrial society gives rise to a new Utopianism, both engineering and psychedelic. Men can be re-made or released, their behavior conditioned or their consciousness altered. *The constraints on the past vanish with the end of nature and things.*"[75]

6. Lash and Urry, in *The End of Organized Capitalism* reinforce these criticisms by discussing "an increase in cultural fragmentation and pluralism, resulting from both the commodification of leisure and the development of new political/cultural forms since the 1960s; the decodification of some existing social forms; the related reductions in time-space distanciation."[76] These qualities characterize the postindustrial and are accepted and even defended by postmodernists.

7. Lash and Urry further point to "the appearance and mass distribution of a cultural-ideological configuration of 'postmodernism'; this affects high culture, popular culture, and the symbols and discourse of everyday life."[77]

Lash and Urry expand on these remarks. In their view, anything in postmodernism that has "elective affinities with disorganized capitalism," their name for postindustrial society, is bad. Postmodernism, they admit, can be both a source of liberation and dissent, as well as a legitimation of the new order. Yet they claim that postmodernism involves "a glorification of commercial vulgarity. . . a promotion of 'authoritarian populism'. . . [that]

reinforces relations of domination," and undermines the Marxist idea of class. Postmodernism rests on an "economy of pleasure and images." It breaks down the distinctions between high culture and pop culture, aestheticizes things too much, and is a version of a neobourgeois culture, which is "pre-eminently consistent with Thatcherism, Reaganism."[78]

Postmodernism's emphasis on cultural hierarchy and the liberation of desire can be used as sources of resistance. This is compatible with radical democracy. Postmodernism thus needs to be taken seriously. Lash and Urry admit that "societies are being transformed from above, from below, and from within. All that is solid about organized capitalism, class, industry, cities, collectivity, nation-states, even the world, melts into air."[79] Many postmodernists agree.

Marxism, Postmodernism, Post-Marxism, and Postindustrial Society

Not all Marxists share the same view about postmodernism. Jameson agrees that postindustrial society is the economic base of postmodernism, but does not think postmodernists endorse late capitalism. Callinicos rejects the thesis that we are in a new postindustrial order. Harvey and Lash and Urry hold the most extreme view that postmodernism is a friend of the postindustrial order.[80] Others[81] argue that postmodernists, because they lack some type of revolutionary metanarrative, notably Marxist, are making society worse because their political strategies and tactics have no effect. This may be true, but has contemporary Marxism fared any better?

Many postmodernists agree with advocates of the postindustrial society that fragmentation, the end of ideology, the end of history, and the mercantilization of knowledge constitute an advance over the metanarratives of modernity, progress, science, class struggle, and a unified, totalized culture. But to accuse postmodernists of glorifying the excesses of late capitalism misreads what they say; they are just as critical of postmodernism as Marxists. Such critics are analogous to those who accused Nietzsche of being a nihilist because he claimed that our age is dominated by nihilism. In fact, postmodernists often emphasize the ambivalent possibilities in any new developments. Marxist critics of postmodernism assume that the postmodernists's analysis of postindustrial society must be wrong and that postmodern misgivings about standard modern strategies of resistance (class struggle, revolution) must also be wrong.

What if postmodernists are right on both counts? By objecting to new social movements, new forms of political resistance, new foci of analysis and action, and recent attempts to undo the separation between high and pop culture in the name of radical democracy and heterogeneity, traditional Marxists appear to be caught in the same position as sociologists who fail to realize that sociological theory was made to address modernity and cannot speak to new developments unless it transforms its categories of analysis. Perhaps the post-Marxists[82] are developing political visions more likely to address present realities and possibilities. Perhaps Foucault's idea of specific intellectuals who can engage in concrete and specific analyses and tactics is better suited to current times. Perhaps the Marxist idea of total revolution has become problematic. This does not mean that postmodernists can ignore the economic and technological dimensions of late capitalist society and culture. They clearly cannot. Class analysis needs to be modified to explain developments within the post-Fordist economy, to take account of the connections among class, race, and gender and the growing dominance of the new class of knowledge elites. But the charge that anyone who questions traditional Marxism is supporting postindustrial corporate capitalism is gravely mistaken. This Marxist shibboleth indicates how Enlightenment dogmas can conflict with the ethos of the Enlightenment. Chapter 8 considers the debate between critical theory and postmodernism in this light.

The End of History and New Social Movements

A good deal of ambivalence surrounds the potential of postmodernist writings for endorsement of or resistance to late capitalism. New themes such as the end of history, the end of the social, the newly emerging technocultures, postcolonialism, feminism, and cultural and media studies[83] present both new opportunities for and challenges to postmodernism. At the bottom of many of these new challenges is the charge that postmodernists are nihilists.

Take, for instance, the end-of-history thesis. One could read this thesis as the view that liberalism has triumphed everywhere and that, as Fukuyama argues,[84] Nietzsche's greatest fear has been realized that the "last man," who is a spiritless, satisfied, and smug braying ass,[85] dominates. If the last man does not dominate, the idea of performitivity does. This means that the end of history culminates in the global victory for the Protestant ethic and the restricted economy of capitalism. Is either one of these views an endorsement of the new world order? Is either one easily classifiable as conservative or radical? If not, does that mean that postmodernists such as Baudrillard and conservatives such as Fukuyama, who both accept the end-of-history thesis as a fact, are indistinguishable? Do structuralism and other forms of anti-humanism end up in the same camp as conservatives inspired by Hegel and Strauss? Would this confirm the suspicions of traditional Marxists and critical theorists about postmodernists, or vindicate the postmodernist idea that every thesis is indeterminate and undecidable? (For traditional Marxists, the end of history is realized when capitalism and the state are destroyed. For Christianity, the end of history comes after Armageddon. The indeterminacy about the ends of man discussed by Derrida is connected to the indeterminacy about these versions of the end of history.)

If the postmodernists are saying that history is over, that there is nothing new, that everything repeats itself, then logocentrism, the disciplinary society, or the totality equals terror equation can never be escaped; these will always manifest themselves in some form. If any attempt to escape is in vain and rests upon some type of unacceptable metanarrative, are postmodernists manifesting the world-weariness that expresses nihilism according to Nietzsche? Will this malaise dominate everywhere? Or just in the West, whose hegemony may be coming to an end?[86]

One could read the end of history as the last act in a philosophy of history that includes humanism and the values and metanarratives that govern modernity, with its oscillations between ideology and utopia, optimism and pessimism, progress and regress. Nietzsche and some postmodernists (notably Derrida, Lyotard, and Foucault) may be trying to overcome the nihilism that is the inevitable outcome of modernism by moving away from the modernist concepts and values altogether. Or, perhaps nihilism only occurs for those who experience nostalgia and regret about the loss of those horizons that define modernity and its metanarratives.

The postmodernists are accused of being both inattentive to history and desiring to explode history. But some postmodernists believe that history is not a continuous narrative that can be neatly told or divided into chapters or ages, such as modern and postmodern. The views of Braudel and his school, whose perspective of the continuum of history makes change "almost imperceptible,"[87] gives the appearance that structuralists ignore history. French postmodernists who have been influenced by Braudel, structuralism, or poststructuralism may appear to be denying history for this reason. The influence of Braudel may give the appearance that postmodernists are rejecting history, when in fact they are emphasizing historical discontinuities so as to bring out the idea that history is not there ready to be discovered.

Habermas argues that postmodernists want to explode history. He compares the avant-garde's desire to explode history as an act of rebellion against modernity with the postmodernists who endorse the end-of-history thesis. But Habermas simply assumes that there is a "historical continuum"[88] that postmodernists want to explode. However, postmodernists believe that historical discontinuities are more important than continuities.

Ambivalence in Feminism and Postcolonialism

Recent debates among feminists about where to stand on postmodernist themes,[89] among writers who explore the potentials of technoculture[90] or post-Fordist flexibilities in the economy,[91] and among those concerned with popular culture and the role of the media in today's world reflect ambivalence about the emerging world order. Many Marxists reject connections between postmodernism and feminism because, without some notion of subjectivity, history, and universal (or at least rational) norms, no feminist critique or revolutionary activity is possible. In this view, postmodernism preserves male dominance, or at least does not do enough to eliminate it.[92] Similarly, many Marxists think that Foucault, Derrida, and others do not move far enough away from white mythologies, or a Eurocentric set of concerns about history.[93] Perhaps the debates considered in this book are merely local and reinforce Eurocentrism, male chauvinism, and colonialism at a time when they should be abandoned.[94] Even though recent work in ethnography, cultural studies, and postcolonialism often rests upon agreement with postmodernism, some writers in these fields accept the view that postmodernism is just another hegemonic, ethnocentric Western doctrine.

Feminism

There are many versions of feminism, ranging from the very conservative to the very radical. There are Marxist feminists, postmodern feminists, liberal feminists, radical lesbian feminists, and African-American feminists who attack white feminists for being racist and elitist. Even feminists within a category disagree about many fundamental ethical, political, and methodological issues. Is there a feminist standpoint epistemology that provides a determinate epistemology for all feminist issues? Can one be a pro-lifer on abortion and be a feminist? Can a male be a feminist? It is not an exaggeration to say that many leading feminists disagree about virtually every major issue.

Yet feminism is a tremendously important intellectual and social force. Feminist contributions to philosophy, literary studies, and the social and behavioral sciences are revolutionizing these fields. But because this book is about postmodernism and the social sciences, remarks about feminism must be circumscribed.

Some feminists favor the idea of Marxist critique and revolution. Others accept the postmodernist criticisms of traditional Marxism. Some feminists seek to reconcile critical theory with some postmodernists, for example, Foucault. Some believe that postmodernism is more radical than Marxism or Marxist feminism, because Marxism holds to traditional categories of analysis and downplays the demands of specific groups in favor of total revolution, whereas the postmodern emphasis on difference, particularity, and antiessentialism about human nature is more conducive to feminist aspirations. Feminists who believe that postmodernism is not acceptable are expressing only one legitimate feminist point of view, which has been challenged.

Ambivalence is a ubiquitous aspect of postmodernity as well as modernity. Perhaps the charges for and against postmodernism are at best premature and at worst pointless and irrelevant to anything but academic politics and old ways of thought. Even debates about political correctness, multiculturalism, and the university are bogged down, leading people both for and against these developments to reinforce the desire or need to be judgmental and to draw the sharp distinctions that postmodernism is challenging. The inability or unwillingness of many participants in the present culture wars to see the value of ambivalence and difference is evidence that the crisis of modernity, the crisis of legitimacy, the legitimacy of modernity are still dominant cultural and political forces. The postmodernist claim that the culture and society that we would do well to abandon without nostalgia or regret is still very much alive. Perhaps this shows that postmodernism cannot fully transcend modernity, or that it is still too early to tell.

Toward a Social Science of Postmodernity

To some extent, postmodernist thought has already had an impact on the social sciences. But if postmodernism suffers from many of the same ambivalences as modernism, how will this improve things? Traditional social scientific theories, categories, perhaps even methods, insofar as they presuppose something like the ideas of modernity, may require either significant modification or abandonment. This may not mean, however, that everything must go. Some notions, such as class and status, may take on more pronounced significance as we move toward a two-class society and a global market and culture. Some other methods, such as the idea of sociology as a kind of writing,[95] may be needed to supplement, if not altogether replace, traditional methods espoused by both naturalists and antinaturalists. Concepts of community, self, society, and the political may have to be resituated, while other concepts, for instance, Gemeinschaft and "progress," may become useless.[96] Regardless, the social sciences must begin to focus systematically on the conditions of postmodern society. Methods and assumptions that promote this goal should be used, whether they come from the classical body of the social sciences or from postmodernism. Assumptions that do not promote this end should be abandoned or appropriately transformed. This is what Bauman's distinction between the sociology of postmodernism and postmodernist sociology means: The aim of sociology (or any other social science) is not methods or techniques. A postmodern social science that is composed of and guided by nothing but the doctrines and methods of Foucault and Lyotard would not help us adequately understand the postmodern world. A social science of postmodernism in which their writings, as well as relevant components of the classical traditions, are instrumental to this goal stands a better chance of doing so.

Notes

1. Featherstone, M. (1988). In pursuit of the postmodern: An introduction. *Theory, Culture and Society, 5*(2-3), 195-216. It is worth noting that Niklas Luhmann, a neoconservative functionalist, shares the same view of the self as many postmodernists. See Luhmann, N. (1986). The individuality of the individual: Historical meanings and cultural roles. In T. C. Heller, M. Sosna, & D. Welleby (Eds.), *Reconstructing individualism*. Stanford, CA: Stanford University Press.

2. Foster, H. (1983). Postmodernism: A preface. In H. Foster, *The anti-aesthetic*, pp. ix-xvi. Seattle: Bay Press.

3. Kellner, D. (1988). Postmodernism as social theory. Some challenges and problems. *Theory Culture and Society, 5*, 239-270, especially, 251ff.

4. O'Neill, J. (1988). Religion and postmodernism: The Durkheimian bond in Bell and Jameson. *Theory, Culture and Society, 5*, 493-508.

5. Lawson, H. (1986). *Reflexivity*. Chicago, IL: Open Court.

6. Several papers appeared in a special issue in 1988 of *Theory, Culture and Society, 5,* devoted to postmodernism: Bauman, Z. Is there a postmodern sociology? (pp. 217-38); Featherstone, M. In pursuit of the postmodern: An introduction (pp. 195-216); Kellner, D. Postmodernism as social theory: Some challenges and problems (pp. 239-70). These papers elaborate on some of the difficulties about postmodernism's ambivalence.

7. Bauman, Is there a postmodern sociology? See also Heller, A. (1991). Sociology as the defetishization of modernity. In A. Heller and F. Fehr, *The grandeur and twilight of radical universalism*. New Brunswick, NJ: Transaction Publishing.

For essays on some of the themes raised by Bauman, see Halliday, T. C., & Janovitz, M. (Eds.). (1992). *Sociology and its publics*. Chicago: University of Chicago Press.

8. In addition to *Theory, Culture and Society*, the reader may consult the following works: Antonio, R. J., & Kellner, D. (1992). *Modernity and social*

theory: The limits of the postmodern critique. Unpublished manuscript; Barker, F., Hulme, P., & Iverson, M. (Eds.). (1992). *Postmodernism and the re-reading of modernity*. Manchester: Manchester University Press and St. Martin's; Barrett, M. (1992). *The politics of truth.* Stanford, CA: Stanford University Press; Bauman, Z. (1992). *Intimations of postmodernity.* New York: Routledge; Best & Kellner, *Postmodern theory;* Beilharz, P. (Ed.). (1992). *Between totalitarianism and postmodernity* (A *Thesis eleven reader*). Cambridge: MIT Press; Boyne, R., & Rattansi, A (Eds.). (1990). *Postmodernism and society.* New York: St. Martin's; Callinicos, A. (1990). *Against postmodernism: A Marxist critique.* New York: St. Martin's; Connor, S. (1990). *Postmodernist culture.* Cambridge, MA: Blackwell; Denzin, N. (1991). *Images of postmodern society.* Newbury Park, CA: Sage; Denzin, N. K. (1984). Postmodern social theory. *Sociological Theory, 4,* 194-204, and exchange with William Bogard, 206-211; Doherty, T. (Ed.). (1993). *Postmodernism: A reader.* New York: Columbia University Press; During, S. (1993). (Ed.). *The cultural studies reader.* New York: Routledge. Featherstone, M. (1992). *Consumer culture and postmodernism.* Newbury Park, CA: Sage; Featherstone, M. (1985). The fate of modernity. *Theory Culture and Society, 2*(3), 131-91; Game, A. (1992). *Undoing the social.* Toronto: University of Toronto Press; Harvey, D. (1990). *The condition of postmodernity.* Cambridge, MA: Blackwell; Jameson, F. (1991). *Postmodernism, or the cultural logic of late capitalism.* Durham, NC: Duke University Press; Jencks, C. (Ed.). (1992). *The post-modern reader.* New York: St. Martin's; Natter, W., Jones, J. P., & Schatzki, T. (Eds.). (1993). *Postmodern contentions.* New York: Guilford; Kellner, D. (Ed.). (1989). *Postmodernism Jameson critique.* Washington, DC: Maisonneuve Press; Lash, S. (1990). *Sociology of postmodernism.* New York: Routledge; Lash & Friedman, *Modernity and identity;* Natoli, J., & Hutcheon, L. (Eds.). (1993). *A postmodern reader.* Albany: State University of New York Press; Rose, M. (1992). *The post-modern and the post-industrial.* New York/Cambridge, UK: Cambridge University Press; Rosenau, P. M. (1992). *Postmodernism and the social sciences.* Princeton, NJ: Princeton University Press; Seidman, S., & Wagner, D. G. (Eds.). (1992). *Postmodernism and social theory* Cambridge, MA: Blackwell,; Smart, B. (1993). *Modern conditions, postmodern controversies.* New York: Routledge; Smart, B. (1993). *Postmodernity.* New York: Routledge; Symposium on postmodernism. (1991). *Sociological Theory, 9*(2), 131-90; Turner, B. S. (Ed.). (1990). *Theories of modernity and postmodernity.* Newbury Park, CA: Sage; Waugh, P. (Ed.). *Postmodernism: A reader.* New York: Routledge; White, S. K. (1992). *Political theory and postmodernism.* New York/Cambridge, UK: Cambridge University Press.

9. Castoriadis, C. (1988). *The imaginary institutions of society.* Cambridge: MIT Press.

10. Giddens, *Constitution of society* and *Social theory and modern society.* See also Austin-Broos, D. J. (Ed.). (1987). *Creating culture.* Sydney, Australia: Allen and Unwin; Borgmann, A. (1992). *Crossing the postmodern divide.* Chicago: University of Chicago Press; Crespi, F. (1991). *Social Action and Power.* Cambridge, MA: Blackwell; Entrikin, J. N. *The betweenness of place: Towards a geography of modernity.* (1991). Baltimore: Johns Hopkins University Press; Crisis in knowledge: Poststructuralism, postmodernism, postmodernity [10th anniversary issue]. (1986). *Art Papers, 10;* Gilmour, J. C. (1992). *Fire on the*

earth: Anselm Kiefer and the postmodern world. Philadelphia: Temple University Press.

11. Unger, R. (1987). *Social theory*. New York/Cambridge, UK: Cambridge University Press.

12. Featherstone, M. (Ed.). (1990). *Global culture*. Newbury Park, CA: Sage.

13. Albrow, M., & King, E. (Eds.). (1990). *Globalization, knowledge and society*. Newbury Park, CA: Sage.

14. Frisby, D. (1986). *Society*. Winchester, MA: Unwin Hyman; Jay, *Marxism and totality*, pp. 510-38; Wardell, M., & Turner, S. P. (Eds.). (1986). *Sociological theory in transition*. Sydney, Australia: Allen and Unwin.

15. Foucault, M. (1977). Revolutionary action: Until now. In M. Foucault, *Language, counter-memory and practice* (p. 233). Ithaca, NY: Cornell University Press.

16. Habermas, *Legitimation crisis*.

17. Deleuze & Guattari, *Anti-Oedipus* and *A thousand plateaus*; Guattari, F. (1984). *Molecular revolution*. New York: Semiotexte. See also Lyotard, J. F. (1992). *Libidinal economy*. Bloomington: Indiana University Press.

18. Laclau, E., & Mouffe, C. (1985). *Hegemony and socialist strategy*. New York: Verso.

19. Arac, J. (Ed.). (1986). *Postmodernism and politics*. University of Minnesota Press; Nelson & Grossberg, *Marxism and the interpretation of culture*; Pangle, T. L. (1991). *The ennobling of democracy*. Baltimore: Johns Hopkins University Press; Ross, A. (Ed.). (1989). *Universal abandon?* Minneapolis: University of Minnesota Press; Ryan, M. (1990). *Politics and culture*. Baltimore: Johns Hopkins University Press; Shapiro, M. (1992). *Reading the postmodern polity*. Minneapolis: University of Minnesota Press; White, *Political theory and postmodernism*.

20. Lyotard, J. F. (1992). *Postmodernism explained*. Minneapolis: University of Minnesota Press; Lyotard, J. F. (1993). *Toward the postmodern*. Atlantic Highlands, NJ: Humanities Press; Lyotard, *The differend*; Lyotard & Thebaud, *Just gaming*.

21. Miller, J. (1993). *The passion of Michel Foucault*. New York: Simon & Schuster

22. Habermas, J. (1982). Modernity: An incomplete project, and Entwinement of myth and enlightenment. See also Fraser, N. (1985). Michel Foucault: A young conservative? *Ethics, 95*, 165-184; Hiley, *Foucault and the question of enlightenment*; Watson, S. (1984). Jurgen Habermas and Jean-Francois Lyotard: Post-modernism and the crisis of rationality. *Philosophy and Social Criticism, 12*, 1-24.

23. Agamben, G. (1993). *The coming community*. Minneapolis: University of Minnesota Press; Blanchot, M. (1988). *The impossible community*. Barrytown, NY: Station Hill Press; Corlett, W. (1989). *Community without unity*. Durham, NC: Duke University Press; Miami Theory Collective, (1992). *Community at loose ends*. Minneapolis: University of Minnesota Press; Nancy, J. (1991). *The inoperative community*. Minneapolis: University of Minnesota Press; Robbins, B. (Ed.). (1993). *The phantom public sphere*. Minneapolis: University of Minnesota Press.

24. On Foucault, see Arac, J. (Ed.). (1988). *After Foucault*. New Brunswick, NJ: Rutgers University Press; Armstrong, *Michel Foucault: Philosopher*; Bernauer,

J. W., & Rasmussen, D. (Ed.). (1988). *The final Foucault*. Cambridge: MIT Press; Boyne, R. (1990). *Foucault and Derrida*. Winchester, MA: Unwin Hyman; Burchell, G., Gordon, C., & Miller, P. (Eds.). (1992). *The Foucault effect*. Chicago: University of Chicago Press; Cousins, M., & Hussain, A. (1984). *Michel Foucault*. New York: St. Martin's; Deleuze, G. (1988). *Foucault*. Minneapolis: University of Minnesota Press; Dreyfus H. L., & Rabinow, P. (1983). *Michel Foucault: Beyond structuralism and hermeneutics* (2nd ed.). Chicago: University of Chicago Press; Fink-Eitel, H. (1992). *Foucault*. Philadelphia: Pennridge; Grene, M. (Ed.). (1986). *Towards a critique of Foucault*. New York: Routledge; Gutting, *Michel Foucault's archeology of scientific reason*; Hoy, D. C. (Ed.). (1986). *Foucault: A critical reader*. Cambridge, MA: Blackwell; Mahon, M. (1992). *Foucault's Nietzschean genealogy*. Albany: State University of New York Press; McNay, L. (1993). *Foucault and feminism*. Boston: Northeastern University Press; Miller, *The passion of Michel Foucault* (Miller points out [p. 310] that Foucault read extensively in the writings of Friederich van Hayek); Poster, M. (1984). *Foucault, Marxism, and history*. Cambridge, UK: Polity; Poster, M. (1989). *Critical theory and poststructuralism*. Ithaca, NY: Cornell University Press; Rousse, J. (1988). *Knowledge and power*. Ithaca, NY: Cornell University Press; Schumway, D. R. (1992). *Michel Foucault*. Charlottesville: University of Virginia Press; Symposium on "The passion of Michel Foucault". (1992). *Salmagundi, 10*, 30-99.

25. Clegg, J. (1988). *Frameworks of power*. Newbury Park, CA: Sage.

26. Foucault, M. (1977). *Power/knowledge*. New York: Pantheon; Foucault, M. (1988). *Technologies of the self*. Amherst: University of Massachusetts Press; Ingram, D. (1986). Foucault and the Frankfurt school: A discourse on Nietzsche, power and knowledge. *Praxis International, 5*, 311-25; Rabinow, P. (Ed.). (1985). *A Foucault reader*. New York: Pantheon.

27. Foucault, M. (1976). *Mental illness and psychology*. New York: Harper-Collins; Foucault, M. (1989). The dangerous individual and Confinement, psychiatry and prison. In *Politics philosophy culture* (pp. 125-52, pp. 178-210). New York: Routledge; Foucault, *Madness and civilization*; Foucault, *Order of things*.

28. Foucault, M. (1979). *Discipline and punish*. New York: Random House.

29. Foucault, M. (1975). *The birth of the clinic*. New York: Random House.

30. Foucault, *History of sexuality*.

31. See the comparisons between Weber and Foucault in Whimster, S., & Lash, S. (Eds.). (1987). *Max Weber, Rationality and Modernity*. Sydney, Australia: Allen and Unwin (pp. 259-292, 293-316, 355-377). Foucault was inclined to reject comparisons between himself and Weber.

32. Baudrillard, J. (1983). *In the shadow of the silent majorities*. New York: Semiotexte; Baudrillard, J. (1983). *Simulations*. New York: Semiotexte. See also Ashley, D. (1990). Postmodernism and the "end of the individual." *Current Perspectives in Social Theory, 10*, 195-221; Baudrillard [Special issue]. (1985). *October, 36*; Best, S. (1989). The commodification of reality and the reality of commodification: Jean Baudrillard and post-modernism. *Current Perspectives in Social Theory, 9*, 23-51; Bogard, W. (1987). Sociology in the absence of the social: The significance of Baudrillard for contemporary thought. *Philosophy and Social Criticism, 14*, 227-42; Bogard, W. (1990). Closing down the social: Baudrillard's challenge to contemporary sociology. *Sociological Theory, 7*, 1-15; Gane, M. (1990). Ironies of postmodernism: The fate of Baudrillard's fatalism.

Economy and Society, *19*, 314-33; Chang, B. C. (1986). Mass, media, mass meditation. *Current Perspectives in Sociological Theory*, *7*, 157-81; Chen, K. (1987). The masses and the media: Baudrillard's implosive modernism. *Theory Culture and Society*, *4*, 71-88; Fankovits, A. (1984). *Seduced and abandoned: The Baudrillard scene*. Sydney, Australia: Semiotexte; Gane, M. (1991). *Baudrillard's bestiary* New York: Routledge, 1991; Gane, M. (1991). *Baudrillard: Critical and fatal theory*. New York: Routledge; Gane M. (Ed.). (1993). *Baudrillard live: Selected interviews*. New York: Routledge; Grosz, E. A., & Foss, P. (Eds.). (1986). *Futur*Fall: Excursions into post-modernity*. Australia: Power Institute of Fine Arts; Hefner, R. (1977). Baudrillard's noble anthropology. *Substance*, *6*, 105-113; Kellner, D. (1989). Boundaries and borderlines: Reflections on Baudrillard and critical theory. *Current Perspectives in Social Theory*, *9*, 5-22; Kellner, D. (1989). *Jean Baudrillard: From marxism to postmodernism and beyond*. Stanford, CA: Stanford University Press; Kroker & Cook, *The postmodern scene*; Kroker, A., & Levin, C. (1989). Cynical power: The fetishism of the sign. *Canadian Journal of Political and Social Theory*, *12*, 123-134; Levin, C. (1989). Baudrillard, critical theory and psychoanalysis. *Canadian Journal of Political and Social Theory*, 12, 170-187; Luke, T. W. (1991). *Screens of power*. Champaign: University of Illinois Press; Norris, C. (1990). Lost in the fun house: Baudrillard and the politics of postmodernism. In C. Norris, *What's wrong with postmodernism?* (pp. 164-94). Baltimore: Johns Hopkins University Press; Pefanis, *Heterology and the postmodern: Bataille, Baudrillard, and Lyotard*; Poster, M. (1982). Semiology and critical theory: From Marx to Baudrillard and M. Hays, Response. In W. V. Spanos, P. Bove, & D. O'Hara (Eds.), *The question of textuality* (pp. 275-88 and 289-93). Bloomington: Indiana University Press. Poster, M. (1988). Introduction. In M. Poster, Ed., *Jean Baudrillard: Selected writings* (pp. 1-9). Stanford, CA: Stanford University Press; Roderick, R. (1989). Beyond a boundary: Baudrillard and new critical theory. *Current Perspectives in Social Theory*, *9*, 3-4; Rubenstein, D. (1989). The mirror of reproduction: Baudrillard and Reagan's America. *Political Theory*, *16*, 582-606; Singer, B. (1989). Baudrillard's seduction. *Canadian Journal of Political and Social Theory*, 12, 139-51; For major influences on Baudrillard, consult Debord, D. (1970). *Society of the spectacle*. New York: Verso; and Debord, D. (1900) *Comments on the society of the spectacle*. New York: Verso.

33. Frisby, *Society*.

34. Baudrillard, *In the shadow of the silent majorities*.

35. Baudrillard, J. (1990). *Fatal strategies*. New York: Semiotexte. See also Baudrillard, J. (1988). *The evil demon of images*. Sydney, Australia: Power Institute Publications; Baudrillard, J. (1990). *Revenge of the crystal*. Sydney: Pluto Press; Baudrillard, J. (1990). *Seduction*. New York: St. Martin's.

36. Lyotard, *The differend* and Sensus communis; Lyotard & Thebaud, *Just gaming*. See also Altieri, C. (1989). Justice and judgment under postmodern conditions. In R. W. Dasenbrock (Ed.), *Redrawing the lines* (pp. 61-90). Minneapolis: University of Minnesota Press; White, S. K. (1987). Justice and the postmodern problematic. *Praxis International*, *6*, 307-19. See also Benjamin, A. (Ed.). *Judging Lyotard*. New York: Routledge; Bennington, G. (1988). *Lyotard: Writing the event*. New York: Columbia University Press; Carroll, *Paraesthetics*; Connor,

S. (1992). *Theory and cultural value*. New York: Routledge; *Diacritics* [Entire issue]. (1984). *14*(3); Readings, *Introducing Lyotard*.

37. Miami Collective, *Community at loose ends*; Nancy, J. (1991). *Inoperative community*. Minneapolis: University of Minnesota Press.

38. Turner, C. (1990). Lyotard and Weber: Postmodern rules and neo-Kantian values. In Turner, *Theories of modernity and postmodernity*, pp. 108-116.

39. Benjamin, *The Lyotard reader*, pp. 314-411; Lyotard, *The differend*.

40. Wittgenstein, L. (1953). *Philosophical investigations*. New York: Macmillan.

41. Keane, J. (1988). The modern democratic revolution: Reflections on Jean-Francois Lyotard's *la conditione postmoderne*. *Chicago Review*, *39*, 4-19; Steele, M. (1990). Lyotard's politics of the sentence. *Culture Critique*, *5*, 193-214.

42. Lyotard, J. F. (1989). The sign of history. In Benjamin, *The Lyotard reader* (pp. 393-410); and Lyotard, J. F. (1984). The unconscious, history, and phrases: Notes on the political unconscious. *New Orleans Review*, *11*, 71-78.

43. Foucault, What is enlightenment?

44. Carroll, Narrative, heterogeneity, and the question of the political: Bakhtin and Lyotard. See also Stam, R. (1988). Mikhail Bakhtin and left cultural critique. In E. A. Kaplan (Ed.), *Postmodernism and its discontents* (pp. 116-45). New York: Verso.

45. Feyerabend, P. (1976). *Against method*; Feyerabend, P. (1979). *Science in a free society*. New York: Verso.

For comparisons between Feyerabend and Lyotard, see Hendley, S. (1992). *Reason and relativism: A Sartrean investigation*. Albany: State University of New York Press; Rosenau, *Postmodernism and the social sciences* (chapter 8). See also Lawson & Appignanesi, *Dismantling truth*.

46. Miami Theory Collective, *Community at loose ends*; Nancy, J. (1991). *Inoperative community*. Minneapolis: University of Minnesota Press.

47. Botwinick, A. (1990). *Skepticism and political participation*. Philadelphia: Temple University Press; Botwinick, A. (1993). *Postmodernism and democratic theory*. Philadelphia: Temple University Press; Shapiro, I. (1990). *Political criticism*. Berkeley: University of California Press.

48. Lyotard, *Postmodern condition*, p. 67.

49. Hannay, A. (1989). Politics and Feyerabend's anarchist. In M. Dascal & O. Gruengard (Eds.), *Knowledge and politics* (pp. 241-62). Boulder, CO: Westview; Hollinger, R. (1980). Freedom, reason, and tradition. *Reason Papers*, *6*, 83-91; Rouse, *Knowledge and power*.

For some useful, but somewhat dated, papers on the debates surrounding the relevant works of Feyerabend, Kuhn, and Popper, see Lakatos, I., & Musgrave, A. (Eds.). (1968). *Criticism and the growth of knowledge*. New York/Cambridge, UK: Cambridge University Press. See also Kneale, W. (1989). Scientific revolutions forever? *British Journal for the Philosophy of Science*, *19*, 27-42.

50. For the relevant postmodernist meanings of anarchism, see Schurmann, R. (1987). *Heidegger on being and acting: From principles to anarchy*. Bloomington: Indiana University Press.

51. Popper, *Poverty of historicism*; Hayek, F. (1946). *The road to serfdom*. Chicago: University of Chicago Press; Hayek, F. (1962). *The counterrevolution in science*. New York: Free Press.

52. Kendall, W. (1975). The "open society" and its fallacies. In D. Spitz (Ed.), *On liberty* (pp. 154-166). New York: Norton.

53. Reich, R. (1989). *The resurgent liberal.* New York: Vintage.

54. Altieri, *Justice and judgment under postmodern conditions.*

55. Callinicos, *Against postmodernism.*

56. Frankel, B. (1987). *The post-industrial utopians.* Madison: University of Wisconsin Press.

57. Harvey, *Condition of postmodernity.*

58. Lash S., & Urry, J. (1987). *The end of organized capitalism.* Madison: University of Wisconsin Press.

59. Jameson, F. (1984). Postmodernism, or the cultural logic of late capitalism. *New Left Review, 146,* 53-92.

60. Frankels, *Post-industrial utopians.*

61. Reich, R. (1987). *Tales of a new America.* New York: Time Books; Reich, R. (1991). *The work of nations.* New York: Knopf; Reich, *Resurgent liberal*; Drucker, P. F. (1989). *The new realities.* New York: HarperCollins; Rothenberg, R. (1984). *The neo-liberals.* New York: Simon & Schuster. See also Bruce-Briggs, B. (Ed.). (1979). *The new class?* New York: McGraw-Hill; Derber, C., Schwartz, W. A., & Magrass, Y. (1990). *Power in the highest degree.* New York: Oxford University Press.

62. The revival of the Protestant work ethic is defended by neoconservatives such as Bell and neoliberals such as Reich.

63. Foster, H. (1984). (Post)modern polemics. *New German Critique, 33,* 67-78. Foster, Postmodernism: A preface; Foster, *The anti-aesthetic.*

64. Bell, D. (1970). Structural changes in the United States. In E. F. Duchene, (Ed.), *The endless crisis: America in the seventies* (pp. 186-93). New York: Macmillan.

65. Marien, M. (1977). Two visions of post-industrial society. *Futures,* 415-31.

66. Rose, *The post-modern and the post-industrial,* p. 31.

67. Lyotard, *Postmodern condition*; Sarup, *Introductory guide to poststructuralism and postmodernism.*

For a defense of Lyotard against Harvey, see Morris, M. (1992). The man in the mirror: David Harvey's "Condition" of postmodernity. *Theory Culture and Society, 9,* 253-279. See also Keatley, A. (1983). Knowledge as real estate. *Science, 222,* 4625; Nelkin, D. (1984). *Science as intellectual property: Who controls research?* New York: Macmillan.

68. Derrida, J. (1982). Of an apocalyptic tone recently adopted in philosophy. *Semeia, 23,* 63-97; Fenves, *Raising the tone of philosophy.*

69. Gane, Ironies of postmodernism; Baudrillard, *Fatal strategies.*

70. Bromley, S. (1990). The politics of postmodernism. *New Left Review, 104,* 129-150.

71. Eagleton, T. (1985). Capitalism, modernism and postmodernism. *New Left Review, 99,* 96-113.

72. Jameson, *Postmodernism, or the cultural logic of late capitalism.*

73. Mandel, E. (1978). *Late capitalism.* New York: Verso.

74. See notes 31 and 38.

75. Bell, *Coming of post-industrial society.* Cited in Frankel, *Post-industrial utopians,* p. 5. The last emphasis is mine.

See also Archer, M. (1990). Theory, culture and post-industrial society. In Featherstone, *Global culture*, pp. 97-121; Badham, R. (1984). The sociology of industrial and post-industrial societies. *Current Sociology*, *32*(1), 1-75; Barnes, T. J., & Ducan, J. (Eds.). (1992). *Writing worlds*. New York: Routledge; Bell, D. (1980). *The winding passage*. New York: Basic Books; Block, F. (1991). *Postindustrial possibilities*. Berkeley: University of California Press; Brzezinski, Z. (1970). *Between two ages*. New York: Viking; Featherstone, J. (1973). A failure of political imagination. *New Republic, 145*, 23-28, and September 22, 1973, 25-28; Feenberg, A. (1992). *Critical theory of technology*. New York: Oxford University Press; Giddens, A. (1989). *The consensus of modernity*. Stanford, CA: Stanford University Press; Gorz, A. (1982). *Farewell to the working class*. London: Pluto Press; Halal, W. E. (1990). The new capitalism. In T. Forester (Ed.). *Computers in the human context* (pp. 427-37). Cambridge: MIT Press; Hall, S., & Jacques, M. (Eds.). (1990). *New times*. London: Lawrence and Wishart; Harvey, D. (1991). Flexibility: Treat or opportunity. *Socialist Review*, 65-78; Huntington, S. P. (1974). Postindustrial politics: How benign will it be?. *Comparative Politics, 6*, 163-92; Kuhns, W. (1971). *The post-industrial prophets*. New York: Harper-Collins; Kumar, K. (1976). Industrialism and post-industrialism: Reflections on a putative transition. *Social Research, 32*, 439-478; Kumar, K. (1978). *Prophesy and progress*. Hammondsworth, UK: Allen Lane; Lane, R. E. (1966). The decline of politics and ideology in a knowledgeable society. *American Sociological Review, 5*, 649-662; Lash, C. (1972). Toward a theory of post-industrial society. In M. D. Hancock & G. Sjoberg (Eds.), *Politics in the post-welfare state* (pp. 36-50). New York: Columbia University Press; Leiss, W. (1989). The myth of the information society. In I. Agus & S. Jhally (Eds.), *Cultural politics in contemporary America* (pp. 282-98). New York: Routledge; Liebowitz, N. *Daniel Bell and the agony of modern liberalism*. Westport, CT: Greenwood; Lipset, S. M. (Ed.). (1979). *The third century: America as a post-industrial society*. Chicago: University of Chicago Press; Kellner, *Critical theory, Marxism and modernity*; Lowi, T. J. (1980). The political impact of information technology. In T. Forester (Ed.), *The microelectronics revolution* (pp. 453-72). Cambridge: MIT Press; Luke, T. W., & White, S. K. (1985). Critical theory, the informational revolution, and an ecological path to modernity. In J. Forester (Ed.), *Critical theory and public life* (pp. 22-55). Cambridge: MIT Press; Luke, *Screens of power*; Prad, A., & Watts, M. J. (1992). *Reworking modernity*. New Brunswick, NJ: Rutgers University Press; Poster, M. (1990). The concept of postindustrial society: Bell and the problem of rhetoric. In M. Poster, *The modes of information* (pp. 21-43). Chicago: University of Chicago Press; Review symposium (on Bell). *Contemporary Sociology: A Journal of Reviews, 2*, 99-109 (including a response by Bell); Ross, A. (1991). Getting the future we deserve. *Socialist Review*, 125-145; Rustin, M. (1987). The politics of post-Fordism: Or, the trouble with "new times." *New Left Review, 101*, 53-77; Sayer, A., & Walker, R. (1992). *The new social economy*. Cambridge, MA: Blackwell; Schroyer, T. (1974). Review of the coming of post-industrial society. *Telos, 26*, 162-176; Soja, E. W. (1989). *Postmodern geographies*. New York: Verso; Offe, C. (1985). *Disorganized capitalism*. Cambridge: MIT Press; Touraine, A. (1971). *The post-industrial society*. New York: Random House; Touraine, A. What is Daniel Bell afraid of? *American Journal of*

Sociology, 77, 469-473; Touraine, *Return of the actor*; Turner, B. S. (1989). From postindustrial society to postmodern politics: The political sociology of Daniel Bell. In J. R. Gibbins (Ed.), *Contemporary political culture* (pp. 199-217). Newbury Park, CA: Sage; Wickham, G. (1990). The political possibilities of postmodernism. *Economy and Society*, *18*, 121-147; Williams, R. (1983). *The year 2000*. New York: Pantheon; Wodward, K. (Ed.). (1980). *The myths of information: Technology and postindustrial culture*. Cambridge, MA: Coda Press.

76. Lash & Urry, *The end of organized capitalism*.

77. Ibid., p. 299. See also Blumenthal, S. (1988). Reaganism and the neokitsch aesthetic. In S. Blumenthal & T. B. Edsall (Eds.), *The Reagan legacy* (pp. 251-94). New York: Pantheon. Many postmodernists reject the distinction between high and low culture, the liberal-conservative theory of mass society, and the elitist aspects of the Marxist idea of the culture industry. See Collins, *Uncommon cultures*; Ross, A. (1989). *No respect*. New York: Routledge; Swingwood, A. (1977). *The myth of mass culture*. New York: Macmillan.

78. Lash & Urry, *End of organized capitalism*, p. 263.

79. Lash & Urry, *End of organized capitalism*, p. 313.

80. See also Bromley, The politics of postmodernism.

81. Ashley, D. (1992). Playing with the pieces: The fragmentation in social theory. In P. Wexler (Ed.), *Critical theory now* (pp. 70-97, esp. 86ff). New York and London: Falmer Press; O'Neill, J. (1990). Postmodernism and (post)Marxism. In Silverman, *Postmodernism—philosophy and the arts*, pp. 69-79.

82. For discussions of postMarxism, see Laclau & Mouffe, *Hegemony and socialist strategy*; Smart, *Modern conditions, postmodern controversies*. See also Eagleton, *Ideology*; Laclau, E. (1990). *New reflections on the revolution of our time*. New York: Verso; McCarney, J. (1990). *Social theory and the crisis of Marxism*. New York: Verso; Ritzer, G. (1991). The changing nature of neo-Marxist theory: A metatheoretical analysis. *Sociological Perspectives*, *34*(3), 359-376; Thompson, *Ideology and modern culture*.

83. Adam, I., & Tiffin, H. (Eds.). (1992). *Past the last post: Theorizing post-colonialism and post-modernism*. Calgary: University of Calgary Press; Benhabib, S. Feminism and postmodernism: An uneasy alliance. *Praxis International*, *11*(2), 137-49; Butler, J. Contingent foundations: Feminism and the question of postmodernism. *Praxis International*, *11*(2), 150-65; Cultural Studies (1990). *October*, *14*(2); Ermarth, E. D., (1992). *Sequel to history*. Princeton, NJ: Princeton University Press; Flax, J. (1990). *Thinking fragments*. Berkeley: University of California Press; Fraser, N. False antithesis: A response. *Praxis International*, *11*(2), 166-77; Fukuyama, F. (1992). *The end of history and the last man*. New York: Macmillan; Harlan, D. (1989). AHR forum: Some reflections on the new history. *American Historical Review*, *94*, 661-98; Harlan, D. (1989). Intellectual history and the return of literature. *American Historical Review*, *94*, 581-609. Himmelfarb, G. (1987). *The new history and the old*. Cambridge, MA: Harvard University Press; Hunt, L. (Ed.). (1988). *New cultural history*. Berkeley: University of California Press; Hunt, L. (1987). History beyond social theory. In M. Krieger (Ed.), *The aims of representation* (pp. 95-111). New York: Columbia University Press; Kaye, H. J. (1991). *The powers of the past*. Minneapolis:

University of Minnesota Press; Manganaro, N. (Ed.). (1992). *Modernist anthropology: From fieldwork to text*. Princeton, NJ: Princeton University Press; Nicholson L. J. (Ed.). (1991). *Feminism/postmodernism*. New York: Routledge; Penley, C., & Ross, A. (Eds.). (1992). *Technoculture*. Minneapolis: University of Minnesota Press; Ross, A. (1990). New age of technoculture. In L. Grossberg, C. Nelson, & P. Treicher (Eds.), *Cultural studies* (pp. 531-66). New York: Routledge; Pangle, *Ennobling of democracy*; Ross, A. (1991). *Strange weather*. New York: Verso; Tomilson, J. (1992). *Cultural imperialism*. Baltimore: Johns Hopkins University; Tong, R. (1989). *Feminist thought*. Boulder, CO: Westview.

84. Fukuyama, *The end of history and the last man*. See also Grier, P. T. (1989). *The end of history, and the return of history*. Santa Barbara, CA: ABC-Clio. For a discussion of similarities between Fukuyama and Baudrillard, see Best & Kellner, *Postmodern theory*, pp. 126-36. For a comparison between Marcuse's version of the end of history, in the guise of technological determinism, and German conservatism, see Offe, C. (1988). Technology and one-dimensionality. In R. Pippin & A. Feekerf (Eds.), *Marcuse, critical theory and the promise of utopia* (pp. 214-225). For discussions of postmodernism and history, see Ankersmit, F. R. (1989). History and postmodernism. *History and Theory, 28*, 137-53; Ankersmit, F. R. (1990). Reply to professor Zagorin. *History and Theory, 29*, 275-96; Attridge, D., Bennington, G., & Young R. (Eds.). (1987). *Poststructuralism and the question of history*. New York/Cambridge, UK: Cambridge University Press; D'Amico, R. (1989). *Historicism and knowledge*. New York: Routledge; Dannhauer B. P. (Ed.). (1987). *At the nexus of philosophy and history*. Athens: University of Georgia Press (pp. 97-115, 178-200, 201-22); Grumley, J. E. (1989). *History and totality*. New York: Routledge; Kosenau, *Postmodernism and the social sciences*; Murphy, W. T. (1990). Foucault: Rationality against reason and history. In P. Windsor (Ed.), *Reason and history, or only a history of reason?* (pp. 126-60). Leicester, UK: Leicester University Press; Negrin, L. (1991). Post-historie: A comparative analysis of decadentism and postmodernism. *Philosophy and Social Criticism, 13*, 57-77; Poster, M. (1982). Foucault and history. *Social Research, 49*, 116-142; Roth, M. S., (1981). Foucault's "History of the Present." *History and Theory, 20*, 32-46; Roth, M. S., (1988). *Knowing and history*. Ithaca, NY: Cornell University Press; Veesr, H. A. (Ed.). (1992). *The new historicism*. Princeton, NJ: Princeton University Press; Zagorin, P. (1990). Historiography and postmodernism: Reconsiderations. *History and Theory, 29*, 263-74.

For a powerful criticism of postmodernist views of history, see Anderson, P. (1992). *A zone of engagement*. New York: Verso; Niethammer, L. (1992). *Posthistorie*. New York: Verso; Rose, G. (1984). *Dialectics of nihilism*. Cambridge, MA: Blackwell. For a recent survey of historical sociology, see Smith, D. (1992). *The rise of historical sociology*. Philadelphia: Temple University Press, 1992. For earlier works, see Abrams, P. (1982). *Historical sociology*. Ithaca, NY: Cornell University Press; Skocpol, T. (Ed.). (1984). *Vision and method in historical sociology*. New York/Cambridge, UK: Cambridge University Press. Structuralists, including structural Marxists, partly owing to their antihumanism, in effect have an end of history thesis. For a good critique of the structuralist view, see Anderson, *Arguments within English Marxism*; Anderson, *In the tracks of his-*

torical materialism; Schmidt, A. (1983). *History and structure*. Cambridge: MIT Press. Postmodernist versions of the end of history thesis, especially Baudrillard's, may be influenced by this aspect of structuralism.

85. Nietzsche, *Thus spoke Zarathustra*.

86. Kaye, *Powers of the past*; Tominson, J. (1989). *Cultural domination*. New York: Routledge.

87. Bernauer, J. W. (1990). *Michel Foucault's force of flight*. Atlantic Highlands, NJ: Humanities Press.

88. Habermas, Modernity: An incomplete project.

89. Benhabib, Feminism and postmodernism: An uneasy alliance; Butler, Contingent foundations: Feminism and the question of postmodernism; Fraser, False antithesis: A response. This topic is discussed in greater length in Chapter 8.

90. See Penley & Ross, *Technoculture*; Ross, New age of technoculture.

91. Harvey, *Condition of postmodernity*; Smart, *Modern conditions, postmodern controversies*.

92. Giroux, H. A. (Ed.). (1991). *Postmodernism, feminism and cultural politics*. Albany: State University of New York Press. See especially the Introduction, pp. 1-59.

93. Young, R. (1990). *White mythologies*. New York: Routledge. See also Lambropoulos, V. (1992). *The rise of Eurocentrism*. Princeton, NJ: Princeton University Press; *Yale French studies,* nos., 82-83 on postcolonial conditions.

94. Gottdiener, M. (1990). The logocentrism of the classics. *American Sociological Review, 55,* 460-62, a response to Collins, R. (1989). Sociology: Proscience or antiscience. *American Sociological Review, 54,* 124-39. See also Collins, R. (1988). *Theoretical sociology*. New York: Harcourt Brace and Company; Ritzer, G. (Ed.). (1989). *Frontiers of social theory* (part III). New York: Columbia University Press; Ritzer, G. (Ed.). (1991). Recent explorations in sociological metatheorizing [Special issue]. (1991). *Sociological Perspectives, 34*(3); Ritzer, G. (1992). *Sociological Theory* (3rd ed.). New York: McGraw-Hill.

95. For a recent example of this genre, see Green, B. S. (1988). *Literary methods and sociological theory: Case studies of Simmel and Weber*. Chicago: University of Chicago Press. See also Agger, B. (1989). *Socio(onto)logy: A disciplinary reading*. Champaign: University of Illinois Press; Agger, B. (1991). *A critical theory of public life*. Cambridge, UK: Falmer Press; Brown, R. H. (Ed.). (1992). *Writing the social text*. New York: Aldine de Gruyter.

96. Berman, P. (Ed.). (1992). *Debating P. C.* . New York: Laurel Books; Goldfarb, J. C. (1991). *The cynical Society*. Chicago: University of Chicago Press; Holton, R. J. (1987). The idea of crisis in modern society. *British Journal of Sociology, 37,* 502-20; Lenz, G. H., & Shell, K. L. (Eds.). (1986). *The crisis of modernity*. Boulder, CO: Westview. On new social movements, see Touraine, A. (1981). *The voice and the eye*. New York/Cambridge, UK: Cambridge University Press; Touraine, A. (1992). Beyond social movements. *Theory Culture and Society, 9,* 125-46; Touraine, *Return of the actor*. See also the entire issue of *Social Research, 52*(4) (1985); Boggs, C. (1986). *Social movements and political power*. Philadelphia: Temple University Press; Bourdieu, P., & Coleman, J. S., (Eds.) (1992). *Social theory for a changing society*. Boulder, CO: Westview; Cohen, J., & Arado, A. (1992). *Civil society and political theory*. Cambridge: MIT

Press; Luke, T. W., *Social theory and modernity*. Newbury Park, CA: Sage; McNall, H. G., Levine, R. F., & Fantesa, R. (Eds.). (1992). *Bringing class back in*. Boulder, CO: Westview; Morris, A. D., & Mueller, C. M. (Eds.). (1992). *Frontiers in social movement theory*. New Haven, CT: Yale University Press; Wright, E. O. (Eds.). (1990). *The debate on classes*. New York: Verso.

8

THE CHALLENGE FROM
CRITICAL THEORY

Postmodernist writers are subject to a number of challenges. Some of these challenges amount to little more than emotional or ideological attacks, from both the left and the right.[1] Many criticisms are misinformed, although postmodernist writing is often extremely dense, and even people with academic backgrounds have trouble following much of it. An additional difficulty is the fact that writers connect social and political issues to debates about postmodernism regardless of whether postmodernist writers or themes do or do not bear on an issue. Examples of this are the debates about political correctness and multiculturalism.

Many postmodernists seem sympathetic to the left at some level, and some have affinities with writers such as Adorno.[2] Many leftist writers hope to join postmodernism in revitalizing Marxism within a post-Marxist framework. Others on the left think that postmodernism and post-Marxism are problematic.

Other factors, such as DeMan's nazism[3] or that of Heidegger,[4] are often taken to indicate that postmodernism is either compatible with any political position or lends itself to retrograde, irrational politics. Some writers believe that postmodernism is totally divorced from politics. Rorty argues that writers such as Nietzsche, Foucault, and Derrida have nothing to say about politics, because for Rorty "politics" means "American liberalism."[5] Rorty relegates postmodernism to the realm of the private, just as poetry is, indeed, more so, because Rorty believes that poets can help change our public vocabularies through their visions.

It is clear, however, that postmodernists such as Foucault, Derrida, Baudrillard, and Lyotard believe that everything is political, although they are attempting to resituate the concept of the political.[6] Because it would take us too far afield to discuss this matter at length, this chapter concentrates on the issues raised by Habermas and his followers,[7] who charge that postmodernists are young conservatives who favor an end-of-ideology approach to politics or a conception of politics that is rooted in the political aestheticism and irrationalism of elitists like Nietzsche[8] and the conservative political theorist Schmitt. Habermas does not make this charge because the postmodernists are not Marxists but because they abandon and denigrate the Enlightenment project, with its metanarratives about reason, science, universalism, progress, and the division of modern culture into spheres.

Habermas and Critical Theory

To discuss Habermas's criticisms of postmodernism, it is necessary to return to the dialectic of Enlightenment, for in coming to grips with Weber and the Frankfurt school, Habermas develops an account of modernity that he brings to bear against the postmodernists.

Habermas believes that Weber and the Frankfurt theorists' account of the rationalization of the world is too one-sided and too pessimistic, and is based on an untenable philosophy of consciousness or subjectivity.[9] For Weber, the rationalization of the world involves its disenchantment, its loss of values and meanings—in short, the iron cage of bureaucracy and instrumental rationality. In this environment, which basically cannot be altered, the individual can only escape into the private sphere by making life choices, by choosing one's own defining values in an existentialist fashion[10] and by developing one's own personality in terms of an inner calling. The individual must choose the ethics of responsibility to meet the demands of the day with integrity. Every responsible person should do likewise, even though (or even because) this entails, for Weber, a war of gods and demons. Weber sees a fragmented world that endangers liberal democracy unless strong charismatic leaders can take control and abide by a Machiavellian political realism, albeit one infused by the ethic of responsibility.

Weber's cultural pessimism, which for Habermas is infused with a subjective view of values and a positivist outlook about knowledge,[11] is taken up by the first-generation critical theorists, the Frankfurt school writers Adorno, Horkheimer, Marcuse, and others.[12] The fact that many of these writers were German Jews, all were Marxists, many had studied with Heidegger, and all were writing at the time Hitler came to power contributed to their cultural pessimism. In their view, not only is the iron cage the inevitable outgrowth of rationalization, but rationalization is the essence of the West; the dialectics of Enlightenment turned reason into a myth (the myth of scientism), and the domination of nature turned into the domination of men and women through exploitation and repression. Only some sort of great refusal (of totality), combined with a messianic hope or an aesthetic outlook, can preserve utopian aspirations, but even then only for an indeterminate future.[13]

For the Frankfurt theorists, science and philosophy, that is, "traditional theory,"[14] are part of the fabric of capitalist society and further and sustain its ideals under the guise of pure, disinterested, objective inquiry. Only a critical theory that unmasks these connections and the inadequacies of the outlook of the masses can provide a way of criticizing modern capitalist culture and retrieve the Enlightenment connections between knowledge and emancipation from exploitation, ideology, and power.

Habermas believes the contrary. He believes that rationalization exemplifies a process of selective evolution. Modern science, technology, and the growth of the "systems sphere" have made for genuine progress, which Habermas accuses Weber and the Frankfurt theorists of neglecting or downplaying. This very progress has led to the colonization of the world and to various crises in the systems sphere and in culture; these crises cast doubt on the legitimacy of modern society, and thus threaten it in various ways. Unfortunately, new, less egocentric, more rational ways of responding to this colonization have not evolved. A decentered approach is needed; for Habermas this becomes a discourse ethics, combined with a democratic model of community as dialogue.[15] This model is similar in many ways to

Dewey's notion of the great community in *The Public and its Problems*.[16]

For Habermas, modernity requires differentiation so that the ethical, aesthetic, and scientific remain distinct. He defends an instrumentalist approach to nature and the natural sciences, and is wary of narrowing the gap between the aesthetic and the political, as Marcuse and Adorno, anticipating Foucault and Lyotard, try to do.[17] In recent years, Habermas has assigned a less subjective, more public role to aesthetics, that of providing an overall connection of the spheres as a way of articulating general criticisms of modern society.[18] But the types of argumentation and discussion in the three spheres have their own logic, which embodies the progressive elements of modernity. Moreover, the idea of a universal, formal ethics, derived from Kant, is necessary if rational critique and reconstruction are to develop. In "New Social Movements"[19] Habermas makes it clear that feminists and other radicals must preserve a loyalty to these Enlightenment ideals, even when their own strategies are particular and local.

In short, Habermas views modernity as an incomplete or unfinished project that began in the 17th century, reached a high point in the Enlightenment and its 19th-century proponents (notably Marx), and was derailed in the 20th century, but, contrary to Weber and the Frankfurt school, has made great progress and should be redeemed. Habermas believes that Nietzsche and his disciples, the postmodernists, go further than Weber and the Frankfurt school theorists, not just in their cultural pessimism (clearly influenced by Weber)[20] but also in their total rejection of reason, the Enlightenment project, modernity, and history in favor of emancipation from power and ideology. According to Habermas, the postmodernists favor a primitivist aestheticism and mythology or a self-referential debunking of reason in favor of a kind of historicism that culminates in the same retrograde aestheticism. The project of the Enlightenment needs to be wed to the tasks of the world; the search for knowledge, justice, and beauty needs to be related to everyday life rather than to experts; and the public sphere, which has been lost in advanced industrial society due to consumer culture, the mass culture industry, and the rationalization of the world through the encroachment of the systems sphere and technological rationality, needs to be revitalized.

Habermas links critical theory to the Marxist critique of ideology and Freudian techniques of psychological emancipation from illusion. His agenda is to search for dialogue that generates democratic practices that can provide rational methods for resisting colonization and legitimize a rationally restructured world. These dialogues would both overcome the introduction of technical rationality into all spheres of life and reconstruct the systems of everyday communication, which suffer from sexist, racist, and homophobic language, egoism, various myths, and an emphasis on blind traditionalism. By taking the functionalist elements of Parson's systems theory and combining these with a more critical approach to Mead's symbolic interactionism, an ideal of communicative rationality can be developed to replace purposive or technical rationality in the areas of politics and morality.[21]

Some Difficulties for Habermas

This sounds fine, but only if one waives objections about the "ideal speech situation" and various components of Habermas's theory of dialogue and consensus that are not just counterfactual but arguably unrealistic. Habermas believes that only the force of an argument is relevant to a dialogue. He neglects differences in argumentative ability and expertise. Here Habermas joins Rawls in assuming that ignorance will yield formal justice.[22] Indeed, even if we waive the postmodernist objections to the Enlightenment ideals of universal reason, the political inadequacies of this version of liberal democracy under present conditions cannot be ignored. Even if Habermas confined his model of political dialogue to the local level, it would be overly utopian, if only because it sidesteps postmodernist analyses of the political.

Benhabib and other Habermasians[23] discuss the legitimate functions of utopianism, despite their agreement with postmodernists about traditional metaphysics. Such talk makes it easier to reject the political programs of many feminists and other new social movements and provides a master strategy against the postmodernists. This strategy is partly related to Habermas's claim that postmodernists are against reason, against the Enlightenment, and in favor of myth and a nostalgic past. In fact, the rhetorical differences between critical theorists and postmodernists are more pronounced than the actual differences; many of the claims by the postmodernists are compatible with the ethos behind critical theory; and Habermas and his followers agree with many of the central themes of postmodernism about metaphysics and about many of the weaknesses in traditional humanism, Marxism, the philosophy of subjectivity, and the philosophy of history.

Feminism and Critical Theory

In a recent paper on feminism and postmodernism,[24] Benhabib, a vigorous defender of Habermas, distinguishes between strong and weak versions of the postmodernist theses about man, metaphysics, and history. Her strong theses are arguably not ones postmodernists hold, as Fraser points out in her response to Benhabib.[25] Benhabib insists that the weaker readings of the postmodernist claims need to be taken seriously and in fact are compatible with critical theory. The need to pinpoint the differences therefore becomes important; these two groups of writers may be able to be combined in ways that strengthen them both.[26]

Benhabib asserts that the strong postmodernist theses of the end of history, the death of the subject, and the death of metaphysics rule out macrolevel analyses and critiques and prevent feminists and others from appealing to emancipatory metanarratives and universal values that could generate a framework for a sober utopian agenda for liberation. The end of this chapter discusses the conflict between postmodern feminism and feminist critical theory. Suffice it to say here that Benhabib never defends the legitimacy of these desiderata.

Habermas, who does defend their legitimacy, has a skewed view of what the postmodernists are up to. He[27] and his defenders[28] continue to develop the following argument: The postmodernists reject the Enlightenment; they reject reason in favor of an appeal to myth, art, romanticism, and primitivism; they have no normative grounds to stand on, or rather cut the ground from under normative criticism and reason by their strategy of rejecting reason entirely; and their conception of politics and power, which envisions microlevel transgressions and interventions, leaves everything as it is. The iron cage of the disciplinary society will always be with us in some form; knowledge and power will always be connected; and Marxist revolution is, if possible, always extremely dangerous.

Habermas on Modernity

For Habermas, the postmodernists carry forward the avant-garde's desire to explode the continuum of history, traditions, norms, and ultimately reason and modernity. In so doing, they develop a position that is tantamount to the views of old conservatives such as Durkheim and Bellah and neoconservatives such as Bell, who attack cultural modernism and want to wed the Protestant work ethic to tradition, religion, anti-Enlightenment values, and a Gemeinschaft concept of community.[29] The postmodernists are young conservatives, according to Habermas, because they reject the metaphysical and religious views of old conservatives and neoconservatives.

These conservative one-sided views of modernity are rooted in a failure to appreciate the selective dialectic of rationalization and the untapped potential of modernity and the Enlightenment project. These views rest on the philosophy of consciousness or subjectivity, which assesses everything from the vantage point of individual consciousness. Hegel takes the first false step in this direction by failing to take up the idea of intersubjectivity and communicative rationality.

Two Hypotheses About Reason and History

Habermas's views of the potentials of modernity and the Enlightenment, even "after the fall[30]", rest upon a view of history that seems unduly essentialist.[31] Simply put, modernity has an essence or potential. Its actual developments do not exhaust its potential developments. The way things have actually worked out is accidental. Hegel could have moved beyond the philosophy of consciousness; the iron cage could have been avoided; the failure to develop more rationalized forms of dialogue was not inevitable; the colonization of the world is only a historical accident. Modernity could have been different and its dark side can still be overcome if late modernity is set along the right path.

Then this unfinished project, that of the Enlightenment, can proceed in the right direction.

Whether Habermas's philosophy of history is defensible is a very real question. Perhaps if he took the postmodernist concern for particularity, contingency, discontinuity, and the task of the "specific intellectual"[32] more seriously, he would not be prone to maintain this view. Is there any evidence for his claims, or is he projecting his Enlightenment metanarrative onto the past 200 years and explaining the disparity between its story and actual developments on the basis of wishful thinking and faith?

In many ways, Habermas repeats the argument of Lukacs in *The Destruction of Reason*[33] that everything since Kant and Hegel has been a falling away from reason and that this is ultimately responsible for our malaise. Alternatively, Lyotard argues that the Enlightenment, in the guise of the French Revolution, was a "sign of history," a manifestation of a hope toward which we must constantly work together.[34]

Do we believe, as Habermas does, that the framework of modernity is still essentially intact or at least retrievable? That the categories and values of modernity that infuse mainstream naturalist and antinaturalist sociology can be left as is and continue to play an explanatory and emancipatory role? Can the doctrines of modernity and the Enlightenment help us today? Can the advocates of counter-Enlightenment be dismissed? Do we really live in an order in which politics, science, and aesthetics are distinct? Must an aesthetic approach to our malaise be irrational? Would harmonizing the three spheres of culture, even if possible, set things right? Can the anti-Enlightenment conservatives attacked by Habermas exist outside the framework of modernity?

Critical Theory and Postmodernism

We must again ask who is following the Enlightenment ethos of looking at the concrete realities of the day in an empirically grounded, relatively detached way. If the realities that define the new world order are closer to the descriptions of it given by Foucault, Baudrillard, and Lyotard, then perhaps their understanding and strategies, including political strategies, are more realistic and rational than those of Habermas and his followers.

By the same token, if postmodernists were more explicit about their values, critical theorists might not be so critical of their writings. Once this type of mutual recognition is opened up as a possibility, critical theorists and postmodernists may be able to join forces.

These two camps have some agreements, although the debates about reason, universalism, knowledge/power, norms, and the political are real enough. Instead of reviewing these debates, it may be more helpful to find the areas of agreement.

Habermas and the critical theorists seem to agree with the postmodernists that the Enlightenment project has not succeeded. Late modern societies are suffering from legitimation crises in science, morality, and politics; the dominant forms of knowledge and power—ideology and economics—are leading away from the ideals of democracy, human freedom, and community. Postmodernists and critical theorists disagree about the theoretical accounts of these developments, political strategies and tactics, what we can and cannot reasonably hope for in the foreseeable future, and their views about whether the new world order is a culmination of what preceded it or something radically different. However, they agree about the need for dialogue, the need to keep alive many voices and points of view, the need to move away from traditional philosophy and metaphysics, the need for thought to be at once rigorous and critical, the need to keep alive, in Lyotard's phrase, "a politics that would respect the desire for justice and the desire for the unknown."[35] They also agree in their understanding of connections among science, power, and the state and the need for new social movements that can pave the way for more participatory democracy and new forms of solidarity, community, and cooperation among different but equal voices. The differences are at the level of metatheory and metanarrative.

Best and Kellner[36] discuss the need to combine forces to develop a multidimensional, multiperspective theory to help us understand the present in more systematic ways; the need to combine the macroanalyses of critical theorists with the microanalyses of postmodernists; and the need to develop a philosophy and an interdisciplinary social science of postmodernity. In addition, postmodernists need to be more explicit about the normative dimensions of their work, particularly their loyalty to the ideas of freedom, democracy, community, and a pluralistic ideal of justice. At the same time, we must ask critical theorists to rethink their loyalties to the Enlightenment project, or at least to look at the present without filtering these events through Habermas's problematic view of history; his penchant for architectonic dialectics and system; and his Kantian concern for neat categories. A multiperspective approach to the social sciences that incorporates these two modified perspectives as well as any other relevant points of view might shed light on the times we are living in.

Postmodern Feminism
Versus Feminist Critical Theory

As Chapter 7 mentions, there is no easy way of resolving the dispute between feminist critical theory and postmodern feminism except for the multiperspective route. (There are many other versions of feminism and feminist contributions to the social and behavioral sciences that are not touched on here.) This section explores the dialectic of the argument between these two versions of feminism to show that the issues between them are either rhetorical or undecidable.

For the Marxist feminists or feminist critical theorists to defeat the postmodern feminists, they would need to show that Marxism or critical theory is a more accurate framework for understanding the present than postmodernism. To show this, the concepts and categories of modern social science and philosophy would have to be defended against criticisms. This is not an easy task.

Feminist critical theorists or Marxists could rightly argue that issues of class, race, and gender are of great concern today and that the Marxist tradition does a better job with this topic than postmodernists, who barely touch it. Why do postmodernists not talk about the general categories of class, race, and gender? Because the postmodernists have made a convincing argument that these modernist concepts are outdated in the postmodern world.

Postmodernist feminists need to take the concerns of Marxist (and other) feminists seriously. The demand that postmodernism be explicit about its norms in the areas of social science and social theory is especially important in the area of feminism and other new social movements. A loyalty to the ethos of the Enlightenment ought to bring sympathy for efforts by postmodern feminists in their deconstruction of the concepts of male, female, gender, and sexuality during a time when racism, sexism, homophobia, hate crimes, rape, and the glass ceiling are of great concern. If the postmodernists are right that everything is political and that the ideals of justice, difference, friendship, community, and freedom need to be resituated, it is only fair to ask postmodern feminists to take these issues seriously and to insist that their norms be made explicit.

The differences between the two approaches to feminism are ones of style, tactics, and rhetoric. Nobody in these two camps denies that women and people of color continue to be treated in unjust ways or that the litany of abuses is not warranted. How are these abuses to be eliminated? By appealing to the Marxist ideal of revolution? By appealing to the ideal speech situation and the universal norms that govern Habermas's model of dialogue? There is a problem with combining these norms with the particular concerns of feminism and other new social movements, whose focus is based on their difference and otherness. On the other hand, it is not clear whether postmodern feminist attempts to deconstruct or resituate gender and sex categories have any real political payoffs. Some form of post-Marxism that combines the approaches of critical theory, postmodernism, and feminism holds out the most promise in this area, as well as the most promise to bridge the gap between critical theory and postmodernism.

Feminist scholarship's role in the social and behavioral sciences (and in the academy in general) is salutary. Postmodern feminists in particular are making important contributions to psychology, social history, economics, sociology, and cultural anthropology. The new ethnography is being used in exciting ways in cultural anthropology as well as in feminist scholarship in psychology and sociology. Feminist scholarship in political science and economics may radically alter these disciplines. Postmodernist feminism may turn out to have more radical effects within social science disciplines than within the traditional political sphere. But the political and social ramifications of this work may turn out to be as politically revolutionary as any Marxist version of feminism, including feminist critical theory.

Notes

1. Anderson, W. T. (1991). *Reality isn't what it used to be*. New York: Harper-Collins; Borgmann, *Crossing the postmodern divide*; Gilmour, *Fire on the earth*.

2. Benjamin, *Problem of modernity*; Dews, P. (1987). *Logics of disintegration*. New York: Verso. There are important affinities between Lyotard and Adorno, as well as between Baudrillard and Adorno.

3. Norris, C. (1988). *Paul DeMan* (chaps. 1 and 6). New York: Routledge; Lehman, D. (1991). *Signs of the times*. New York: Simon & Schuster; Waters, L., & Godzich, W. (Eds.). (1989). *Reading DeMan reading*. Minneapolis: University of Minnesota Press.

4. Farias, V. (1989). *Heidegger and nazism*. Philadelphia: Temple University Press; Neske & Kettering, *Martin Heidegger and national socialism*; Wolin, *The Heidegger controversy*.

5. Rorty, *Contingency, irony, and solidarity*.

6. Given the connections among ideas such as community, society, self, and justice, which postmodernists want to rethink, it is not surprising that the political must also be rethought. The best discussion of this topic is White, *Political theory and postmodernism*. See also McGowan, *Postmodernism and its critics*.

7. Habermas, J. (1981). Modernity versus post modernity. *New German Critique, 22*, 3-14; Habermas, J. (1989). *The new conservatism*. Cambridge: MIT Press; Habermas, *Philosophical discourse on modernity*; Habermas, Modernity: An incomplete project. See also Bernstein, *Habermas and modernity*; Dews, P. (Ed.). (1986). *Habermas: Autonomy and solidarity: Interviews with Jurgen Habermas*. New York: Verso.

For major works on the topic of critical theory versus postmodernism by Habermasians, see Agger, *Critical theory of public life*; Benhabib, S. Cornell, D. (Eds). (1987). *Feminism as critique*. Minneapolis: University of Minnesota Press; Bernstein, *The new constellation*; Braaten, J. (1992). *Habermas's critical theory of society*. Albany: State University of New York Press; Calhoun, C. (Ed.). (1992). *Habermas and the public sphere*. Cambridge: MIT Press; Cohen & Arato, *Civil society and political theory*; Dews, *Logics of disintegration*; Frank, M. (1989). *What is Neostructuralism?* Minneapolis: University of Minnesota Press; Hohen-dahl, P. U. (1991). *Reappraisals*. Ithaca, NY: Cornell University Press; Holub, R. C. (1992). *Jurgen Habermas: Critic in the public sphere*. New York: Routledge; Honneth, A. (1992). *The critique of power*. Cambridge: MIT Press; Honneth, A., & Joas, H. (Eds.). (1991). *Communicative action*. Cambridge: MIT Press; Honneth, A., McCarthy, T., Offe, C., & Wellmer, A. (Eds.). (1992). *Philosophical interven-*

tions in the unfinished project of enlightenment. Cambridge: MIT Press; Ingram, D. (1987). *Habermas and the dialectic of reason.* New Haven, CT: Yale University Press; Ingram, D. (1987). Legitimacy and the postmodern condition: The political thought of Jean-Francois Lyotard. *Praxis International, 6,* 286-305; Ingram, Foucault and the Frankfurt school; Ingram, *Critical theory and philosophy*; Jay, *Marxism and totality*; Kellner, *Critical theory, Marxism and modernity*; McCarthy, *Ideals and illusions*; Rasmussen, D. B. (1990). *Reading Habermas.* Cambridge, MA: Blackwell; Roblin, R. (Ed.). (1990). *The aesthetics of the critical theorists.* Lewiston, PA: Edwin Mellon Press; Wellmer, A. (1991). *The persistence of modernity.* Cambridge: MIT Press; Wexler, *Critical theory now*; White, S. K. (1988). *The recent work of Jurgen Habermas.* New York/Cambridge, UK: Cambridge University Press.

For criticisms of Habermas that range from partial to wide-ranging sympathy for postmodernism (but not necessarily total rejection of critical theory), see Ashley, D. (1990). Habermas and the completion of "the project of modernity." In Turner, *Theories of modernity and postmodernity*, pp. 88-108; Bernstein, J. M. (1989). The causality of fate: Modernity and modernism in Habermas. *Praxis International*, 407-25; Cornell, D. (1992). *The philosophy of the limit.* New York: Routledge; Dallmayr, F. (1988). Habermas and rationality. *Political Theory, 15,* 553-79, with response by R. Bernstein, Fred Dallmayr's Critique of Habermas, 580-93; Dallmayr, F. (1989). The discourse of modernity: Hegel, Nietzsche, Heidegger (and Habermas). *Praxis International*, 377-403; Gasche, R. (1988). Postmodernism and rationality. *Journal of Philosophy, 85,* 528-38; Hoy, D. C. (1988). Foucault: Modern or postmodern? In Arac, *After Foucault*, pp. 12-42; Hoy, D. C. (1989). Splitting the difference: Habermas's critique of Derrida. *Praxis International, 8,* 447-65; Norris, C. (1989). Deconstruction, postmodernism and philosophy: Habermas on Derrida. *Praxis International*, 426-46; Poster, M. (1984). *Foucault, Marxism and history.* Cambridge, UK: Polity; Poster, M. (1990). *The mode of information.* Chicago: University of Chicago Press; Poster, *Critical theory and poststructuralism*; Rachjman, J. (1985). *Michel Foucault: The freedom of philosophy.* New York: Columbia University Press; Rachjman, J. (1988). Habermas' complaint. *New German Critique, 14,* 163-91, Rachjman, J. (1988). Foucault as parrhesiast: His last course at the College de France. In Bernhauer, *Final Foucault*, pp. 213-30; Rachjman, Flynn, Foucault and the politics of postmodernity; van den Berg, A. (1990). Habermas and modernity: A critique of the theory of communicative action. *Current Perspectives in Social Theory, 10,* 161-93; White, S. K. (1986). Foucault's challenge to critical theory. *American Political Science Review, 80,* 420-32.

8. Habermas, *Philosophical discourse on modernity.*

9. Habermas, *Theory of communicative action* and *Philosophical discourse on modernity.*

10. For a reading of Weber as an existentialist see Lachmann, L. M. (1970). *The legacy of Max Weber.* Portsmouth, NH: Heinemann.

11. Habermas, *Theory of communicative action* and *Philosophical discourse on modernity.*

12. Habermas, J. (1979). *Communication and the evolution of society.* Boston: Beacon Press; Habermas, J. (1983). *Philosophical-political profiles.* Cambridge:

MIT Press; Habermas, J. (1989). *Moral consciousness and communicative action*. Cambridge: MIT Press.

13. Connerton, *Tragedy of enlightenment*; Friedman, *Political philosophy of the Frankfurt school*; Jay, *Dialectical imagination*; Jay, *Marxism and totality*.

14. Bauman, Z. (1975). *Towards a critical sociology* New York: Routledge; Dubiel, H. (1986). *Theory and politics: Studies in the development of critical theory*. Cambridge: MIT Press; Fay B. (1975). *Social theory and political practice*. Winchester, MA: Unwin Hyman; Fay B. (1988). *Critical social science*. Ithaca, NY: Cornell University Press; Horkheimer, M. (1972). Traditional and critical theory. In Horkheimer, *Critical theory* (pp. 188-243); O'Neill, J. (Ed.). (1976). *On critical theory*. New York: Seabury; Schroyer, T. (1973). *The critique of domination*. New York: George Braziller.

15. Habermas, *Communication and the evolution of society, Theory of communicative action, Philosophical discourse on modernity*. See also Benhabib S., & Dallmayr, F. (Eds.). (1990). *The communicative ethics controversy*. Cambridge: MIT Press; Guess, *Idea of a critical theory*; Honneth & Joas, *Communicative action*; McCarthy, T. (1978). *The critical theory of Jurgen Habermas*. Cambridge: MIT Press; Universalism vs. communitarianism [Special issue]. (1988). *Philosophy and Social Criticism, 14*.

16. Dewey, J. (1929). *The public and its problems*. New York: Capricorn. For comparisons between Dewey and Habermas, see Antonio, R., & Kellner, D. (1992). *Communication, democratization, and modernity: Critical reflections on Habermas and Dewey*. Unpublished manuscript; Keane, J. (1984). *Public life in late capitalism*. New York/Cambridge, UK: Cambridge University Press. On Foucault, Lyotard, and the connections between aesthetics and politics, see Bernstein, J. M. (1991). *The fate of art*. University Park: Pennsylvania State University Press; Carroll, *Paraesthetics*; Readings, *Introducing Lyotard*; Eagleton, T. (1991). *The ideology of the aesthetic*. Cambridge, MA: Blackwell.

17. See Alford, F. (1985). *Science and the revenge of nature: Marcuse and Habermas*. University Presses of Florida. See also Habermas, J. (1970). *Toward a rational society*. Boston: Beacon Press; Habermas, J. (1971). *Knowledge and human interests*. Boston: Beacon Press; Habermas, J. (1988). *On the logic of the social sciences*. Cambridge: MIT Press; Whitebook, J. (1979). The problem of nature in Habermas. *Telos, 40*, 41-69.

18. Ingram, D. (1987). Philosophy and the aesthetic mediation of life: Weber and Habermas on the paradox of rationality. *The Philosophical Forum, 9*, 329-56; Ingram, D. (1990). Completing the project of enlightenment: Habermas on aesthetic rationality. In Roblin, *Aesthetics of the critical theorists*, pp. 359-422; Ingram, *Habermas and the dialectic of reason*. See also Warnke, G. (1988). David Ingram's Habermas and the dialectic of reason. *Praxis International, 7*, 91-98.

19. Habermas, J. (1981) New social movements. *Telos, 22*, 33-37. See also Calhoun, *Habermas and the public sphere*; Fraser, N. What's critical about critical theory? The case of Habermas and Gender (reprinted in Benhabib & Cornell, *Feminism as critique*, pp. 31-55); Habermas, *Structural transformation of the public sphere*.

20. Benjamin, *Problem of modernity*; Friedman, *Political philosophy of the Frankfurt school*; Ingram, *Habermas and the dialectic of reason*.

21. Habermas, *Theory of communicative action: Vol. 2*, and Ingram, *Habermas and the dialectic of reason*.

22. Rawls, J. (1971). *A theory of justice*. Cambridge, MA: Harvard University Press; Rawls, J. (1993). *Political liberalism*. New York: Columbia University Press. See also Benhabib, S. (1989). Liberal dialogue versus a critical theory of discursive legitimation. In N. Rosenblum (Ed.), *Liberalism and the moral life* (pp. 143-56). Cambridge, MA: Harvard University Press; Benhabib, S. (1980) *Procedural and discursive norms of rationality: The search for the normative grounding of political theory*. Unpublished manuscript; Benhabib & Dallmayr, *Communicative ethics controversy*; Honneth & Joas, *Communicative action*; White, *Recent work of Jurgen Habermas*.

23. Benhabib, S. (1992). The utopian dimension in communicative ethics (reprinted in D. Ingram & J. Simon-Ingram, (Eds.), *Critical theory: The essential readings*. New York: Paragon (pp. 388-400); Benhabib, Feminism and postmodernism: An uneasy alliance; Heckman, S. J. (1992). *Gender and knowledge*. Boston: Northeastern University Press.

24. Benhabib, Feminism and postmodernism: An uneasy alliance.

25. Fraser, False antithesis.

26. Best & Kellner, *Postmodern theory*; Fraser, N., & Nicholson, L. J. (1991). Social criticism without philosophy. In Nicholson, *Feminism/postmodernism*, pp. 15-35; Ingram, D. *A reply to Flynn and McCarthy: Foucault and Habermas*. Unpublished manuscript; Kellner, *Critical theory, Marxism and modernity*.

27. Habermas, Modernity: An incomplete project and *Philosophical discourse on modernity*.

28. Dews, *Logics of disintegration*; Frank, *What is Neostructuralism?*; Hohendahl, *Reappraisals*; Honneth, *The critique of power*; Wellmer, *The persistence of modernity*.

29. Habermas, J. (1990). Neoconservative cultural criticism in the United States and West Germany. In Bernstein, *Habermas and modernity*, pp. 78-95; Habermas, Modernism: An incomplete project;

30. Habermas, J. (1992). What does socialism mean today? The revolutions of recuperation and the need for new thinking. In R. Blackburn (Ed.), *After the fall: The failure of communism and the future of socialism* (pp. 25-46). New York: Verso. See also Habermas, J. (1989). Twenty years later. *Dissent, 36*, 250-256.

31. Bernstein, Causality of fate; Rachjman, Habermas' complaint.

32. Foucault, M. (1977). The political function of the intellectual. *Radical Philosophy, 17*, 12-15; Foucault, M. (1980). Two lectures. In Foucault, *Power/knowledge: Selected interviews and other writings, 1972-1977*. See also Merod, J. (1987). *The political responsibility of the intellectual*. Ithaca, NY: Cornell University Press.

33. Georg Lukacs, *The Destruction of Reason*. Atlantic Highlands, NJ: Humanities Press, 1981; Tom Rockmore, *Irrationalism: Lukacs and the Marxist View of Reason*. Philadelphia: Temple University Press, 1992.

34. Lyotard, The sign of history; Lyotard, J. F. (1988). Interview. *Theory Culture and Society, 512*, 277-309.

35. Lyotard, *The Postmodern Condition*, p. 67.

36. Best & Kellner, *Postmodern theory*.

For other pertinent discussions, see Agger, B. (1990). *Decline of discourse.* Agger, B. (1992). *Discourse of domination.* Evanston, IL: Northwestern University Press; Agger, *Critical theory of public life*; Jay, M. (1993). *Force fields.* New York: Routledge; Wexler, *Critical theory now.*

9

POSTMODERNISM

An Overview

This chapter offers a brief overview of postmodernist themes by providing answers to the questions about postmodernism posed in the Introduction.

Is postmodernism against the Enlightenment? As Chapter 1 argues, the answer to this question is yes and no. If one is talking about the doctrines (by now dogmas) that grew out of the Enlightenment—positivism, value neutrality, scientism (blind faith in science and technology), cost-benefit analysis, utopian and dys-utopian philosophies of history, the idea of totality and unification, the search for a scientific and technological Gemeinschaft—then postmodernism is clearly against the Enlightenment. If one is talking about the ethos of honesty and probity, criticism and analysis, the rooting out of dead dogmas, the constant examining and surpassing of current assumptions and practices in the name of emancipation from dangerous dogmas, then postmodernism is not against the Enlightenment; it carries forward the critical ethos of Kant, Nietzsche, and Freud.

However, for some postmodernists the question "Are you for or against the Enlightenment" needs to be rejected rather than answered. This illustrates one postmodernist theme: Set aside, in Nietzschean fashion, the old tablets and questions and the yes-and-no answers to them to overcome the dialectics of modernity that result in the very type of nihilism the postmodernists are accused of sustaining.

169

Is postmodernism a form of irrationalism or nihilism? "Nihilism," at least according to Nietzsche, takes a variety of forms. The nihilism that is destructive, that brings about a loss of meaning and value to whatever cannot withstand rational scrutiny and yields world-weariness is, for Nietzsche, the culmination of the doctrines of modernity. These doctrines constitute the basis for both Enlightenment and counter-Enlightenment thought. To be sure, the ethos of Enlightenment, as a continuation of the will to truth, will destroy whatever cannot withstand examination. But this is destructive nihilism only if we still think there must be something unquestionable to cling to or if we think that it is irrational to cling to anything in this way. Although Nietzsche maintains that we cannot live without illusions, he does not believe that such illusions must be sick, dangerous, irrational, or negative. These illusions provide guideposts for creating our-selves and culture. Moreover, they must not be compatible with beliefs that are refuted by science. This is Nietzsche's version of "aesthetic Socratism," combining aesthetics (healthy illusions) with the scientific outlook to avoid unhealthy beliefs and hori-zons. It is only in this way that knowledge can serve life. Nietzsche does not advocate a form of irrationalism or primitiv-ism, but rather claims that the ideal of truth and knowledge at any price (the ascetic ideal) is harmful and dangerous to life.

Attempts within modernity to defend values such as human-ism, science, positivism, radical egalitarianism, or social engi-neering only reinforce deconstructive nihilism, according to Nietzsche, because these values are the secularization of the Western values that produce nihilism. We must rethink, recon-textualize, and resituate values that are healthy and create others like them. We must abandon those elements of our heritage that do not affirm and enhance life by continually examining the limits of our current beliefs in the spirit of play and experimen-tation. Only then, as Zarathustra puts it, can we remain faithful to the earth.

Postmodernism invites us to rethink the notions of self, soci-ety, community, reason, values, and history that dominate mo-dernity, and to do so without nostalgia or regret and without utopian aspirations for what we create under conditions of postmodernity.

Eventually, in Nietzsche's view, a new "completed" and "active" nihilism will emerge, along with a more mature type of human being who will be able to create healthier values and cultures. Nobody can say whether this is possible in a postmodern world, when and how and for whom it might happen, or with what consequences. Although there have been few gestures in this direction in the social sciences (as opposed to philosophy or art or literature), it is not fair to dismiss this outlook at this early stage.

However, postmodernists may suffer from a related defect, also diagnosed by Nietzsche: a kind of Olympian detachment and withdrawal from involvement in the world, or a failure to keep a relationship between "involvement and detachment." Nietzsche, Weber, Freud, Mannheim, Rorty, Foucault, and Derrida are prone to this shortcoming, the life of Mannheim's free-floating intellectual. Perhaps this is the price postmodernist intellectuals—perhaps all intellectuals since Plato—who adopt the ethos of Enlightenment have to pay. The Nietzschean query "How much truth can an individual stand?"might be too much for many to worry about. Perhaps postmodernists have a strength that most intellectuals do not to accept the harshness of unvarnished truth and to reject the ascetic ideal. However, postmodernists are not free-floating intellectuals but rather specific intellectuals engaged in the political activity of testing the limits of doctrines and practices. Chapter 10 argues that this is the vocation of the postmodernist scholar.

If more human beings learn to grow up (in Freud's sense), there might not be quite the same need for intellectuals, and presumably little reason for occasion nostalgia, regret, or utopianism. The idea of life as continual experimentation and play may not be feasible for everybody, not even all intellectuals, but there is no way to project how many people can grow to be like this or what the general effects of such a life on society and culture might be. Intellectuals, being overly reflective, may be the least likely group to relinquish utopian aspirations or resentment. But this does not vitiate the Freudian project of an ethics of total honesty. If the price for a postmodern world that avoids the weariness of Nietzsche's last man is the disappearance of the traditional intellectual, it may be worth it.

One can argue that the price for this sort of nihilism is irrationalism. To give up the utopian underpinning of science, reason, and universalism in morals in favor of aesthetic excess, play, experimentation, irony, perhaps even myth, would be dangerous and retrograde. It even seems unrealistically utopian, at least for a postmodernist. However, if Lyotard is right, these underpinnings have already disappeared in favor of the mercantilization of knowledge.

In any case, is this nihilism, or would it mean that we have outgrown nihilism, rooted as it is in the spirit of seriousness and the failure of utopianism? What is meant by "irrationalism" here? What does reason demand? These questions uncritically involve the arsenal of concepts that define modernity as surveyed in Chapters 1 through 4. Thus, the terms "rational" and "irrational" are defined either by pro-Enlightenment, promodernity assumptions or else by anti-Enlightenment, antimodernity comparison of modernity with, say, the Greeks. Whatever does not fit these definitions becomes irrational. Even romantics, Dostoyevsky's underground rebel, and Sartre, all of whom seem to defend the irrational, arguably reject the Enlightenment view of reason. Perhaps they are buying into it and merely negating it.

Weber's discussion of these issues is important in many ways. Modern instrumental or formal rationality may be our fate. But it may also be substantively irrational from all other points of view, comparative history, life, and traditional, valuational, and affective rationality and action.

Even if postmodernists rejects all of Weber's ideal rational action types, that does not make them irrationalists. Another motif in postmodernism is the notion of "dedifferentiation": blurring the distinction between reason and unreason, literature and philosophy, science and art, aesthetics and politics. Perhaps postmodernism is moving toward a dedifferentiated approach to the fundamental concepts, values, and assumptions of modernity. Perhaps it asks us to combine involvement and detachment, to look at ourselves and our values in a clinical, reflective manner.

The writings of postmodernists are rigorous and demanding, exhibiting an ethos of probity, so they do not manifest any sort of irrationalism. But they do concern themselves with "the other side of reason": points of view and voices of women, people of color, third-world people, European counter-Enlightenment traditions, and other non-Europeans who have been marginalized by the dominant ideas of reason and the privileged hierarchies that go with them. The dogmas of the Enlightenment have made these other points of view irrational by definition. The postmodernists attempt to widen the horizons of reason by limiting the influence of one powerful but narrow and dogmatic notion of what constitutes reason.

Although many postmodernists reject or downplay many of the methods used by both naturalists and antinaturalists (owing in part to the metaphysical doctrines about humans and society that underlie their pro- and antimodern outlooks), they do favor some methods, for example, radical hermeneutics, the new ethnography, textuality, deconstruction, and archeology and genealogy. Foucault makes use of the concepts of archeology and genealogy. He is interested in studying the contingent origins of our current beliefs and practices and their effects on us. Archeology allows him to uncover these beliefs and practices and their origins; genealogy allows him to uncover their embodiments in regimes of power. Foucault takes our practices and beliefs, and thus our history, to be discontinuous. He rejects the idea that the origins of a practice or belief tells us anything about its present status. He believes that uncovering alternatives to existing systems can point out the limits of reason and offer possibilities of transgression, even if we cannot retrieve those other systems for ourselves.

For Foucault, all of this serves the ethos of Enlightenment, the critique of the present limits of reason, which he takes from Kant. By uncovering the assumptions and history behind our current practices and beliefs, by showing their contingent and discontinuous history, their connections with relations of power and domination, and the way in which power is both enabling and constraining, Foucault continues Kant's radical project. In the tradition of Nietzsche, Weber, and Freud, Foucault believes this activity must be continuing, rigorous, clinical, and as unbiased as possible to be effective.

Foucault avoids moral judgments about what is good or bad. For him, it is more important to recognize that everything is dangerous. The limits of reason need to be examined and transgressed all the time, without hope that we will reach a utopian society, although a society that is less repressive than ours is always a possibility. In any event, because power is enabling as well as constraining, testing the limits of reason and the history of the present will always yield new possibilities for action.

Lyotard uses Kantian strategies and concepts; for instance, the search for paradoxes and paralogisms, reliance on ideas (such as justice, knowledge, community, and knowledge) that cannot be fully articulated, emphasis on differences (the differend), and heterogeneous language games to prevent totality and terror (the silencing of the voices of difference) and to promote knowledge, community, and justice.

Theory is thus important to postmodernists, but the task of theory, and its basic orientation, is not the universal truth of the Enlightenment but specific to the demands of the day. One must be more rigorous and honest than defenders of the dogmas of the Enlightenment can allow themselves to be; we need to examine our questions and assumptions critically and test their limits. This is a very Socratic enterprise. Like Socrates, Lyotard, Derrida, and Foucault carry the arguments wherever they lead. This may be dangerous, but it is not irrational.

Does postmodernism abandon the ideas of society and the social? Does postmodernism reject the idea of the self? Does postmodernism relinquish the search for community? Once again, the answer is both yes and no. These concepts, as embodied in modernity, cultural modernism, and philosophy, must be re-thought and resituated, in ways that are explored in detail in Chapters 7 and 8.

To some extent, the postmodernists avoid the debates about modernity, unless it is to examine them reflectively and clinically only to surpass them. The guiding questions of these debates, "Are you for or against modernity, the Enlightenment, reason, and progress?" and "Is modernity good or bad?" are rejected. Postmodernists agree with Bauman's claim that modernity is ambivalent. They want to recontextualize the self, society, community, history, and politics within a framework that bypasses all these questions and debates and emphasizes otherness, plurality, the local, the specific, difference, perspective, and the contingent.

It does not matter whether we say that postmodernism is the radicalization and completion of certain tendencies within modernity or cultural modernism or that it is a radical break or discontinuity or that it is, in part, both. The key point is that it is the rigorously self-reflexive clinical examination of modernity, inspired by the ethos of Enlightenment probity. However, these questions get us nowhere and are basically unimportant. Enlightenment and counter-Enlightenment and promodernity and antimodernity views share common assumptions, dualisms, values, and conceptions about self, society, community, history, politics, reason, progress, method, and freedom. Postmodernism distances itself from everything in modernity, just as the person unconcerned with religion distances herself or himself from all religious points of view, including that of the atheist, and all controversies that surround the various positions within a religious worldview.

This does not mean that postmodernism rejects everything in and about modernity. It means that postmodernism recontextualizes many of its ideas while abandoning the assumptions that underlie modernism. This approach keeps the ethos of probity alive. Because these efforts to resituate modernist ideas are just beginning, it is too early to characterize fully, let alone evaluate, such efforts.

Does postmodernism attack the modern ideas of freedom, reason, and emancipation? The ethos of the Enlightenment is designed to enhance these values. The whole point of the postmodernist enterprise is to increase human understanding and possibilities. But postmodernists do not try to justify such values or ground them. In this respect they radicalize Nietzsche and Freud by refusing to give justification or theories for what they are doing or the values they defend.

Unfortunately, by doing so, postmodernists leave open the possibility of being caught in Weber's iron cage, of assuming that any totality or unification is just another variant on the disciplinary society. Following Weber, all postmodernists can give us are strategies and tactics for keeping the iron cage at bay. By refusing to talk about general norms, goals, or hopes, are they exhibiting that weariness about life and history that Nietzsche associates with incomplete nihilism, which is content to resituate many of the old values? Even if they are not Mannheimian free-floating intellectuals, there is always the risk that they will become indifferent observers and not participants. The postmodernist scholar's vocation of probity may well have this result.

Taking a longer perspective, it is not obvious what effect the refusal to offer either hope or consolation will have. Nietzsche died in 1900, Freud has been dead for over 50 years, and we still do not understand or can assess what they were driving at. If Nietzsche is right, none of us is in a position to say what a genuinely post-nihilistic culture would look like or whether the emerging global culture would be, for better or worse, postnihilistic. Is Fukuyama right in claiming that such a culture will perpetuate the last man, or is the postmodernists' hope that something more life enhancing will emerge closer to the truth? We do not know, so we cannot dismiss the postmodernist radicalization of the Nietzsche-Freud ethics of honesty, even if we cannot fully understand its meaning or ramifications.

What becomes of politics within a postmodernist outlook? The above observations raise the issues of postmodernism and the political and the normative—of power, ideology, critique, and action. Political positions within modernity run the gamut from anarchism and socialism to liberalism, conservatism, and fascism. The social sciences have been influenced by all of these ideas, but the policy sciences are not the only place where these gods and demons have battled. Postmodernists believe that the political has to be rethought, in tandem with all the key ideas of self, society, community, justice, friendship, authority, freedom, law, power, knowledge, truth, unity, and reason. If the effect of this is to make everything political, perhaps that is inevitable. Postmodernists believe that everything always has been and will be political. But once one abandons modernity's ideas and distinctions and focuses on the interactions between knowledge and power, on the local level and on the institutional contexts that dominate power/knowledge relations in our disciplinary society, this idea is put into a new light. Chapter 10 explores some of these issues in greater depth in an attempt to answer the question of how postmodernism is changing the social sciences.

Is postmodernism the cultural ideology of late capitalism and postindustrial society? Does postmodernism take anything seriously, or does it turn everything into a game? This is not to say that postmodernists take nothing, including politics, seriously. They follow Nietzsche in dancing over the spirit of gravity; they believe in affirmation through difference and reject the theoretical and political projects of modernity that they see as two sides of one coin. Yet their intellectual work is colored by a political posture that is clearly rooted in a deep feeling for the outsider and downtrodden. Post-Marxism, which seeks to combine elements of Marxism with liberalism and postmodernism, feminism, and postcolonialism to engender radical democracy, is a manifestation of this postmodernist concern.

Unlike writers who never challenge assumptions and prejudices, postmodernists are rigorously, even ruthlessly, honest, probative, and historically specific. They are thus more realistic than the allegedly more rational, serious writers. Yet postmodernists, perhaps for this very reason, are less indifferent to involvement in combatting real theoretical and social injustices. The postmodern intellectual may be more ready to do this than the traditional "universal" intellectual, who sees everything from an abstract point of view, because the postmodernist is an interpreter, not an Olympian legislator.

Does postmodernism reject the ideas of objective reality, truth, and knowledge and thus try to overthrow modern science and technology? Postmodernists do not reject reality, science, and technology, nor are they Luddites, aesthetes, idealists, or pragmatists, although motifs from the last three philosophies are often meshed in postmodernist writings. Postmodernists, along with a host of other antirealists, explore the ways in which language, power, social factors, and history shape our views about reality, truth, and knowledge. They favor Nietzschean perspectivism, which rejects the idea of the world in itself, of objective reality, as rooted in our longest lie: the belief in God. Examining science, philosophy, and literature in light of these factors is not a project that is new to postmodernists. Their antifoundationalist, constructivist views are present within modernity; this aspect of postmodernism is clearly a radicalization of what has been part of modernity all along. Postmodernists simply carry forward these views more thoroughly and without nostalgia or regret for lost realist ideals of objectivity and truth.

10

HOW POSTMODERNISM IS CHANGING THE SOCIAL SCIENCES

The social sciences have been inseparable from ideological and political factors since their beginning. In this century, institutional factors and professionalization have exaggerated this separation.

Many modern intellectuals, including leading social scientists, either feel alienated from modernity or wish to legitimize it. Marxists and conservatives typically feel alienated from modernity and liberals typically wish to legitimize it. The search for Gemeinschaft by the left and the right is connected to this dissatisfaction with modern culture. Liberals, as heirs to the Enlightenment, want neither a utopia nor the nostalgic return to a premodern society. This attitude has culminated in two liberal ideological theses, the end-of-ideology thesis of the 1960s and Fukuyama's end-of-history thesis of the 1990s.

The alienation of modern intellectuals is also connected to the dominance of the "conflict versus consensus" dualism of modern sociology (the problem of order) and to the ideal of the intellectual as a legislator of culture, that is, a part of the ruling elite.

Postmodernism seeks to move beyond this ideological context in the social sciences. Postmodernists advocate a version of Weber's science as a vocation that can be called "the vocation of the postmodern scholar." In this view, the social scientist is an interpreter, not a legislator. Even in the role of specific intellectuals, postmodern scholars do not have the vocation of proposing or dictating values or solutions to social problems, defending what is going on, or issuing calls for revolution. It is their vocation to pursue the ethos of Enlightenment in order to promote understanding in a way that allows the values of freedom, difference, and affirmation to operate as fully as possible so that individuals can have the maximum opportunities to construct their own lives and communities.

The Normative Structure
of the Social Sciences

Is modern social science rooted in liberal or conservative political aspirations? Some writers, such as Seidman,[1] take the former line; others, notably Nisbet,[2] take the latter. Others, such as Hearn[3] and Strasser,[4] argue that both of these modern political outlooks influenced the founding of the modern social sciences. In any event, the social sciences have clearly been normative or ideological from the beginning.

It is once again useful to invoke the Enlightenment versus counter-Enlightenment distinction. Defenders of the Enlightenment typically want to use knowledge to enhance "the human estate." Promodernists wish to transform society from its reliance on tradition, religion, and literature into a society where reason will rule and where utopia may be achieved. In Bacon's words, the social sciences could contribute to the relief of the human estate by promoting a rational society governed by science, technology, liberal democracy, and utilitarianism or scientific socialism. Liberalism and socialism or Marxism becomes the ideological framework of and justification for the social sciences.

Counter-Enlightenment thinking typically accompanies a conservative or reactionary ideology. Antimodernity and antinaturalist methods are often used to support the construction of or a return to some real or imagined Gemeinschaft rooted in premodern values.

Conflict Versus Consensus

Another approach to understanding the affinities between the modern social sciences and ideology is the conflict-versus-consensus models of sociological theory.[5] Strasser describes these models as, respectively, "progressive" and "integrative" or "stabilizing." His description has a ring of truth as a historical observation. One can line up conflict theorists, such as Marx, and consensus theorists, such as liberals Parsons and Durkheim, along a continuum that ranges from utopian aspirations for radical change to various meliorist reform programs to an equilibrium and adjustment model that assumes "the system" is acceptable as it is and provides self-adjusting mechanisms for dealing with the relatively minor (if never-ending) problems of adjustment to "normalcy." The various attitudes toward the Enlightenment and the counter-Enlightenment—pro- and antimodernity and naturalist and antinaturalist—are enmeshed in these ideological contexts and attitudes.

Liberalism, in particular reformist liberalism (with certain forms of democratic socialism as a limiting case), has clearly been the dominant ideology in the social sciences, at least in the United States. It will be helpful to discuss this in more detail.

The Social Sciences and Liberalism

To tell a complete story[6] of the connections between academic social science, sociology, cultural anthropology, psychology, political science, history, and economics and modern reformist liberalism, one would have to discuss the rise of the corporate state and corporate liberalism;[7] the influence of Social Darwinism;[8] the professionalization of the social sciences;[9] the move from radicalism to reformism in Germany and the United States away from the American Social Science Association,[10] which was dominated by "sociologists of the chair,"[11] radical and reformist journalists, clergy, and nonprofessional social scientists; the establishment of the modern university and the professionalization of the social and behavioral sciences;[12] the rise of the theory of the democratic elite;[13] the Progressivists' vacillation over elitism versus democracy;[14] the rise of the Social Science

Research Council and its involvement with various foundations for the benefit of corporate elitism;[15] the movement from advocacy to objectivity as the social sciences became professionalized and enmeshed in universities and competition for power, money, and prestige;[16] the rise of scientism and the search for objectivity in the social sciences;[17] the origins of the policy sciences, economic planning, and the managerial elite;[18] the end-of-ideology thesis and Cold War liberalism;[19] Parsons's attempt to nationalize the social sciences during the Cold War;[20] the rise of postindustrial society and neoconservatism;[21] the Fukuyama's end-of-history thesis;[22] debates about the "new class" and the role of intellectuals as scientific and technological experts[23] in a technological society;[24] and, most recently, the revitalization of Spencer's Social Darwinism and the Protestant ethic, the end of the welfare state, the accompanying "rhetoric of reaction,"[25] and the emergence of the new world order, globalization, and corporatism at home and abroad under the guise of a worldwide victory for market capitalism, human rights, and democracy. The latter amounts to a victory for the Machiavellian brand of political realism that stems from Weber and manifests itself in this country as revisionist or elitist democracy beginning with Morgenthau, Lasswell, and others in the 1930s.[26]

It is impossible to touch on all of these topics here, let alone treat them systematically or comprehensively. This chapter provides a brief interpretation of the connections between academic social science and the ideology of reformist liberalism.

The Corporate State
and Liberal Social Science

The rise of the corporate state in the late 19th century produced many social, political, economic, and psychological problems, especially in the cities. The first generation of social scientists in this country, like many of their contemporaries in Germany, France, and England (including Weber and Durkheim) wanted to deal with these problems in fairly radical ways. Many were socialists or associated with the Christian Social Gospel movement, and most were from the WASP elite, who had a vested interest in preserving their power and status in an increasingly secularized society but who were usually well intentioned and wished to aid the masses. Social Darwinism also played a crucial role, but even many of the Social Darwinists had views that were compatible with reformism, if not liberalism.

A number of events conspired to defeat the reformist or radical aspirations of these early social scientists. The growing dominance of the corporate state and corporate liberalism was one factor. Eventually corporatism turned the country in Durkheimian directions. A knowledge elite educated the people, engaged in policy advice, helped in national planning, and limited democracy in favor of rule by experts. These people may have been liberals; but, beginning with the Progressives, their liberalism was that of the democratic elite, who distrusted the masses and did not believe in government by the people. So corporate liberalism, when combined with the social and policy sciences,[27] led to politics by experts. These corporate liberals are the heirs of Comte and Saint-Simon.[28]

Social Darwinism led to eugenics,[29] the Testing Movement,[30] and the rise of the "architects of adjustment,"[31] the behaviorists' term for what social scientists called "social control." The social sciences would provide the knowledge and resources, as well as the advice, so that America could become a Durkheimian Gemeinschaft where everyone would fit in, play a role, and contribute. The unfit, notably the poor, would be helped to adjust. Lasswell uses Freud to psychoanalyze the unfit and rebellious, that is, those who do not think the system is in order as it is.[32]

The rise of universities and the professional social sciences, as well as the firing of some of the more radical reformers[33] and deviants, put a damper on real reform. From this point, in the name of professionalization, social scientists had to take the established order as a given and as good, and advocate only piecemeal adjustments. In practice, only disagreements about technical matters, for adjudication by experts, were allowed. This was the victory of Weber in America, even though Weber himself was much more prone to advocacy in practice than either his own doctrines allowed or his American followers had the stomach for.

Ross sums up the situation in *The Origins of American Social Science*:

. . . the professionalizing process itself had acted to discourage radicalism and dampen fundamental conflict. Professionalism required at least the appearance of objectivity, an elusive attribute that generally meant absence of bias and hence neutrality as between biased contending parties. In the heated political context of the Gilded Age . . . the historical economists' overt ethical stance, sympathy with labor, and tendencies toward socialism made their objectivity suspect and endangered the professional project. . . . Even before the public attack on Ely . . . his professional peers pressed him toward moderation and they ultimately abandoned him. . . . In case after case of university pressure brought against social scientists in the 1880s and 1890s, the conservative and moderate professional leaders carefully parceled out their support, making clear the limited range of academic freedom and the limited range of political dissent they were willing to defend. A degree of professional autonomy was achieved by narrowing its range.[34]

The social sciences moved from advocacy and reform to quietism, acceptance, and objectivity, as if accepting the status quo were objective and value free. (This is the main blind spot in much of academic social science even today.) From then on, mainstream social scientists would try to develop objective methods (statistical analysis of objective data, cost-benefit analysis), while claiming that such methods would lead to knowledge that is needed for genuine reform.

The Americanization of the Iron Cage

A good case can be made for the claim that the social and behavioral sciences have helped turn the United States into a Weberian iron cage in the form of a Durkheimian corporate state. The growing elitism and scientism and the ruse of value neutrality as a defense of the status quo, most dramatically defended under the guise of the end of ideology, and in the allegedly morally neutral policy sciences, have contributed to this state of affairs. The recent claims that the crisis in our society stems from too much democracy and too much liberal-inspired modernism and narcissism[35] are but defenses of corporate liberalism. Currently, the dominance of "objective" social science in the universities arguably is a resurgence of conservative tendencies that underwrite the new rhetoric of reaction.

On the other hand, the cultural wars being fought by the Christian right and the extreme left over political correctness, hate speech, free speech, multiculturalism, and against white males goes to the other extreme and raises the specters of tribalism, chaos, and violence in the name of justice and equality. This is at least as dangerous as the neoconservatism or timidity of academic social science. Perhaps this is why many scholars have dubbed the defenders of political correctness the McCarthyites of the left. It is also why many social scientists are so violently opposed to postmodernism. For some reason, postmodernism is often associated with extremists. But it is not clear what connections, if any, the more extreme writings of Derrida, Foucault, and Baudrillard have with these movements, unless they have been misused, as the Nazis misused Nietzsche's writings earlier this century.

Postmodernism and the Social Sciences

It is within this context of the dominance of liberalism and more extreme recent developments that we need to consider postmodernism. We need to ask, along with the postmodernists, whether liberalism, reformism, reaction, nihilism, and radicalism have exhausted themselves; whether the social sciences, spawned by modernity, can cope with the major transformations that are now occurring in the postindustrial information society. Then we must examine whether postmodernist themes resemble the end-of-ideology thesis of the 1960s and the end-of-history thesis of the 1990s.

Those who accuse modern intellectuals of oscillating between an outworn ideological yearning for Gemeinschaft or the Greek polis and a technological utopianism inspired by Marxism or socialism are correct in pointing out the dangers in ideological extremism in the social sciences. But what if the social sciences (and just about everything else, for that matter) are already political? What if the modern social sciences always have been normative in supporting or rationalizing radical, reactionary, or reformist forces? What do we do then? Adopt some version of Gouldner's reflexive sociology and engage in the sort of ideological wars that Weber's doctrines try to minimize? Insist that social scientists become interpreters rather than legislators or gatekeepers? Admit, with Foucault, that everything is dangerous, but focus attention on the specific dangers in our own disciplinary society, dependent as it is on the social and behavioral and policy sciences? Move in Habermas's direction of a critical social science that tries to harmonize the systems sphere of technology, economics, and bureaucracy with a democratic culture? Or should we accept even more radical, perhaps more pessimistic, options such as Baudrillard's claim of the end of the social and society? Does postmodernism signal the end of history, politics, democracy, and ideology as well as the end of the social and society?[36] Are there tendencies within modernity (capitalism, objectivism, scientism, instrumental reason, inadequate views of the social, or incorrect methodologies) that culminate in the end of the social and the end of man? Does modern humanism, the view that actors make their own history but in ways not of their own choosing, lead to the death of all these modern notions? Does the current oppositional culture of political correctness move us further away from these difficulties than neoconservative advocations of the new world order? What can we learn from the postmodernists about knowledge, power, and politics that might help us see the connections between the social sciences and ideology in more useful ways?

This book argues that the postmodernist conception of the social scientist's vocation in a postmodern world is incompatible with the ideologies that make up the political context of modern social science. The ethos of Enlightenment, of a probity that is specific, contextual, and yet reflexive, is what this vocation advocates. The social sciences of postmodernity must adopt this neo-Weberian vocation if they are to promote a realistic understanding of the postmodern condition. There will be time enough for debates about ideology, politics, and advocacy when such a social science helps clarify the new world order that is coming into existence.

Many social scientists feel threatened by postmodernism or a social science that takes postmodernism seriously. There are obvious conjectures about generational conflicts, power and prestige, ego-involvement with one's own theories and life's work, new developments in the universities and the professions, misunderstandings (such as those that blame the acts of the new tribalists on postmodern writers), the desire to hold onto the role of gatekeeper and legislator, the difficulty of coping with conflicting demands from all sides to transform the disciplines, the perceived loss of one's favorite ideology, method, or pet theory, and so forth. But the postmodern world will not go away. The issues raised by postmodernists will not go away. Coming to terms with postmodernism does not mean throwing out everything in the classic body of writings, but finding ways to make old and new ideas work together in specific contexts. Unless the social sciences find a place for the study of postmodern conditions and the writings of postmodernists, the social sciences as we have known them will become marginalized or perhaps even disappear.

Some positive suggestions for harmonizing the old and the new are called for.

Human Nature

To harmonize the old and new, human nature, a concept at the heart of the social sciences, must be abandoned, as should many of the conceptions of self, subjectivity, and agency that grew out of theories of human nature. But antihumanism and nominalism do not mean that a concern for understanding individuals would play no role in a social science of postmodernity. On the contrary. There would be more emphasis on the constructivist and fluid aspects of how selves are created and enriched. The various ideas about the self would be resituated into contexts that abandon many of the concepts, theories, and norms that define the self within modernity, such as egoism, rational choice theory, and behaviorism, as well as various ideas about normality and deviance.

Postmodernist works in psychology, economics, and history must emphasize different concepts of what a person is and can be. These disciplines should be less deterministic and quantitative, and less interested in prediction and control than they often have been. Some common assumptions about rationality, decision making, and individual values require modification or abandonment.

Society

The social, the political, and community are concepts that must be recontextualized in light of postmodernist concerns about plurality, otherness, and difference. These key concepts of sociology, political science, and history might be transformed in such a way as to give these disciplines a more fluid, constructivist perspective. Moreover, more interdisciplinary work, which appreciates the insights of literature and the voices of the marginalized, will be possible once scientism is set aside as a remnant of modernity's assumptions.

History and Cultural Anthropology

These fields of study must undergo radical transformation if the ideas of evolution, progress, primitive, and advanced societies are to be abandoned. Consideration of the end-of-history thesis and the new forms of global economics and culture might have a sanguine effect on the somewhat Whiggish and ethnocentric outlook of modern social science.

Methodology

Methodology should become more eclectic, flexible, and less central to the subject of the social sciences. There should be less emphasis on quantitative techniques (data analysis, for example) and more reliance on ethnography, description, narration, interpretation, and literature. The unfortunate tendency to make method the end all and be all of the social sciences is a product of modern assumptions about truth and objectivity. Deconstruction, genealogy, archeology, and analyses from different individuals and groups would promote greater specific understandings and increase appreciation of differences and variety while avoiding judgmental conclusions. The processes and mechanisms that enhance and constrict human possibilities could become more well known. The voices of the many others should be heard as a result of new developments in ethnography.

Although many of these approaches, methods, and assumptions are not new to postmodernism, the prominence they would have, when coupled with the abandonment of the ideological underpinnings of naturalist and antinaturalist methods in modern social science, might produce a joyful science that would increase our understanding of human possibilities under conditions of postmodernity.

Skinner, Heidegger, and Nietzsche view human beings as a set of specific possibilities. If we can learn to move beyond the stress associated with the newly emerging postmodern world, we may be able to develop fresh possibilities that would give us a new sense of wisdom attendant on the realization that there is a bright side to the fact that all that is solid *does* melt into air.

Notes

1. Seidman, S. (1983). *Liberalism and the origins of European social theory*. Berkeley: University of California Press. See also Bellamy, R. (1992). *Liberalism and modern society*. University Park: Pennsylvania State University Press; Hawthorn, G. (1976). *Enlightenment and despair*. New York/Cambridge, UK: Cambridge University Press; Westby, D. L. (1991). *The growth of sociological theory*. Englewood Cliffs, NJ: Prentice Hall.

2. Nisbet, R. (1966). *The sociological tradition*. New York: Basic Books.

3. Hearn, *Reason and freedom in sociological thought*.

4. Strasser, S. (1976). *The normative structure of sociology*. New York: Routledge. See also Turner, S. P., & Kasler, D. (Eds.). (1992). *Sociology confronts fascism*. New York: Routledge.

5. See Rhoads, *Critical issues in social theory*; Strasser, *Normative structure of sociology*.

6. Bramson, L. (1961). *The political context of sociology*. Princeton, NJ: Princeton University Press; Bannister, R. C. (1987). *Sociology and scientism*. Chapel Hill: University of North Carolina Press; Cravens, H. (1985). *History of the social sciences*. In S. Kohlstedt & M. Rossiter (Eds.), *Historical writing on American science* (pp. 183-209). Baltimore: Johns Hopkins University Press; Furner, M. (1975). *Advocacy and objectivity*. Lexington: University of Kentucky Press; Gans, H. J. (Ed.). (1990). *Sociology in America*. Newbury Park, CA: Sage 1990; Haskell, T. (1977). *The emergence of professional social science*. Champaign: University of Illinois Press; Ricci, D. (1984). *The tragedy of political science*. New Haven, CT: Yale University Press; Ross, D. (1990). *Origins of American social science*. New York/Cambridge, UK: Cambridge University Press; Seidelman,

R., & Harpham, E. (1985). *Disenchanted realists*. Albany: State University of New York Press; Turner, B., & Turner, S. P. (1990). *The impossible science*. Newbury Park, CA: Sage; Vidich, A. J., & Lyman, S. M. (1985). *American sociology*. New Haven, CT: Yale University Press.

7. Lustig, J. (1982). *Corporate liberalism*. Berkeley: University of California Press.

8. Cravens, H. (1988). *The triumph of evolution*. Baltimore: Johns Hopkins University Press; Degler, C. N. (1991). *In search of human nature*. New York: Oxford University Press; Kevles, D. J. (1985). *In the name of eugenics*. Berkeley: University of California Press; Schwartz, B. (1985). *The battle for human nature*. New York: Norton.

9. Furner, *Advocacy and objectivity*; Haskell, *Emergence of professional social science*; Ross, *Origins of American social science*.

10. Kasler, D. (1983) In search of respectability: The controversy over the destination of sociology during the conventions of the German sociological society: 1910-1939. In *Knowledge and society: Studies in the sociology of culture past and present: Vol. 4* (pp. 227-72). Greenwich, CT: JAI Press; Kasler, *Max Weber*; Kloppenberg, J. T. (1988). *Uncertain victory*. New York: Oxford University Press; Mommsen, W. J., & Osterhammel, J. (Eds.). (1987). *Max Weber and his contemporaries*. Winchester, MA: Unwin Hyman (pp. 71-98).

11. Schwedinger H., & Schwedinger, J. (1974). *Sociologists of the chair*. New York: Basic Books.

12. Furner, *Advocacy and objectivity*; Haskell, T. (Ed.). (1984). *The authority of experts*. Bloomington: Indiana University Press; Haskell, *Emergence of professional social science*; Hatch, N. (Ed.). (1987). *The professions in America*. Baltimore: Johns Hopkins University Press; Vesey, L. (1967). *The emergence of the American university*. Chicago: University of Chicago Press;

13. Bachrach, P. (1967). *The theory of the democratic elite*. Boston: Little, Brown.

14. Buenker, J., Burnham,J., & Crunden, R. *Progressivism*. Rochester, VT: Schenkman Books; Forcey, C. (1961). *Crossroads of liberalism*. New York: Oxford University Press; Kaplan, S. (1956). Social engineers as saviors: The effects of World War I on some American liberals. *Journal of the History of Ideas, 16*, 347-69; Noble, D. (1958). *The paradox of progressive thought*. Minneapolis: University of Minnesota Press.

15. Haskell, *Authority of experts*.

16. Furner, *Advocacy and objectivity*.

17. Bannister, *Sociology and scientism*.

18. Fischer, F. (1990). *Technocracy and the politics of expertise*. Newbury Park, CA: Sage; Heineman, R., Bluhm, W. T., Peterson, S. A., & Kearney, E. N. (1990). *The world of the policy analyst*. Chatham, NJ: Chatham House; Lasswell, H. D., & Lerner, D. (Eds.). (1951). The policy sciences. Stanford, CA: Stanford University Press.

19. Abbott, P. (1980). *Furious fancies* Westport, CT: Greenwood; Ball, T. (1990). The politics of social science in postwar America. In F. May (Ed.), *Recasting America* (pp. 76-92). New York: Routledge; Brick, H. (1986). *Daniel Bell and the decline of the radical intellectual*. Madison: University of Wisconsin Press; Fowler, R. B. (1978). *Believing skeptics*. Westport, CT: Greenwood; Lipset,

S. M. (Ed.). (1969). *Politics and the social sciences*. New York: Oxford University Press; Wald, *New York intellectuals*.

20. Buxton, W. (1985). *Talcott Parsons and the capitalist nation-state*. Toronto: University of Toronto Press; Klanser, S., & Lidz, V. (1986). *The nationalization of the social sciences*. University of Pennsylvania Press; Turner, B. (Ed.). (1991). *Talcott Parsons: Theorist of modernity*. Newbury Park, CA: Sage.

21. Aaron, R. (1966). *The industrial society*. New York: Simon & Schuster; Bell, *Coming of post-industrial society*; Frankel, *Post-industrial utopians*; Huntington, Postindustrial politics; Kuhns, *Post-industrial prophets*; Touraine, *Post-industrial society*.

22. Fukuyama, F. (1989). The end of history. *The National Interest, 16*(3), 3-28, with responses; Fukuyama, *End of history and the last man*.

23. Bruce-Briggs, *The new class*; Derber, Schwartz, & Magrass, *Power in the highest degree*; Fischer, *Technology and the politics of expertise*; Gouldner, A. (1979). *The future of the intellectuals and the rise of the new class*. New York: Oxford University Press.

24. Gouldner, A. (1973). *For sociology*. New York: Basic Books.

25. Auletta, K. (1982). *The underclass*. New York: Vintage; Hirschmann, A. O. (1991). *The rhetoric of reaction*. Cambridge, MA: Harvard University Press.

26. Factor & Turner, *Max Weber and the dispute over reason and value*; Lasswell, (1936). *Who gets what, when, how*. New York: McGraw-Hill; Lasswell (1950) *Power and society*. New Haven, CT: Yale University Press; Morgenthau (1958). *Dilemma of politics*. Chicago: University of Chicago Press; Morgenthau (1970). *Scientific man and power politics*. Chicago: University of Chicago Press; Proctor, *Value free science?*; Rosenthal, J. H. (1991). *Righteous realists*. Baton Rouge: Louisiana State University Press; Smith, M. J. (1990). *Realist thought from Weber to Kissinger*. Baton Rouge: Louisiana State University Press; Waxman, C. I. (Ed.). (1968). *The end of ideology debate*. New York: Simon & Schuster.

27. Callahan, D., & Jennings, B. (Eds.). (1983). *Ethics, the social sciences and policy analysis*. New York: Plenum. Fischer, *Technology and the politics of expertise*; Tong, R. (1989). *Ethics and policy analysis*. Englewood Cliffs, NJ: Prentice-Hall.

For a disturbing study of the role of social scientists and the federal government, see Horowitz, I. L. (Ed.). (1974). *The rise and fall of project camelot*. Cambridge: MIT Press.

28. Fischer, *Technology and the politics of expertise*.

29. See note 8 above.

30. O'Donnell, J. M. (1985). *The origins of behaviorism*. New York: New York University Press; Sokol, M. J. (Ed.). (1990). *Psychological testing in American society*. New Brunswick, NJ: Rutgers University Press.

31. Napoli, D. (1981). *Architects of adjustment*. Port Washington, NY: Kennikat Press.

32. Lasswell, H. (1930). *Psychopathology and politics*. New York: Viking.

33. Ross, *Origins of American social science*.

34. Ibid., pp. 117-118. The reference is to Furner, *Advocacy and objectivity*, chapters 4, 5, and 7.

35. Bell, *Cultural contradictions of capitalism*; Lasch, *Culture of narcissism*.

36. Baudrillard, *In the shadow of the silent majorities*.

INDEX

Althusser, Louis, 89-90
Antihumanism, 85-86, 111-116

Baudrillard, Jean, 128-129
Bauman, Zygmunt, 124-126

Critical theory, 80-85, 154-162

Derrida, Jacques, 96-107
Descartes, Rene, 23-25

Elitism, 48-50, 182-184
End of history, 137-138
Enlightenment, 7-20, 159-162, 169-172

Feminism, 139-140, 162-168
Foucault, Michel, 15-20, 127-128
Freud, Sigmund, 82-83

Geminschaft vs. Gesellschaft, 26-26

Habermas, Jürgen, 153-159
Heidegger, Martin, 111-112
Hermeneutics, 98-103
Hobbes, Thomas, 21-22
Humanism, 29-30, 111-112
Human nature, 116-117

Ideology, 69-71
Intellectuals, 124-125, 177-179

Kant, Immanuel, 9-11
    postmodernist critique of, 11-14

Lacan, Jacques, 90-92
Levi-Strauss, Claude, 87-89
Liberalism, 181-183
Logocentrism, 97-107
Lyotard, Jean-Francois, 129-131

Marxism, 81-82, 131-135
Mass culture, 48-50
Methods, 53-63, 173-174
Modernism, 40-42
Modernity, categories of, 28-30
Modernization, 1-3

Nietzsche, Friederich, 15-20, 103-106
Nihilism, 69-71, 171-173

Postindustrial society, 130-133

Reason, 57-59
Relativism, 66-69

Sassure, Ferdinand, 86-87, 113-117
    modern ideas of, 42-48. See also
    Antihumanism
Social sciences, 3-4, 179-190
    postmodernism, 124-130, 184-190
Society, conflict vs. consensus
    models, 180-181
Structuralism, 80-82

Value freedom, 71-75
Values, 59-60

Weber, Max, 64-65
Weltanschauung, 97-98

ABOUT THE AUTHOR

Robert Hollinger is an Associate Professor of Philosophy at Iowa State University, where he has taught philosophy of the social and behavioral sciences since 1974. He received a B.A. in philosophy from Brooklyn College in 1966 and a Ph.D. in Philosophy from the University of Wisconsin in 1972. He also has taught at Mankato State University, Minnesota, and Clark University, Massachusetts. He has served on numerous graduate committees in sociology, psychology, economics, history, political science, anthropology, English, and professional education. He coedited (with Stephen P. Turner) a special issue of *Qualitative Sociology* (1980) and collaborated with William F. Woodman (Iowa State) and Deb Lemke (Western Carolina State) on two papers that were presented at meetings of the Midwest Sociological Society: one on the origins of the concept of rationality, the other on Max Weber and scholars in the iron cage of the contemporary university. He is currently completing a book called *The Dark Side of Liberalism: Elitism Versus Democracy*, and is coediting with David Depew (California State University at Fullerton) an anthology, *Pragmatism: From Progressivism to Postmodernism*.

192